International H

CW01498338

Solidarity and Justice in Health Care

International Health Law

Solidarity and Justice in Health Care

Edited by

A.P. den Exter

Maklu
Antwerpen - Apeldoorn

A.P. den Exter (ed.)
International Health Law. Solidarity and Justice in Health Care
Apeldoorn - Antwerpen
Maklu
2008

258 pag. - 24 x 16 cm
ISBN 978-90-466-0200-3
D/2008/1997/30
NUR 828

Maklu
Koninginnelaan 96, 7315 EB Apeldoorn, The Netherlands, info@maklu.nl
Somersstraat 13/15, 2018 Antwerpen, Belgium, info@maklu.be
www.maklu.eu

USA & Canada
International Specialized Book Services
920 NE 58th Ave., Suite 300, Portland, OR 97213-3786, orders@isbs.com, www.isbs.com

UK and Ireland:
R. Bayliss, 81 Milehouse Road, Plymouth, Devon PL3 4AE

Contents

Maklu

Preface

André den Exter

International Health Law Solidarity and Justice in Health Care

In the twenty-first century, complex health care problems have remained unsolved. Conflicts between public interests and individual rights, evolving public health crises in low income countries, the challenge of regulating health professionals, and the effects of globalization on health (care systems) dominate the contemporary debates in this field. In a way, these problems expose the (regulatory) weaknesses of health systems responding to these questions. As a result, health lawyers and policy makers should - more than in the past - focus on underlying normative values in health care.

One of these core values includes the right to health care. Access to health care services has been generally accepted as a fundamental human right. Numerous international and national legal documents have defined both the content and scope of such a right, whereas the judiciary has played a crucial role in strengthening the enforceability of (individual) health care claims. As the health crisis deepened, efficiency became the mantra of health system reforms, aimed at guaranteeing an effective health system. Reforms, such as the 'marketization' of the social health insurance system and/or health services, combined with patients' increasing need for medical care, scarcity of (financial) resources, and, consequently, the need for prioritizing choices in health care, have challenged the key element of a strong health system: the right to health care.[1] What is important is the identification of the right to the highest attainable standard of health as underpinning value of an effective, integrated and accessible health system (p. 6).

Interpreted as *equal* access to necessary health care facilities, the notion of access to care raises various fundamental questions, such as how to interpret equal access? Clearly, it includes the absence of unjust discrimination but it is not synonymous with absolute equality.[2]

Equitable access implies effectively obtaining a necessary degree of health care, but then, what can be considered as necessary and who decides? According to the Biomedicine Convention's explanatory report, equitable access to

---

[1] Human Rights Council. Promotion and protection of all human rights, civil, political, economic, social and cultural rights. Report of the special reporter on the right to everyone to the enjoyment of the highest attainable standard of physical and mental health, A/HRC/7/11, 31 January 2008.

[2] Explanatory report. Convention for the protection of Human Rights and dignity of the human being with regard to the application of biology and medicine. Oviedo 4.IV.1997, ETS No. 164 (Convention on Human Rights and Biomedicine), as confirmed by the Special reporter's report ... 'responsive to the particular health needs', p. 11-12.

health care should be in accordance with the person's *medical* needs.3 This implies that it is up to the treating physician to decide what is necessary in each individual case, merely based on medical and medically reducible criteria.

Equal access also implies to be solidary with the person in need. However, in case of illegal refugees and other vulnerable groups, equal access or solidarity with those in medical need, is not generally accepted. Refugees' access to health care has been restricted by national law, and often interpreted as emergency care only. As such, the solidarity concept in health care does not cover *international* solidarity, at least, not to the same extent.

But even at national level, the solidarity notion is under pressure. Solidarity in financing health care is traditionally based on (a combination of) income and risk solidarity arrangements. However, the increased interest in introducing market elements in both the financing and provision of health services, the ongoing debate on own payment mechanisms, de-listing medical services from the social insurance package, the debate on life style related premiums, and the suggestion of (additional) personal saving initiatives (medical saving accounts), clearly reflect a change in the solidarity notion from an unconditional '*Solidarität zwischen Fremden*', transforming in a more restricted or 'conditional' type of solidarity.4 Whether or not such a development is in line with international social security law remains to be seen.

Solidarity, as a condition of equal access to health care, refers to the notion of (social) justice. Social justice implies a redistribution of goods, whereas differences in treatment require justification. Rawls defended in "*A Theory of Justice*" inequalities in (medical) treatment on the difference principle, according to which inequalities are justified only if they are designed to bring, and actually do bring the greatest possible benefit to others who are less well off.5 A more plausible theory, however, was developed by Walzer, claiming that the variety of goods requires different distributive criteria (e.g., desert, qualification, need, political loyalty, free exchange), uneasily coexisting. Distributive justice searches for principles internal to each distributive sphere; within each own sphere there are different distributive criteria.6 Within the sphere of health care (security and welfare), need is the distributive criterion, derived from Marx's famous maxim: "To each according to his needs, from each according to his ability", which has been revised as: From each according to his ability (or his resources); to each according to his socially recognised needs (p. 91). These socially recognised needs are based on shared values of needs and health. Since individual needs are infinite, the Biomedicine Convention already explained needs as *medical* needs, i.e. it is the treating physician who decides on inequalities in access to health care, based on medical criteria and the professional standards. Since the resources are scarce, hard choices on (de)listing health services have to be made, which have to be political choices. As such, the idea of need is subject to political limitation (p. 67), setting the

---

3   *Ibid.*
4   As suggested by the Dutch Council of State in its report 'Tenable solidarity in health care systems'(in Dutch), Signalementen RVZ Zoetermeer, 2005.
5   See J. Rawls, *A Theory of Justice* (Oxford: Oxford University Press, 1971), p. 105-106.
6   M. Walzer, *Spheres of Justice: a defense of pluralism and equality*, (New York: Basic Books, 1983), p. 4 ff.

8

boundaries of the sphere of health care in detail. By doing so, multilateral legal documents such as the social rights conventions and minimum standards conventions function as standard-setting instruments in health policy decision-making (as explained by Schoukens in his contribution "*The Right to Access Health Care: Health Care according to International and European Social Security Law Instruments*").

Objective international health Law

International Health Law. Solidarity and Justice in Health Care explores the underlying normative values of health systems from a global and local perspective. Leading academics around the world were invited to explain the key elements of health systems, analyse contemporary issues and key factors shaping health care, while taking into account the principles on health care access. Formulated as international treaty norms, the notions on justice and solidarity colour and explain the meaning of the fundamental right to health care.

By explaining the global and local context of contemporary health systems in terms of access, solidarity and justice, *International Health Law* could (ultimately) contribute to reduce health inequities and strengthen health systems. Analysis of evolving problems (e.g. increased private initiatives on health care markets and its effects on equal access, human rights concerns and health system reforms, etc.) shows a clear relationship with the health principles. For instance, a health system discriminating individuals or certain groups conflicts with the ideas on justice and equal access. Even more, analysis reveals that health system reforms and health care rights are interdependent. One cannot be realised successfully without taking into account the other dimension.[7] Those research outcomes on health system reforms enable health policy makers to reformulate initial reform strategies where necessary. Secondly, analysing health care access jurisprudence could be relevant to health lawyers in other legal systems, being confronted with health inequalities and health system deficiencies.

Well aware of the limited role in improving the health standard and reducing inequalities in health, one could question the focus on health care. Indeed, poverty remains the main cause of disease, but it is also a factor which is beyond the immediate control of medicine and health care.[8] No doubt that combating poverty must remain one of the foremost objectives.[9] Nonetheless, there is no reason why we should not achieve a health system that reaches eve-

---

7   As confirmed be the Human Rights Council report, supra note 1.
8   Echoing the 19th century pioneers of social medicine Henry Sigerist, quoted in *Inequalities in Health*. Report of a research working group (the Black report), published by the Department of Health and Social Security (DHSS), UK, 1980, p. 3.
9   About the recognition of the shared benefits of economic development to health improvement, see: B. Mason Meier and A.M. Fox. "Development as Health: Employing the Collective Right to Development to Achieve the Goals of the Individual Right to Health." *HRQ* 30 (2008) 259-355.

rybody, health and sick, rich and poor.[10] It is the reason why the contributors narrowed the health conception to health care.

Structure

This volume brings together examples of legal (and other) writing covering access to health care. What unites all the chapters is the concern on this fundamental right. Structured by continent, the volume starts with the global perspective on health care access, subsequently, covers various examples of access to health care and system reforms, while addressing (different conceptions of) solidarity and justice. Apart from examining country experiences, the authors provide an interesting and valuable contribution to the (inter)national legal and health policy debate on guaranteeing equal access to health care facilities, resisting a market or consumer-driven movement.

The book begins with the exploration of the legal contours of the right to access to health care under international law, by Paul Schoukens. Here the emphasis is on realising health care access under both international social security law, and international human rights law. Traditionally, the first conventions set minimum standards for social security risk, including access to health care, and pursue the "harmonisation" of social health care systems. Maintaining the value of these conventions, the main challenge will be re-thinking the standard-setting instruments, combined with measuring accessibility and health care outcomes. International human right treaties create legal obligations for States to promote and protect human rights. As it appeared from the case law, the judiciary is increasingly testing the compatibility of social security norms with human rights principles (e.g., respect of private and family life, inhuman treatment, property, etc.). One may welcome this pragmatic approach of the judiciary by interrelating individual and social rights, however, it is not without consequences. Schoukens questions the court's ability to recognise the specific nature of collective rights: redistribution of health care resources between citizens, hence the collective interests of society as such.

Part Two covers several contributions focussing on two health care systems in Europe that are diametrically opposed: the Dutch social health insurance scheme and the National Health System in the United Kingdom. From a different perspective, the authors emphasize both the collective (Buijsen and Newdick), and the individual dimension (Den Exter) of health care access. Needless to say that due to the variety of European health care systems, the outcomes as described does not necessarily reflect 'the European approach' on justice and solidarity in health care.

In "The Meaning of 'Justice' and Solidarity' in Health Care" Martin Buijsen argues that the health care sector can be characterised by a strong notion of justice. Justice, as already mentioned by Aristotle, is related to equality: justice should serve equality, especially in the interest of the weak and needy. Therefore, just distribution in the sphere of health care is based on need rather then 'merit'. In line with Walzer's theory on *"spheres of justice"*, Buijsen examines

---

10   H. Sigerist, *Civilisation and Disease*, (Ithaca: Cornell University Press, 1943), p. 239-240.

the exact meaning of justice in health care by taking the example of the latest health system reforms in the Netherlands. Examples such as introducing patients co-payments (the so-called no-claim refund), the bonus points for an organ donors scheme, and priority treatment arrangements made clear that in the - scarce - debates on distributive justice, the need criterion was painfully avoided, the "inability for moral argumentation", quoting Buijsen. The relationship with solidarity is explained as follows: Solidarity in the normative sense, is unmistakably linked to justice, as it refers to the (biblical) duty to care for the poor, implying a certain degree of force and constraint, leading to ethical and political choices (in health care). In terms of equal access to social health insurance, however, Buijsen claims the need criterion on the benefit side cannot be dissociated from the merit principle on the premium side. Consequently, reform proposals ignoring that separation violate solidarity in the strict sense.

The following contribution, "*Litigating Health Care Access in the Netherlands: Challenging International Treaty Law.*", complements the legal-philosophical approach by Martin Buijsen. André den Exter explores the judiciability of the right to access to health care in the Netherlands under international law. Traditionally, the judiciary has interpreted access to health care in terms of health insurance entitlements. Under the (new) Health Insurance Act, the insured may claim the types of care as entitlements provided by (contracted) health providers. From the analysis it becomes clear that besides conceptualising the health care right, international legal norms including EC trade rules have been used to enforce such a positive right in terms of benefit entitlements.

How different is the approach of Christopher Newdick when discussing solidarity in his contribution "*Solidarity, Rights and Social Welfare in the NHS – Resisting the Tide of Bioethics?*". He argues that 'calls for courts to become more actively involved in the substantive allocation of finite public resources should be resisted'. Here, he analyses the nature and content rights to solidarity via the experience of resource allocation in the National Health Service in the UK. Contrary to popular currents of contemporary bioethics, it argues for a stronger sense of institutional ethics capable of balancing individual claims to substantive rights with the need for solidarity and social cohesion in the community as a whole.

Part Three. Unlike the continental approach on patient mobility in the EU, the Canadian Supreme Court took a different activist approach in the famous case on waiting times and the role of private health insurance, i.e. the *Chaoulli* case (2005). In "*Health Care Rights in Canada: The Chaoulli Legacy*", Flood and Xavier discuss the government's response to this controversial court ruling by liberalizing the law relating to private health insurance. Furthermore, since *Chaoulli* has inspired a range of different claims to health care based on the Canadian Charter of Rights and Freedoms, the authors examine three types of recent challenges to the Canadian health system.

Tim Jost offers in his contribution "*Health Care Access in the United States. Conflicting Concepts of Justice and Little Solidarity*" a particular vision of a peculiar health care system. "At its best, American health care is the best in the world".[11] Notwithstanding its achievements, about 17.5 percent of the population at any one time is uninsured, getting less health care then the insured, and get it later, when it is often less effective. Jost advocates a different approach to expand access to health care (insurance). Many Americans, however, do not support expansion of public programs to cover the uninsured. According to an influential health policy group, the "consumer-driven health care" advocates, the primary health policy problem is not underinsurance, but rather over insurance since health insurance greatly reduces the price of health care services to the consumer. 'Infected' by the European solidarity concept, Jost criticises consumer-driven health plans (so-called health saving accounts) since these plans will support the relatively wealthy Americans.

The next chapter "*Health in Chile: Is the Government Doing Everything it Can to Achieve Social Justice?*", written by Silvia Borzutzky, examines the main characteristics and problems of Chile's health care system. Here, the emphasis is on the so-called 'Plan AUGE' implemented in 2004. Confronted with the Pinochet legacy and its market oriented politics, the AUGE-plan contains an innovative approach restoring solidarity and equitable access to health care.

Part Four focuses on the AIDS pandemic in the African continent. Here, it becomes clear that protecting and promoting human rights is becoming one of the key means in preserving the health of individuals and populations. Using the AIDS pandemic as a lens, the authors evaluate government health policies, as well as the jurisprudence from the South African Constitutional Court challenging the right to health. Notably, the South African Constitutional Court's jurisprudence provides a path-breaking illustration of the social justice potential of an enforceable right to health. The South African experience suggests that enforcing health rights may in fact contribute to greater degrees of collective solidarity and justice. The novel rights paradigm locates individual civil and social rights within a communitarian framework drawing from the traditional African notion of 'ubuntu,' which denotes collective solidarity, humaneness and mutual responsibilities to recognize the respect, dignity and value of all members of society. In "*Justice and Justiciability: Advancing Solidarity and Justice through South Africans Right to Health Jurisprudence*", Lisa Forman explores these aspects of the Constitutional Court's unfolding jurisprudence on the right to health, sending a clear message to other legal cultures regarding the justiciability of social rights and positive duties. 'It illustrates the potential for a judicial role in enforcing rights that answers pragmatic concerns about their zero sum claims and indeed about the institutional competence and democratic legitimacy of judicial review of social policy'.

Like South Africa, most health systems in sub-Saharan Africa (sSA), are struggling the HIV/AIDS pandemic. One of the solutions fighting this health crisis is by scaling up delivery of anti-retroviral treatment (ART). In "*The Impact of ART Scale-up on Health Systems (De-)Strengthening in Sub-Saharan Africa: Justice and Justification*", Stephanie Nixon and Nina Veenstra explore how the scale-up of expensive HIV treatment in sub-Saharan Africa (sSA) could impact their health systems and discuss the value of solidarity as a guiding

---

[11]   Federal Trade Commissions/Department of Justice. Improving Health Care: A Dose of Competition. Washington DC, 2004, p. 1.

principle for anti-retroviral treatment (ART) scale-up. Based on their research, they conclude that the current expansion of access to ART may run counter to many aims of strengthening health systems (e.g., investments in HIV prevention programs). They call for a reflection on the public duties in health care and suggest a range of concrete lessons for moving forward.

The final part, part Five, covers contributions from Australia and two Asian countries: South Korea and China. In particular the Asian health system reforms give a clear picture about the current situation. Until now, contemporary dilemmas and future direction of these health systems remained largely unknown outside this region. This is why we are pleased to have on board two key contributions opening the Asian health care markets.

Starting with an interesting contribution on Medicare, Australia's universal health insurance scheme, *Steven Duckett* claims that Medicare has been bedevilled by a contest of values about support for universal versus targeted or segmented policy approaches or the role of the market sector. Duckett observes a lack of consensus about the relative roles of the public and private sector in health care, nor is there consensus on the role of government. The nature of the government response represented a challenge to Medicare's egalitarian ethos, as being discussed in *"The Continuing Contest of Values in the Australian Health Care System"*.

In *"Public Identity, Private Behaviour – Causes, Consequences, and Remedies for Health Sector Reforms in China"*, Vivian Lin and Hongwen Zhao describe the various stages of health sector reforms in China, starting with the 'First health revolution', just after the founding of the People's Republic of China in 1949. The egalitarian health development, addressing the availability, accessibility and affordability of health care, was replaced by unsuccessful market reforms, undermining solidarity and causing social unrest notably in rural areas. After the failure of privatising health care, destroying the previously successful Chinese health system, the latest changes introduced the concept of 'market socialism': reintroducing the role of the state in health care, while strengthening health care rights by guaranteeing access to medical insurance to all. This chapter addresses the causes, consequences and remedies to the health reforms, focussing on issues of justice and equity and the emerging discussion of health rights.

For more then 30 years, South Korea has built an impressive national health insurance system. Celebrating their anniversary, the current Korean health care system has focused on problems of inadequate and inequitable access to health services. Minah Kang Kim analyses these problems in her contribution *"Access to Health Care in Korea"*. Despite the universal insurance scheme, a significant part of the population (e.g., below the poverty line, elderly and those living in rural areas), face accessibility problems. One of the reasons is the tight definition of accessibility. In short, the Korean system was diagnosed as: 'having a wide coverage of the population, shallow benefit provision, and a high cost-sharing element' (Mossialos 2007). The underlying problem, however, is the lack of consensus about defining 'necessary' care, covered by the insurance scheme. Absence of consensus reflects the ideological debate on whether health care should be considered as a public or private good. Advocating the idea of health care as a public good, Kim emphasises the need for a more principle debate on the role of private initiative in this sector.

June 2008

Part One

International Treaty Law and Access to Health Care

Chapter 1

The Right to Access Health Care: Health Care according to International and European Social Security Law Instruments

Paul Schoukens*

Introduction

Health and especially the access to health care are considered by many as a fundamental cornerstone of our societies. The number of national and international documents discussing the quality of health care, the sustainability of health care systems and the accessibility of the health infrastructure is increasing rapidly. Yet in this growing attention for health and health care, the entitlement aspect, i.e. the accessibility issue has been somewhat overlooked. Often it is assumed that there is a general principle of universal access, meaning that all should have access in the same way. It may be interesting to confront this assumption with the legal reality as it is has been written down in international conventions. Indeed, with this contribution we would thus like to investigate upon the legal contours of the right to health care as it is being articulated in international legal instruments. Essentially, we will try to find out how these instruments concretely shape the right to have access to health care.

Before tackling this question, we first need to delineate clearly the scope of this contribution. As already mentioned, health (care) is multifaceted and trying to approach each of the facets would bring us too far. Here, the emphasis will mainly be upon the guarantee of accessibility to health care, and thus not upon the right to health in its aspect of "freedom"; the latter aspect touches upon the right to control one's health and body, including sexual and reproductive freedom, and the right to be free from interference, such as the right to be free from torture, non-consensual medical treatment and experimentation.

With regard to the entitlement aspect, the main attention will go to the citizens' access to health care, which is realised through social security systems (more specifically social health care insurances, but also national health care systems pursuing the goal of accessibility by providing free health care services to the citizens). Consequently, we will mainly address international and Euro-

---

*   The author would like to thank his colleague Danny Pieters for a critical review of the article.

pean social security conventions which give legal contents to the right to (access to) health care.

The duty for states to develop (a minimum of) health facilities of a certain quality level will not be addressed as such. Hence, less attention will be given to the aspects of public health care, like preventive health, the conditions under which health facilities can be established and the legal obligations under which a health practitioner should practice. As we are mainly looking at accessibility, we will neither touch upon the international conventions establishing standards in the field of occupational safety and health. Most of these international agreements have been concluded under the auspices of the *International Labour Organisation* and mainly address the collective relations between employers and workers. As international labour law rules they fall out of our strict ambit of health accessibility guaranteed though social security.

As to the instruments under investigation we have chosen for two types of conventions which are enacted by organisations of two different levels. As to the territorial level, we distinguish between the universal/international conventions that have been enacted in the framework of the United Nations (including the specific agency of the *International Labour Office*) on the one hand, and the regional agreements developed by the Council of Europe. The latter organisation is in Europe still the main guardian for the respect of the fundamental rights (including social rights). For the purpose of this contribution the rules of the European Union will in principle be left untouched. Although the creation of the internal market (the economic freedoms) does have a serious impact upon the (national) health care systems in Europe, the European Union as such did not develop legal standards in the field of access to health care. Strictly speaking it is even not empowered to do so, unless for the access to health care for migrant EU-citizens (articles 12, 17, and 42 EC-Treaty). As will be explained later, this part of international social security law, touching upon the co-ordination of systems and access to foreign health care systems, will not be dealt with.

As to the types of conventions, we will have first a look at the traditional social rights conventions and investigate which articles are relevant for the right to health care. Concretely we will deal with the International Covenant on Economic, Social and Cultural Rights and the European (Revised) Social Charter. Both are the socio-economic counterparts of the human rights instruments in place (viz. the Universal Declaration of Human Rights and the European Convention for the Protection of Human Rights). Next to these social rights conventions, we will investigate how relevant the traditional standard-setting instruments are for the right on health care. As their title already suggests, these conventions have set minimum standards for the traditional social security risks, (the access to) health care being one of them. The reason for this detour has to do with the tight links that exist between the social rights instruments and the minimum standard conventions. The latter give indeed more concrete contents to the general proclaimed right to social security. It is therefore interesting to look how the right to access to health care (a part of the right to social security) is being concretely shaped in those instruments. Next to the general standard-setting conventions, such as the ILO-Convention 102 and the European Code of Social Security, we also deal with the sectoral conventions elaborating the standards of one particular risk. Relevant for us are the ILO-Conventions that set minimum rules in the field of health care, i.e. Convention No. 121 touching among others upon medical services to be provided in cases of labour accidents and professional diseases, No. 130 on medical care and No. 189 on maternity health benefits.

Both types of conventions, i.e. the social rights conventions and the minimum standard conventions, pursue as objective the "harmonisation" of social security systems, including social health care systems. The idea is that they want to have effect upon the national systems, by bringing them closer as regards their specific contents. This objective is opposed to the so-called co-ordination of social security systems which can be found in a numerous amount of international agreements. The latter type of conventions focuses upon migrating persons who, due to their migration, risk to loose parts of their social security entitlements. In a way, they touch partially upon the "access" to health care as well, i.e. the issue of access of migrating persons to foreign health care systems. Dealing with this rather technical part of the right to health care (abroad) would lead us however too far. Hence, those instruments will not be investigated.

After having analysed the social rights conventions and the standards-setting instruments, we will focus upon the relevance of human right conventions regarding the right to access to health care. Although strictly speaking those conventions are not of a nature to create social rights, they may still be legally relevant for social security systems, and specifically for social health care systems. Indeed, in recent years we can discern a tendency in which judges start to screen national social security rules on their compatibility with fundamental human right principles, as being laid down in international conventions. This tendency can be observed especially in relation to the European Convention of the protection for Human Rights. Hence, in the final part we will look at the potential impact of this instrument on the accessibility to health care. The case law developed by the European Court of Human Rights will play a major role here.

In the concluding part we try to summarise the concrete meaning of these conventions for the right to health care. Especially their interrelation, and if possible their conflicting relationship will get major attention.

1. The right to (access) health care as a social right

In this part we will analyse in some more detail some social rights conventions and their legal meaning with regard to the right to health care. First we will discuss the International Covenant on Economic, Social and Cultural Rights, a United Nations' instrument. It will be followed by a description of the relevant articles of the European (Revised) Social Charter, which is the socio-economic counterpart of the European Convention for the Protection of Human Rights in the Council of Europe.

At the international level: the right to access to health care according to the International Covenant on Economic, Social and Cultural Rights

The International Covenant on Economic, Social and Cultural Rights has been adopted as a multilateral treaty by the United Nations General Assembly on December 16, 1966. It came into force on January 3, 1976. The treaty has been signed by 155 states of which 149 ratified it. The Covenant develops some of the rights contained in the Universal Declaration of Human Rights especially fundamental rights of a more social economic nature, such as the right to work and the right to social protection.[1] For our focus, it gives a more concrete content to articles 22 and 25 of the Universal Declaration of Human Rights which respectively proclaim the right to social security and the right to health care.[2] Although more will be said about these rights at a later stage, the obligations for the state parties are set in rather cautious and conditional way. For instance it is not expected that the signatory states subscribe all social rights from the outset. The principal obligation is reflected in article 2 of the Covenant, which stipulates that states take steps *"with a view to achieving progressively the full realization of the rights recognised"* in the Covenant. Thus, it is considered that the full implementation of these social rights can in general not be achieved in a short period. Furthermore, for the implementation of those rights, the country's financial and economic possibilities are taken into account as well (article 2, par. 1: each state takes the necessary steps *"to the maximum of its available resources"*).

Compliance by states with their obligations under the Covenant and the level of implementation of the rights and duties in question are monitored by a specific Committee on Economic, Social and Cultural Rights. The committee, essentially bases its judgement about the compliance on national reports sent in by the state parties. However, it is also entitled to make use of other information sources. Many of the interpretations about the social rights that relevant for this contribution are based upon the reports of this Committee.[3]

Before embarking upon the analysis, it should be mentioned that the right to access health care is mainly developed in article 12 of the Covenant (right to health care). Not much is to be found in this relation in the article dealing with

---

[1] The International Covenant on Civil and Political Rights does the same for the fundamental human rights of the Universal Declaration.

[2] Article 22 stipulating: *"[e]veryone, as a member of society, has the right to social security and is entitled to realization, through national effort and international co-operation and in accordance with the organization and resources of each State, of the economic, social and cultural rights indispensable for his dignity and the free development of his personality"*. Article 25 stipulating: in its first paragraph: *"[e]veryone has the right to a standard of living adequate for the health and well-being of himself and of his family, including food, clothing, housing and medical care and necessary social services, and the right to security in the event of unemployment, sickness, disability, widowhood, old age or other lack of livelihood in circumstances beyond his control"*.

[3] Especially the following report has been used as a major source of information: Committee on Economic, Social and Cultural Rights, *Substantive issues arising in the implementation of the International Covenant on Economic, Social and Cultural Rights. General Comment No. 14*, E/C.12/2000/4, 11/08/2000.

the right to social protection (article 9).4 Consequently it will be to a large extent left out from the description.

The right to access health care interpreted

Article 12 of the International Covenant on Economic, Social and Cultural Rights one reads:

> "1. The States Parties to the present Covenant recognize the right of everyone to the enjoyment of the highest attainable standard of physical and mental health.
>
> 2. The steps to be taken by the States Parties to the present Covenant to achieve the full realization of this right shall include those necessary for:
>
> [...];
>
> (c) The prevention, treatment and control of epidemic, endemic, occupational and other diseases.
>
> (d) The creation of conditions which would assure to all medical service and medical attention in the event of sickness".

Following the Committee's interpretation, article 12 refers to a wide range of socio-economic facts that should promote conditions in which people can lead a healthy life.5 The article refers mainly to the requirement of "availability" of health care, as an inclusive right extending not only to timely and appropriate health care but also to the availability of underlying determinants, such as safe food, nutrition, housing, healthy occupational conditions, and education.6

More in the scope of our interest, the right to health care refers as well to "accessibility". Health facilities, goods and services have to be accessible to everyone without discrimination, within the jurisdiction of the State Party. Accessibility has, in the Committee's view, four overlapping dimensions: the absence of discrimination, physical availability, economic availability and information.7

First of all states should not discriminate between persons when organising access to health care services: health facilities, goods and services must be accessible to all, especially the most vulnerable or marginalized sections of the population, in law and in fact, without discrimination on any of the prohibited grounds. States have thus a special obligation to provide the necessary health care coverage to those who do not have sufficient means. Hence, measures facilitating access to health care for these groups are of major importance, which

---

4   Stipulating: *"The States Parties to the present Covenant recognize the right of everyone to social security, including social insurance"*.
5   *General Comment No. 14*, 2.
6   *Ibid*, 2.
7   *Ibid*, 3.

can imply that a policy showing positive discrimination in this respect could be allowed.

Forbidden are rules or government actions that are of an indirect discriminatory nature. Inappropriate health resource allocation can indeed lead to discrimination that may not be overt. For example, investments should not disproportionately favour expensive curative health services which are often accessible only to a small, privileged fraction of the population, compared to primary and preventive health care benefiting a far larger part of the population.[8]

Finally, governments should prevent any discrimination on internationally prohibited grounds in the provision of health care and health services. By virtue of article 2.2 and article 3, the Covenant proscribes any discrimination in access to health care and underlying determinants of health, as well as to means and entitlements for their procurement, on the grounds of race, colour, sex, language, religion, political or other opinion, national or social origin, property, birth, physical or mental disability, health status (including HIV/AIDS), sexual orientation and civil, political, social or other status, which has the intention or effect of nullifying or impairing the equal enjoyment or exercise of the right to health.

Secondly, health care should be physical accessible: health facilities, goods and services must be within safe physical reach for all sections of the population, especially vulnerable or marginalized groups, such as ethnic minorities and indigenous populations, women, children, adolescents, older persons, persons with disabilities and persons with HIV/AIDS. Accessibility also implies that medical services and underlying determinants of health, such as safe and potable water and adequate sanitation facilities, are within safe physical reach, including in rural areas. Accessibility further includes adequate access to buildings for persons with disabilities.

Thirdly, health care should be affordable and thus economically accessible. Payment for health-care services, as well as services related to the underlying determinants of health, has to be based on the principle of equity, ensuring that these services, whether privately or publicly provided, are affordable for all, including socially disadvantaged groups. Equity demands that poorer households should not be disproportionately burdened with health expenses as compared to richer households.

Finally, regarding "accessibility", the population should be informed about their rights, meaning that access to information is sufficiently guaranteed. Accessibility includes the right to seek, receive and impart information and ideas concerning health issues. However, accessibility of information should not impair the right to have personal health data treated with confidentiality.

Next to availability and accessibility, health care delivery is being made subject to the conditions of "acceptability" and "quality". Whereas the first condition refers to the fact that the health care delivery should be respectful of medical ethics and should be culturally appropriate, the second one presupposes a decent quality attainment.

---

[8]   *Ibid*, 5.

As with the other rights in the Covenant, the right to health imposes three types or levels of obligations on state parties: the obligations to *respect*, to *protect* and to *fulfil*.9 The obligation to *respect* requires States to refrain from interfering directly or indirectly with the enjoyment of the right to health. States should e.g. refrain from denying or limiting equal access to health care to some groups of the population (e.g. detainees or prisoners, minorities, asylum seekers or illegal migrants) to health care. The obligation to *protect* requires States to take measures that prevent third parties from interfering with article 12 guarantees. This can interpreted in the following way: states should ensure that e.g. privatization of the health sector does not constitute a threat to the availability and quality of health facilities. Finally, the obligation to *fulfil* requires States to adopt appropriate legislative, administrative, budgetary, judicial, promotional and other measures towards the full realization of the right to health. This entails e.g. the provision of a social health system which is covering health care for all in an affordable way. In this regard it is a concrete translation of the right to social protection as laid down in the articles 22 of the Universal Declaration of Human Rights and article 9 of the International Covenant on Economic, Social and Cultural Rights.

Finally, some attention should also be given to Comment No. 3 made by the Committee on Economic, Social and Cultural Rights.10 This Comment confirms that state parties have some core obligations to be fulfilled in order to be, at least, in line with the essentials of each of the rights enunciated in the Covenant. With regard to the access to health care, these core obligations include at least:

(a) To ensure the right of access to health facilities, goods and services on a non-discriminatory basis, especially for vulnerable or marginalized groups;
(b) To ensure access to the minimum essential food which is nutritionally adequate and safe, to ensure freedom from hunger to everyone;
(c) To ensure access to basic shelter, housing and sanitation, and an adequate supply of safe and potable water;
(d) To provide essential drugs, as from time to time defined under the WHO Action Programme on Essential Drugs;
(e) To ensure equitable distribution of all health facilities, goods and services.

Interestingly, the core obligations mainly refer to the accessibility of health determinants rather than to some basic health care provisions (with the exception of basic drugs). Furthermore, it is stipulated that what is available regarding health care, should be distributed in a non-discriminatory and in a redistributive manner. As we will see immediately, this distinction of core duties and other duties has some consequences with regard to the interpretation of the legal obligations.

---

9   *Ibid*, 8.
10 Committee on Economic, Social and Cultural Rights, *Substantive issues arising in the implementation of the International Covenant on Economic, Social and Cultural Rights. General Comment No. 3*, E/C. 14/12/1990.

As to the undertaken obligations and legal enforceability

The Covenant is mainly addressing the signatory states. They should make the necessary efforts to implement the obligations they have taken up by signing the Covenant. The Covenant provides for progressive realisation of the goals as being described in the various articles (see article 2 par. 1 of the Covenant). In other words, regarding the access to health care, states fulfil their duty when they take initiative to implement a health care system that makes health care accessible to all, even when that goal has not been fully realised yet. The interpretative authorities acknowledge e.g. the constraints that limited resources can bring along. More important is that states take the necessary efforts to implement these rights in the best possible manner. In that way the Covenant is to a large extent a declaration of intent.

Yet some obligations are more concretely defined. States parties have immediate obligations in relation to the right to health, such as the guarantee that the right will be exercised without discrimination of any kind (art. 2 par. 2 Covenant) and the obligation to take steps (art. 2 par. 1 Covenant) towards the full realization of article 12. Such steps must be deliberate, concrete and targeted towards the full realisation of the right to health. With regard to the latter obligation, this means that regressive measures taken in relation to the right to health are not permissible. If any deliberately regressive measures are taken, the State party has the burden of proving that they have been introduced after the most careful consideration of all alternatives and that they are duly justified by reference to the totality of the rights provided for in the Covenant in the context of the full use of the State party's maximum available resources.[11] In the same manner, a State which is unwilling to use the maximum of its available resources for the realisation of the right to health is in violation of its obligations under article 12. If resource constraints render it impossible for a State to comply fully with its Covenant obligations, it has the burden of justifying that every effort has nevertheless been made to use all available resources at its disposal in order to satisfy, as a matter of priority, the obligations outlined above. Furthermore it should be stressed that a State party cannot, under any circumstances whatsoever, justify its non-compliance with the core obligations of article 12 (as listed in Comment No. 3).

Consequently, apart from these immediate obligations, a violation of article 12 will thus does not easily occur. But even then, the question remains what sanctions can be taken against states that are not fulfilling their obligations? In essence, the Committee cannot do more than asking or urging the state to correct the situation. There is no possibility of imposing fines or applying similar sanctions. As this may attract states to sign the Covenant (hence the success of the instruments), the implementation of the rights may be at peril (thus undermining the practical meaning of the rights).

Furthermore the obligations as formulated in the Covenant are usually of a too general nature to be applied directly by citizens before a national court. They do lack direct effect. In essence the Covenant asks the states to do their best to have a system in place that provides health care to all in an equitable

---

11   *General Comment No. 14*, 8.

manner. When more concrete obligations are at stake, such as the non-discriminatory provision of health care, it will be very unlikely that (national) courts will apply the article on health care. The Committee of Social, Economic and Cultural Rights is quite clear on this issue: it asks for an incorporation and translation of the Covenant in the domestic legal order, so that violation of the right to health, or at least its core obligations, can be challenged directly before the national courts.[12] Without such incorporation, courts most probably will refrain from applying directly the provisions of the Covenants. This goes as well for the right to access to health care as being embedded in article 12.

At the European level: the right to access to health care according to the European (Revised) Social Charter

The main instrument which we should investigate here is the (Revised) European Social Charter which has been enacted by the Council of Europe. At the level of the Council of Europe, it is the counterpart of the European Convention for the protection of Human Rights. Although the latter is certainly the centrepiece of the organisation – all its member states have to accept it when acceding to the organisation – the Council of Europe was from the outset also very committed to the enactment of social rights. As early as 1950 it began to work out multilateral instruments in the field of harmonisation. One of the centrepieces is the European Social Charter, which after having been signed in 1961, came into on 26 February 1965.[13] It corresponds at European level to the International Covenant on Economic, Social and Cultural Rights as well as to certain articles of the Universal Declaration of Human Rights. In 1996, a revised version of the Social Charter was, next to the existing one, being put forward for signature.[14] The revised version contains some new social rights, which reflect better modern social policy thinking (e.g. the combat of social exclusion). For this contribution the Social Charter and the Revised Social Charter will be analysed together as the articles of both documents, relevant to the topic, are largely corresponding. They are also jointly interpreted by the European Committee of Social Rights which is the competent institution to follow up the implementation of these social right documents by the signatory parties. Especially, the Committee's assessment documents have been a major source of information for the further analysis of the right to health care in accordance with the Social Charter.[15]

The right to health care embodied in several articles

The right to health care is proclaimed in article 11 of the (Revised) Social Charter. It stipulates: *"[e]veryone has the right to benefit from any measures enabling him to enjoy the highest possible standard of health attainable"*. Yet probably more

---

12   *Ibid*, 14.
13   Signed by 32 states in Europe; ratified by 27 of them.
14   Signed by 41 states but only ratified by 23 of them. It came into force on July 1 1999.
15   In particular has been used: European Committee of Social Rights, *Digest of the case law*, Strasbourg December 2006, Council of Europe.

relevant for this contribution, focusing upon the right to have access to health care, are the articles dealing with the right to social security (article 12) and the right to social and medical assistance (article 13). Article 11 of the (Revised) Social Charter is mainly focusing upon the "freedom" aspect (the right to control one's health) and the public health aspect (especially the preventive health care). Hence, we will touch less upon this article for the description of the legal contours of right (to access) health care. The same goes for the articles 3 (Revised) Social Charter, 7 (Revised) Social Charter, 8 Revised Social Charter and 23 Revised Social Charter as they focus respectively upon safe an healthy working conditions for workers, the protection of children against physical and moral hazards (incorporating e.g. the minimum age of admission to employment, the prohibition to have persons younger than 18 years employed in dangerous or unhealthy jobs, etc), the labour protection for pregnant women or mothers who just gave birth to a child and the specific protection of elderly.

The right to (access) health care as a social right

The right to access to health care as a part of the right to health (article 11)
Similarly to the International Covenant on Economic, Social and Cultural Rights, the Social Charter considers the right to health as a prerequisite for the preservation of human dignity. In that way, it complements the articles guaranteeing human dignity, as laid down in the European Convention for the Protection of Human Rights (articles 2 and 3).

Article 11, par. 1 stipulates that *"with a view to ensuring the effective exercise of the right to protection of health, the Parties undertake, [...] to take appropriate measures designed inter alia to remove as far as possible the causes of ill health"*. Although the emphasis has been put upon the obligation to conduct a policy in the field of public health in general and preventive health in particular, one can discern as well from this article the principle that health care should be made accessible to everyone.[16]

Generally, in the view of the European Committee of Social Rights, the right of access to care requires that:
-   The cost of health care should be borne, at least in part, by the community as a whole; conversely it means that part of the costs can be transferred upon the patient (e.g. through the technique of own contributions).
-   However, care must not represent an excessively heavy cost for the individual. Steps must therefore be taken to reduce the financial burden on patients from the most disadvantaged sections of the community.
-   Arrangements for access to care must not lead to unnecessary delays in provisions. Access to treatment must be based on transparent criteria, agreed at national level, taking into account the risk of deterioration in either clinical condition or quality of life.
-   There must be adequate staffing and facilities. [17]

---

[16]   *Ibid*, p. 91.
[17]   *Ibidem*, p.92.

Interesting are the observations made by the European Committee of Social Rights concerning the efficiency of a health care system. A number of key health indicators are applied to see whether a given health care system is functioning appropriately. *"The Committee recalls that the state of mother and child health is a key indicator as to whether the health system as a whole is functioning well or not in a given country. A particular high infant mortality rate (in casu 18,6 deaths per 1000 live births) raises the problem of conformity with article 11 of the Charter".* [18] And in the same line: *"[t]he Committee stresses that maternal mortality is an avoidable risk that States Parties must deal with if they are to comply with Article 11 of the Charter. Considering in particular the level of development of the French health care system, it holds that all necessary measures should be taken in order to achieve the risk as near as possible to zero".*[19] Concerning the coverage of the health care system, the Committee has provided some other interesting interpretations as well: *"[t]he health care system must offer care accessible to the largest number, which presupposes sufficiently broad coverage of the population, and at the best universal coverage, and "the bearing by collective bodies of all, or at least a substantial part, of the cost of health care services".*[20] As we will see later on, this interpretation of article 11 goes much further than the minimum conditions for coverage stipulated within the framework of article 12 of the Social Charter (formulating the right to social security). More particularly in relation to waiting lists, the following was decided: *"The Committee is aware that the fact that waiting lists are getting longer has more than one cause and may in particular reflect growing demand and expectations of the population. However, the Committee notes that the duration of waiting times is long in absolute terms, that the situation is not improving and that simultaneously the number of hospital beds continues to decrease. It considers that on the basis of these data, the organisation of health care in the United Kingdom is manifestly not adapted to ensure the right to health for everyone."* [21]

Equal access should be provided, but in assessing whether the right to protection of health can be effectively exercised, the Committee pays particular attention to the situation of disadvantaged and vulnerable groups. Hence article 11 gives further concrete body to article E (which formulates the general non-discrimination principle for the application of the (Revised) Social Charter). [22] Indeed, article E stipulates that *"[t]he enjoyment of the rights set forth in the Charter shall be secured without discrimination on any ground such as race, colour, sex, language, religion, political or other opinion, national extraction or social origin, health, association with a national minority, birth or other status"*. Access to health care can thus not be (directly or indirectly) conditioned on the basis of one or more of these criteria. At the same time the Committee calls for a specific protection for the weakest groups in society. Here we come close to the interpretation of article 12 of the International Covenant on Economic, Social

---

[18]   *Ibid*, p. 232, Conclusions Romania.
[19]   *Ibidem*, Conclusions France.
[20]   *Ibidem*, 233, Conclusion Cyprus.
[21]   *Ibidem*, 233, Conclusions UK.
[22]   Article E draws inspiration from article 14 of the European Convention on Human Rights. It takes up the principle of non-discrimination which was set forth in the Preamble of the 1961 Social Charter, and incorporates it into the main body of the revised Charter.

and Cultural Rights by its Committee. For persons without sufficient resources a proper provision has been included in article 13 of the European Social Charter (right to medical and social assistance).

The right to access to health care as a part of the right to social security (article 12)

The general principle of access to health care is developed more in detail in article 12 of the (Revised) Social Charter, viz. with regard to the structural organisation of a social health care system. In other words article 12 sets conditions for shaping a health system that grants on the basis of solidarity, large parts of its population access to health services and facilities. Article 12 par. 1 guarantees the right to social security. It stipulates: *"[w]ith a view to ensuring the effective exercise of the right to social security, the parties undertake to establish or maintain a system of social security"*. Within the meaning of article 12 par. 1 a social security system should comply with the following general criteria. Firstly the social security system should cover the traditional risks, among which we find, next to the risks of unemployment, old age, sickness and family,[23] the risks related to health care (medical care, employment injury and maternity). Secondly, this right to social security is to be guaranteed to workers (including self-employed people) and their dependants. A significant part of the population should be covered for health related risks; for employment injuries a significant part of the working population is to be covered.

Along with its mere existence, the social security system should guarantee an effective right to social security with respect to the benefits provided under every branch. This means that benefits of a certain level are to be guaranteed. As specified in paragraph 2 of article 12, the signatory parties undertake to maintain a social security system at a satisfactory level, which is at least equal to that necessary for the ratification of the "minimum standards" conventions (i.e. the ILO Convention 102 to which article 12 of the Social Charter is referring; the European Code of Social Security to which the revised Charter refers).[24] In that way, the minimum standards of the Code and the ILO Convention 102 give more body to the general right to social security as stipulated in the Social Charter. Both conventions do indeed set minimum standards for the traditional social risks, including health care. When a party to the Social Charter fulfils the minimum standards of the ILO Conventions 102 and the Code, that state is considered to be in line with article 12, par. 2. If a state is not party to those conventions, it has to show that its social security system is at least of the level of the minimum standards as laid down in Convention 102 and the Code. Although these standards will be explained further on with regard to the health care related risks, we can already mention that states do not

---

23   This list does not mention invalidity and survivors' benefits; only if they exist these benefits should be taken in to account. See *Digest of the case law*, p. 92.

24   For the income replacement benefits an alternative condition is formulated by the European Committee of Social Rights, referring to 50% of the median equivalised income. This reference criterion is however not applicable upon health care benefits which are of a different nature (i.e. cost compensating). See *Digest of the case law*, 2006, p. 98.

have to fulfil the minimum requirements of all nine social risks. For the ILO-Convention 102 it suffices to have fulfilled the requirements of at least three contingencies; for the Code one needs to be in line with the standards of at least six risks. However, for the application of the Code, health care counts for two, and old age for three. Apparently, organising a health care system along the lines of the "minimum standards" instruments is given more weight than e.g. the introduction of a decent family benefit scheme.

Furthermore, the social security system in place should only be changed for the better. In accordance with article 12 par. 3 the states should progressively raise the social security system to a higher level. Yet, important in the field of health care, measures to consolidate public finances may be considered as a means to contribute to the maintenance and sustainability of the social security system. It is this possible that health care entitlements are levelled down in order to safeguard in the end the financial sustainability of the whole system. Still, any modification should not be of the kind that it undermines the effective social protection. Moreover, it should not transform the social insurance scheme into a mere basic social assistance system.[25]

The right to access to health care as a part of the right to social and medical assistance (article 13)

The right to access to health care should also be guaranteed to people without adequate resources. Article 13 stipulates in its first paragraph that "*[w]ith a view to ensuring the effective exercise of the right to social and medical assistance, the Parties undertake to ensure that any person who is without adequate resources [...] be granted adequate assistance, and, in case of sickness, the care necessitated by his condition*". The provision of assistance should go further than the moral duty of charity; the scheme should grant individuals in need a subjective right to an assistance benefit. Contracting parties are not merely empowered to grant assistance as they think fit; they are under an obligation which they may be called on in court to honour.[26] Consequently the right to (medical) assistance must constitute an individual right laid down in law and be supported by an effective right of appeal.[27]

Article 13 does not say which form social assistance should take. However, regarding medical assistance, everyone who lacks adequate resources must in the event of sickness receive the care necessitated by his or her condition free of charge. Medical assistance in this regard refers to free or subsidised health care or to grants that enable persons to pay for the care required by their condition. The Committee has not determined so far what exactly the assistance must cover, nor whether it is limited to treating illness. In the interpretation statements we can read that "*it is not within its competence to define the nature of the care required, or the place where it is given*".[28] However, the seriousness of the

---

25 *Ibid*, p. 100.
26 *Ibid*, p. 104.
27 See for e.g. for a country violating this right of appeal in the case of social assistance: European Committee of Social Rights, *Digest of the case law*, comment article 13, p. 251.
28 *Ibid*, p. 104; and -, Conclusions XIII-4, Statement of interpretation on Article 13, p. 54-57.

illness cannot be a factor in refusing to grant medical assistance.[29] Furthermore, as is generally stipulated for all assistance benefits, the level must be "appropriate", i.e. making it possible to live a decent life and to cover one's basic needs. It must be provided for as long as the situation of need persists. It is not clear whether this means that the entitlement conditions can be more limited when compared to persons who are socially insured for health care. Can a state e.g. limit the health accessibility for needy persons to a basic package that is less extensive than the general health insurance package? One should refer here to a previous interpretation comment made by the Committee on article 12, stating that the right to social security (and hence the right to health care access) should address especially the weakest segments of the population. Does this then preclude states from providing a less developed health care scheme for persons on assistance? A specific protection for needy persons does in my view not mean that the same protection should be guaranteed as the one foreseen in the social health care scheme. It should be in the first place adapted to their specific needs. This could e.g. mean that in some cases even a more extensive entitlement is being provided (taking into account the needy situation), but that it is at the same time much more conditioned (to preclude e.g. abusive behaviour or in order to monitor integrative behaviour). The latter could also mean that a covered package of another kind is being granted for persons on assistance.

As to the personal scope, reference is also made to the foreigners staying on the territory of the signatory state. To this purpose article 13 should be co-read with the Appendix to the Charter, dealing with the application of the listed social rights upon foreigners: *"foreigners who are nationals of Contracting Parties and are lawfully resident or working regularly in the territory of another Party and lack adequate resources must enjoy an individual right to appropriate assistance on an equal footing with nationals"*. The fourth paragraph of article 13 does confirm this principle but at the same time goes one little step further, at least following the rather broad interpretation by the Committee: all foreigners staying on the territory should have access to at least urgent social and medical assistance.[30] The scope of this paragraph goes thus further on two particular points. First of all it is sufficient that the person is staying on the territory; residence is not required. Secondly, it is covering all foreigners and not only the nationals coming from another signatory state. In the case FIDH v. France, based upon a collective compliant (see below) the Committee even decided that under certain conditions health treatment should be guaranteed to illegal migrants.[31] The material scope is however more restrictive. States are required to provide for those persons care sufficient to cope with an immediate state of need (including accommodation, food, emergency and clothing). The provision of urgent medical care must be individually governed, looking at the particular state of health of the person concerned.[32] Reports are required to indi-

---

29   *Ibidem.*
30   *Ibidem*, p. 110.
31   European Committee of Social Rights, 5 September 2003, Collective complaint from FIDH v. France.
32   As such: *Digest of the case law, ibid*, p. 110.. See as well the case FIDH v. France (decision of 5 September 2003), where it has been decided that the right to health care for children of ille-

cate, especially for the states in which health care is not free of charge, how many persons receive medical assistance in each reference period and to provide information on the amount of funds devoted to medical assistance and the percentage of the social welfare expenses they represent.33 In other words the level of the medical assistance is not controlled on an individual basis but on the basis of the overall sums spent on it. How the evaluation is concretely carried out, is not specified though.

As to the undertaken obligations and legal enforceability

Compliance with the (Revised) Social Charter is monitored through a system of supervision requiring each contracting state to submit a report every two years to an independent committee of experts (i.e. the *European Committee for Social Rights*). This Committee's conclusions are submitted for examination to a Governmental Committee, composed of representatives of the governments of the signatory parties with observers from European federations of employers and trade unions.34 The Parliamentary assembly has the right to examine and comment the conclusions as well, and the Committee of Ministers has the power to make recommendations to a member state which it considers to be in breach with the obligations of the Charter. If the Committee of Ministers decides that a state has not fulfilled its undertakings, it invites that state to take the necessary measures and to ensure compliance. Yet real sanctions can hardly be taken. Interestingly, the Governmental Committee is much more restrictive in its interpretations of the Social Charter than the European Committee of Social Rights. The latter goes indeed rather far in its interpretations of the social rights listed in the Charter; its statements sometimes do not find a clear linkage with the rights described. It is indeed questionable whether the Committee has been empowered to develop the legal contours and obligations of the Charter. However, the fact that the Governmental Committee is much more sober in its interpretation, and is thus declining to a large extent the rather far reaching conclusions of the Committee of Social Right, shows that the interpretation powers of the latter Committee are being undermined.

The provisions of the Social Charter are stipulated too generally to be self-executing. Especially with regard to the articles on social security (commented upon above) there is no concrete evidence that national courts would apply them directly in a case.35 Finally, it should be mentioned that the European

---

gal immigrants and unaccompanied minors is restricted to necessary care, whereas adult illegal immigrants have only a right to emergency medical care, included in life-threatening situations.

33   *Ibidem.*

34   Some states also accepted the additional Protocol to the Social Charter providing a system of collective complaints (9 November 1995). On the basis of this procedure recognised trade unions, employers' organisation or NGO's can launch a complaint about a state that is not fulfilling its obligations of the Charter, directly to the European Committee of Social Rights. The Committee can then transfer its assessment of the complaint directly to the Committee of Ministers.

35   By contrast, the articles related to the right to organise (article 5) and the right to take collective action, including the right to strike (article 6) are applied sometimes directly in national

Court of Human Rights does not have the competency to interpret the provisions of the (Revised) Social Charter. However this did not withhold the Court to refer in its case law indirectly to the interpretation comments of European Social Charter made by the European Committee of Social Rights. An example of such a cross-reference to the European Social Charter can e.g. be found in the case *Poirrez*, in which the Court had to assess whether the nationality condition in French legislation in order to become entitled to a disabled adult's allowance, was in contravention with article 14 of the European Convention (non-discrimination) taken in conjunction with article 1 of Protocol No. 1 (protection of property rights). [36],[37] Nevertheless, a direct interpretation or assessment of the European (Revised Social Charter) is not within the competency of the European Court. Hence one cannot but conclude that the legal effect of this social right instrument seems of a rather limited nature.

Some preliminary conclusions regarding the social rights instruments

Although different weights are being given to the concrete legal implications, when it comes down to the right to access to health care, both fundamental rights instruments mainly impose upon the signatory states a general obligation to have a (social health) system in place which guarantees in a non-discriminatory and equitable manner access to health care to their populations.

The provisions mainly address the states and are formulated rather generally. The Covenant especially stresses the right to access to the health determinants (food, nutrition, etc); the Social Charter mainly focuses upon the need to have a proper social protection system in place. States have to show that they undertake the necessary efforts to reach the objectives set. When obligations are defined more concretely (e.g. with regard to the core obligations or with regard to the non-discriminatory provision of health care), one cannot but conclude that there is no intention to grant the provisions direct applicability. Specific supervisory procedures exist on the basis of which the efforts undertaken by the states are assessed.

As to the contents (how should the system be shaped?) the provisions remain rather vague or, as for instance is the case for the Social Charter, do refer to other instruments which set standards for the matter concerned. Interesting here is the role of Committees that supervise the reports sent in by the signatory states and hence interpret the provisions of the Covenant and Charter. Here, more concrete interpretation guidelines are often to be found on how the right to access to health care should look like. States should e.g. not act in a discriminatory manner and should in principle offer a universal coverage but

---

case law: see in this respect: K. Kapuy, D. Pieters and B. Zaglmayer, *Social security cases in Europe: The European Court of Human Rights*, (Antwerpen: Intersentia, 2007), p.3.

36   ECHR, 30 September 2003, *Koua Poirrez v. France*, Appl. 40892/98.

37   See consideration No. 29, where the Social Charter and especially its interpretation by the Committee is being listed as "relevant domestic law" to be taken into consideration: European Committee of Social Rights, Conclusions regarding France's compliance with Article 12 of the Charter (15th report, reference period 1997-1998; Conclusions XV-1, Volume 1, p. 277, Council of Europe editions, 2000):

with special attention for the weakest parts of the population. This means among others that cost sharing should be used in a limited manner for these groups. The health care system providing to the population access to health care should be of public nature and states should prevent that private insurances take too big a portion in its organisation. Other interpretation rules refer to waiting lists or to the effectivity of the system, which is being measured on the basis of health outputs.

Although these interpretation guidelines give some more concrete guidance with regard to accessibility, they risk undermining the fundamental rights in the long run. Many of them go far beyond what is being stipulated in the fundamental rights' instruments. They do not interpret a concept or sentence but simply add new provisions or rules to the fundamental rights' instruments. The committees are however not empowered to do so and consequently their authority is at peril. Signatory parties reject their interpretations, especially when they do not originate in the text of the document. The fact that e.g. the Governmental Committee is hardly taking over the supervisory conclusions of the Committee of Social Rights for the purpose of the application of the European Social Charter is clearly evidence to this. Also the Committee interpreting the International Covenant on Economic, Social and Cultural Rights went apparently too far in its interpretation competence. In its growing "jurisprudence", it had to make clear again what the right to access to health care was about in essence, when formulating the core obligations in Comment No. 3. It had to make sure that at least those obligations were being followed up, thus undermining itself indirectly the pursuance of the other obligations which it had discerned in the text of the Covenant.

2. The right to health care as being defined by "minimum-standards" instruments

Introducing the minimum standards as being defined by ILO Convention 102 and the European Code of Social Security

In 1952 the International Labour Organisation proposed for signature to its member states an instrument containing minimum standards in the field of social security: the ILO Convention No. 102.[38] Technically speaking, the Convention lists the major nine contingencies which, at least at the period of launching the Convention, were considered to be the traditional social security risks. Concretely speaking, standards were put in place for the following contingencies: medical care, sickness, unemployment, old-age, employment injury, family burden, maternity, invalidity and survivorship. Regarding health care, the standards developed for medical care, maternity and employment injuries are of relevance. The latter two contingencies contain indeed provisions in relation to both the cash benefits (income replacement) and the benefits in kind (medical care), the latter being slightly of a more demanding nature than the standards found in the general part related to medical care.

---

[38]   Since its entry into force the Convention has been ratified by 41 ILO Member States.

The European Code of Social Security (1964), the "minimum standards" instrument which the Council of Europe puts forward for its member states, has been modelled very closely on the ILO-Convention.[39] The Code repeats the ILO-provisions with some minor modifications. It is more demanding though, as it imposes the signatory states to be in line with at least six contingencies, whereas the ILO-Convention 102 only asks for minimum three. Next to that, an additional Protocol[40] to the Code has been drafted.[41] This protocol requires higher standards to be respected. In a way, the Protocol was designed for those states within Europe that already had a system place that easily outreached the standards of the ILO Convention 102.

Taking into account the rather huge economic and social differences between the member states, the standard conventions are set up in rather flexible manner this in order not to be totally out of reach for the poorer countries, but to retain at the same time some relevance for the more developed systems. This explains e.g. the partial acceptance of the minimum standards, i.e. at least for some but not for all contingencies. Furthermore the Conventions are formulated in such a way that they set only "minimum" standards. This means that by definition states can do better, if they wish to. Moreover, many provisions are designed in a so-called relative way. Standards assessing e.g. the level of the benefits are put in relation to the national realities, i.e. national average wages. An old age benefit should e.g. be at least of the level of 40% of what a standard beneficiary is earning in the country.[42] Applied to health care, the level of the own contributions that states may impose upon the patients covered, is often set as a maximum percentage of the national cost of a given health care product.[43] Regardless of some exceptions, absolute harmonisation standards, such as e.g. a universal minimum benefit of a given level, are not applied.

Besides the general provisions, which contain among others the definitions of some concepts, the obligations to be taken up by the signatory states, standards on the administration and financing, and the grounds on the basis of which states are allowed to suspend benefits, the different contingencies have been structured in a similar way. First of all, the minimum number of persons to be covered for the given contingency is defined ("personal scope" of the schemes). Subsequently, we find provisions about waiting periods, qualifying periods, the duration of payment of benefits, and other conditions governing the access to the benefits ("material scope" of the schemes); finally, provisions can be found that are designed to test the level of the benefits. To that purpose a reference income is defined in a separate part (part XI: articles 65, 66 and

---

39 Signed by 25 member states to the Council of Europe, followed by 20 ratifications.
40 Signed by 13 states; ratified by the following 7: Belgium, Germany, Luxembourg, the Netherlands, Norway, Portugal and Sweden.
41 The Revised Code (6 November 1991) which modernised the provisions of the standard Code will not be discussed here, since it has not been ratified by any of the member states of the Council of Europe so far.
42 To that purpose, rules have been established to single out the standard beneficiary in the signatory state: see articles 65, 66 and 67.
43 As it is being done in the Protocol to the European Code of Social Security; see further below.

67) against which the benefits are set off. The main idea is that each benefit should reach a minimum income replacement level (see schedule to part XI, to be found at the end of the ILO Convention and Code). The latter is however not of relevance for medical care, as it is focusing upon the income replacement benefits.

Subsequently, we will describe the provisions of the ILO-Convention 102 and the Code that are relevant to our topic ("access to health care"); the description is done simultaneously because of the similarities between both instruments. The standards mainly address the aspect of access to health care. In other words they mainly focus upon the health care scheme as a part of social security. First, an overview is given of the health standards, for each (relevant) contingency: the standards are presented as they can be found in the general chapter on health care. Then we will focus upon the specific health care standards as they are stipulated in the chapters on maternity and employment injuries. Finally we will look at some more advanced standards as being laid down in the Protocol to the Code and the ILO-Conventions, which are specifically designed per contingency.

Minimum standards for access to health care

Standards formulated in the general health care section
The section on health care starts with a definition. In article 7, health care is delineated as the *provision of benefits in respect of a condition requiring medical care of a preventive or curative nature*. Each state, having accepted this part of the convention, must secure for its covered citizens access to health care services, both preventive and curative. Health care comprises any morbid condition, whatever its cause, including pregnancy, confinement and their consequences. As to what should be understood by "morbid condition", the ILO gives some further guidance: a condition may be considered as morbid as long as it necessitates medical care. Generally speaking, medical care has to be afforded with a view to maintaining, restoring or improving the health of the persons protected and their ability to work and to attend to their personal needs.[44] Hence, the definition remains rather general and does not give, except for the reference to preventive care, much concrete guidance as to what kind of health care services should be provided.

To obtain more information on what kind of health care services are to be offered, we need to look at article 10 (material scope). Concretely the persons protected must enjoy the following health care benefits: general practitioner care, including domiciliary visits; specialist care; essential pharmaceutical supplies as prescribed by medical or other qualified practitioners; and hospitalization where necessary. In the case of pregnancy and confinement it is clearly outlined that pre-natal, confinement and post-natal care, either by medical practitioners or by qualified midwives, is to be guaranteed, and where necessary, hospitalisation. Although this description gives us some further direction in the sense that the health care systems should cover general care, specialised care provided in hospitals, essential pharmaceuticals and maternity

---

44   ILO, *Standards for the XXIst Century*, Geneva, 2005, p. 17.

care, it all remains quite vague. Consequently, the fulfilment of this (part of) the material scope does not pose big problems to most of the states. Important is that a state is able to indicate that the general categories of health care services – outpatient care, inpatient care, maternity care and a list of covered pharmaceutical supplies – are available to its covered population. Next to that we can read in article 10 that the (essential) pharmaceuticals are only to be covered by the system when prescribed by health professionals. Furthermore, covered hospitalisation cost does not include maintenance, nursing and other auxiliary services; we are talking strictly about the health care costs.45 The Committee of Experts, interpreting both the ILO-Convention 102 and the Code (see below under legal enforceability), does not give much additional information in this respect, nor does the interpretatory report to ILO Convention and Code.

Also the provision dealing with the level of the own contributions – the part of the covered health care that the patient has to pay directly to the health care provider - is rather generally stipulated. Article 10, paragraph 2 rules that national legislation may require beneficiaries to share in the cost of any medical care received (except for medical care granted in the situation of maternity). The amount of the co-payment that is allowed, is however not specified. The article merely states that "*the rules concerning such cost-sharing shall be so designed as to avoid hardship*". The Protocol to the Code gives some more concrete indications here (see below under advanced standards). However, in the general standard-setting instruments the criterion "to avoid hardship" is rather difficult to assess. In general, the Committee of Experts, supervising the application of these instruments, will pay more attention to categories of people who are chronically sick or to persons with restricted means, as these categories are of the ones that risk facing hardship. A problematic issue is how one should measure the concrete amounts of own contributions. Does one add together all the different amounts in a cross-benefits way and hence measures the total amount of own contributions in general? Or does one, as e.g. applied in the Protocol to the Code, consider the different categories of care separately? Care services differ indeed extensively from each other what costs are concerned: 25% own contributions for a long hospitalisation does mean in absolute terms something different than 33% to be paid by a patient for a routine dental care. So far, no clear answer can be given with regard to this question. The Committee of Experts is rather inclined to extrapolate the technique used in the Protocol to the general standards.

As the list of the medical services to be covered is not being precise – it works with general health categories – the provisions with regard to the own contributions have above all a perverse effect: a state is better to have a specific treatment not covered at all than to have it covered only partially. In the last case, it risks to come into conflict with article 10, as the relatively high cost charged to the patients may be considered to push them into hardship. In the first case – the health service is not covered at all – there is no conflict with the

---

45   See in this respect E. Imesch, "The European Code of Social Security: General structure and those parts of the Code not relating to pensions", in Council of Europe (ed.), *Compilation social security training course*, 1998, (63), 68.

standards, as long as other general or specialist medical services are foreseen in the health system.

Another question is related to the personal scope: which persons should minimally be covered? Article 9 dealing with the personal scope, is again formulated in a rather flexible way: *"[t]he persons protected shall comprise:*

a. *prescribed classes of employees, constituting not less than 50 per cent of all employees, and also their wives and children; or*
b. *prescribed classes of the economically active population, constituting not less than 20 per cent of all residents, and also their wives and children; or*
c. *prescribed classes of residents, constituting not less than 50 per cent of all residents."*

The flexibility in the description has to do with the different health care systems that are in place in Europe, if not to say in the rest of the world. If only (some categories of) employees are covered, then at least 50% of all employees should be covered, including their dependent family members. In case the health care system covers more than only employees, the minimum standards depend upon the kind of system in place: if the system is of a professional kind – covering economically active people, such as employees, self-employed persons and civil servants – the state has to make sure that eventually 20% of the residents are covered; if the system is of a universal kind at least 50% of the residents should be covered. In other words, universal health systems can be targeted, in the sense that they cover only persons with limited means. The minimum percentages seem rather low: which health care system would not be able to fulfil such criteria, even in less industrialised countries? Still, we have to take into account that some states face serious problems because large segments of their economically active population are working in the hidden economy. This is specially a problem for professional health systems, as these "hidden" workers, in my opinion, should be taken into account in the respective reference categories of the residents (20% to be covered) and of the employees (50% to be covered). As they are not in a formal work situation, they will not be socially insured for health care. Hence when there is a large hidden economy, it will become difficult to reach the standards.

Entitlement to benefits may be made subject to the completion of a certain qualifying period, the period of which is considered necessary to preclude abuse (article 11). The qualification period may consist of a period of contribution, a period of employment, a period of residence or a combination of those. Still, no other criteria are given to determine how long such period may take concretely. From the reports of the Committee of Experts, in general qualifying periods of 6 months are being tolerated. Once entitled, the medical benefits must be provided throughout the contingency, with the exception that the duration of the benefit may be limited to 26 weeks in each case. Such a limitation is not allowed in the case of pregnancy and confinement and their consequences. Next to that medical care may not be suspended while the beneficiary continues to receive sickness benefit, and national legislation must extend the duration of the benefit in the case of diseases recognised as entailing prolonged care.

Specific health standards in relation to maternity and employment injuries

In case the morbid condition is due to an employment injury (labour accident or professional disease) higher standards are imposed (see Part VI). In such cases, medical care shall comprise: general practitioner and specialist in-patient care and specialist out-patient care (including domiciliary visiting), dental care, nursing care at home or in hospital (or other medical institutions), maintenance in hospital, convalescent homes, sanatoria or other medical institutions, pharmaceutical and surgical supplies, including prosthetic appliances and care provided by paramedics as may at any time be legally recognised (possibly under supervision of a medical or dental practitioner). The list of services to be covered is thus described more extensively. The provisions about the material scope are more restrictive: no qualifying period is allowed, nor is the application of own contributions. Furthermore, the benefit should be granted during the contingency (no time limit). As to the personal scope, the standards are formulated in terms of employees (at least 50% to be covered). Other (professional) groups can thus be left uncovered.

Also in relation to medical care granted under the maternity contingency (part VIII), the standards repeat to a large extent the provisions about medical care under the general Part. Yet, the application of own contributions is not allowed and the medical benefit must be provided throughout the contingency and may not be granted for less than 12 weeks. In case of complications, the period should be extended as well. Finally regarding the personal scope, 50% of the employees should be covered for this contingency. Of those covered employees all women should be given access to maternity benefits, meaning all working women and, with regard to the medical benefits, also all the women who are depending upon a covered employee.

Advanced standards

As mentioned before, some instruments contain higher standards. In the framework of the Council of Europe these additional standards have been incorporated into the Protocol to the Code. Article 9 demands a higher number of protected persons: respectively 80% of all employees (including their dependant family members), 30% of all residents and 65% of all residents, depending whether one works with a health care scheme for employees, professionally active persons or a universal health care scheme. As to the guaranteed services, the following have to be offered as well: all necessary hospital care (thus including cure services, nursing care and auxiliary services), all necessary (and thus not only essential) pharmaceuticals of a non-proprietary nature, and all essential proprietary preparations, conservative dental care for the children, and all pharmaceutical supplies in case of maternity care. (article 10, par. 1). Furthermore medical care must be granted throughout the contingency, except that hospital care may be limited to 52 weeks in each case or to 78 weeks in any consecutive period of three years. In the second paragraph of article 10, concrete maximum shares are stated in case one makes use of cost-sharing.

These are 25% for care provided by general practitioners, specialists outside the hospital and for hospital care; for pharmaceutical supplies 25% on the average, so some products can be charged more if for others lower own contributions are asked; and for conservative dental care 33,3%. In case of maternity care, only own contributions (amounting in average to maximum 25%) can be charged for pharmaceutical supplies.

Taking into account the assessments of the Expert Committee, especially this more concretely defined provision causes numerous problems to the ratifying states. A country like Belgium e.g., which has increasingly introduced cost sharing measures over the last decades in order to keep the rising health care budget under control, continuously struggles to convince the supervisory instances that it keeps the own contributions within the tolerated levels, even after having invested a lot in the introduction of maximum caps for health care costs (own contributions) for the chronically ill and the persons with moderate and low means.[46] The fact that those measures are designed in a rather complicated and non-transparent manner does not help the cause. Interesting to note is that already for 20 years now, Belgium has been invited by the Committee of Ministers to reduce its too high cost sharing levels.[47] Apparently, the supervisory bodies show the necessary patience in case of contravention (see more about this below under the heading legal enforceability).

Within the framework of the ILO, more advanced standards with regard to health care are to be found in the so-called "single contingency" instruments that set standards for one particular risk: Convention No. 130 (medical care), Convention No. 121 (employment injury) and Convention No. 183 (maternity). Interesting to note is that some countries (such as e.g. Finland) preferred to accept these conventions, rather than to accede to the general Convention No. 102.

Compared to the "mother convention", the standards about the personal scope are defined more broadly. Convention No. 130 talks e.g. about covering all employees, including apprentices, and their dependants in case of health care systems covering employees, and about 75% of all economically active people (including their dependants) when such kind of system is in place. If health care is granted through a universal system it should cover at least 75% of the residents. Conventions No. 121 (employment injury) and No. 183 (maternity) demand a full coverage of all employees, respectively dependant wives of such employees.

As to the services, Convention No. 130 (medical care) additionally provides the coverage of dental care and medical rehabilitation, including the supply, maintenance and renewal of prosthetic and orthopaedic appliances. Convention No. 121 (employment injury) demands that in case of serious labour acci-

---

46   See e.g. Council of Europe, Resolution CSS(2006), 1 on the application of the European Code of Social Security and its Protocol by Belgium, Adopted by the Committee of Ministers on 6 September 2006.

47   See for other examples of legislation conflicting with the medical care standards: A. Otting, "The supervisory machinery for implementation of the Code: Introduction, working methods and practical examples" in Council of Europe (ed.), Social security training course on the study of standard-setting instruments of the Council of Europe in the field of social security; Compendium of working documents, 2000, (113), p. 121-123.

dents, emergency treatment services should be made available at the place of work; for slight-injuries not entailing a discontinuation of work, follow-up treatments should be guaranteed as well to the patient. Convention No. 183 goes much further in the description of the guaranteed maternity services. For instance much attention is given to rights for breastfeeding mothers, with regard to health protection, employment protection and non-discriminatory behaviour from the side of the employer.

As to the duration of the medical services, more stringent provisions have been included as well. Convention No. 130 (medical care) starts from the principle that medical care is to be granted as long as the contingency takes. A limitation to 26 weeks is only authorized where the beneficiary ceases to belong to the categories of protected persons and the sickness started while the beneficiary still belonged to such categories. As to the charging of own contributions, Convention No. 130 stipulates that, next to avoiding hardship, cost-sharing should not prejudice the effectiveness of medical and social protection.

As to the undertaken obligations and legal enforceability

The compliance of the signatory states with the minimum standard instruments of the Council of Europe (i.e. the Code) and of the International Labour Organisation is supervised on the basis of a specific procedure. Once the minimum standard convention has been ratified, the member states are required to submit regular reports on their implementation and application. These reports follow a standard framework that reflects the relevant obligations of the ILO-Convention 102/Code and at the same time asks for concrete proof (statistical material) indicating that the minimum standards are being applied in practice. The reports are then examined by a *Committee of Experts on the Application of Conventions and Recommendations*, constituted within the framework of the ILO. The committee consists of independent experts chosen by the Governing Body of the ILO. Nevertheless, it also supervises the minimum standards promulgated by the Council of Europe, as the provisions of the European Code of Social Security are similar to the ones of the ILO Convention 102. The Committee's decisions are not only based on the government reports, but also on other available information such as observations supplied by trade unions and employers' associations. With regard to the ILO-Conventions, the report of the Committee is then submitted to the International Labour Conference. Within a specific *Conference Committee on the Application of Conventions and Recommendations*, the representatives of governments, workers and employers – with equal voting rights - discuss the national reports of the Committee of Experts and eventually make a proposal for a final assessment report that is consequently adopted by the International Labour Conference. For the application of the Code, the Committee of Experts is forwarding the reports to the *European Committee of Experts on Standard-Setting Instruments*, a body composed of senior officials from the social security ministries of each of the member states to the Council of Europe. The committee is empowered to adopt and transmit its conclusions to the Committee of Ministers (of the Council Europe). The Committee of Ministers is to decide, with a two-thirds majority, whether each contracting Party has fulfilled its obligations under the Code. If it comes to a negative conclusion, it invites the state concerned to take the measures necessary to ensure that the obligations are met again. The supervisory procedures in place are thus of a rather "diplomatic" nature. The idea is not to impose real sanctions on a defaulting state but to establish a dialogue in order to help to overcome its non-compliance with the set standards.[48]

Taking into account the nature of the minimum standards, most of the provisions are not concrete nor detailed enough stipulated in order to be self-executing. Still, there are some examples, although very exceptional, of national courts applying directly some of the provisions of these minimum standard conventions. Best known in this respect are two rulings of the Swiss Federal Insurance Court of 25 August 1993 and 21 February 1994[49], in which the Court held that the Code is not only binding for the contracting parties, i.e. the governments, but that its provisions may be self-executing in so far as they are sufficiently clear and precise and leave no element of political evaluation or discretion. Consequently the Court ruled that the provision in case was prevailing over the national legislation. The cases dealt with article 68 of the Code, which sets standards for the suspension of the benefits payment, more concretely by enumerating the possible grounds of suspension. The Swiss Federal Insurance Tribunal considered that article 68, sub f of the Code, which authorises the suspension of benefits only when the contingency has been caused by wilful misconduct on the part of the person concerned is directly applicable and prevails over the corresponding provisions of national law to the extent that the provisions of the federal law allowed (at that moment) the reduction of benefits in the event of serious misconduct committed through negligence. In these cases, the insured workers that were concerned, were being reproached gross negligence at the moment of the labour accident occurred.

More recently, the *Centrale Raad van Beroep* (Central Appeals Court) in the Netherlands made an interesting judgement applying directly some provisions of the Code related to the contingency of employment injury (art. 31, 32 and 34).[50] The case dealt with a worker who had become incapable to work as a result of a work accident. As a result of the accident, the man was confronted with serious psychiatric problems and was permanently residing in a psychiatric clinic for medical treatment. According to the relevant Dutch legislation (i.e. the Dutch law for long-term special medical care –AWBZ), the person was obliged to pay a monthly contribution for this treatment. In the procedure, the question was asked if that Dutch law provision was in accordance with the European Code. The articles 31, 32 and 34 of the Code (Part VI) rule that each member state shall secure, in case of a morbid condition due to a work related injury, that the benefit for the worker shall be medical care, which comprises general practitioner and specialist in-patient care and out-patient care. More-

---

48 See for a more extensive description of the procedures at stake, including some examples showing that states do take efforts to come in line again with the standard instrument, in case of non-compliance: Otting, *Ibid*, p. 134-136.
49 *Ibid*, p. 117-123
50 Centrale Raad van Beroep, 8 September 2006, as being commented by Th. de Vries, "Problems with the (interpretation of) Conventions from a judge's point of view", in F. Pennings (ed.), *The Role and Interpretation of International Social Security Conventions*, to be published.

over, it is not allowed to charge own contributions (see also above). The Central Appeals Court judged that the articles 32 and 34 give concrete rules for the persons protected to claim medical care. Hence, the Court considered these articles to be of a self-executing nature. Consequently, the Court judged that the contribution the worker had to pay for his medical care was in violation of the articles 32 and 34 of the Code. As support for its interpretation, the Court also refers to a resolution of the Ministers of the Council of Europe in which is written: "*Since the code makes no provision for sharing by insured persons in the cost of medical care in cases of occupational injury, it should be made clear [that a specific law about contributions] applies in practice only to the victims of non-occupational accidents*".[51]

Some preliminary conclusions regarding the "minimum-standards" instruments

One can conclude about the minimum standards in the field of health care, that they are somewhat outdated and too generally stipulated. Furthermore, one can doubt whether they eventually have a concrete effect upon our social health care systems. Taking into account the listed health services that are to be covered, one can wonder whether the standards still reflect modern health care thinking, which is focusing increasingly upon integrated health care. Probably more troublesome is the very general stipulation of the services in care categories. One can deduct from the provisions that in general a health care system should cover in general primary care and specialised care, and this both through outpatient services and hospital services. This stipulation has been formulated too generally to have a concrete effect upon the proper organisation of health care systems. As we mentioned before it can, when read together with the provisions about the amount of the chargeable own contributions have perverse effects: states are sometimes better off not to have a service covered than to have it only partially paid for.

Although exceptionally, national courts consider minimum standard provisions to have a self-executing character, and even when it is considered that over time, states have to adapt their system in case it conflicts with the standards, one can but raise questions about the concrete effect of these instruments upon the health care systems.[52] The provisions are not formulated in such a way as to draw concrete obligations from them. Similarly to what we have seen in relation to the Social Charter, the Expert Committee sometimes shows a tendency to create additional and more concrete (sub-)standards; yet in such cases we notice a tendency of rejection by most of signatory states. The Committee indeed does not have the authority to do so, as they are only mandated to supervise and in the best scenario to interpret the standards. Most striking though is that the standards are not translating anymore what is concretely living in most social health care systems: making qualitative health care accessible to all persons, in an economically acceptable manner. A more mod-

---

[51]   *Ibid.*
[52]   As is for instance the case for the concretely defined maximum levels of own contributions in the Protocol to the Code. See also in this respect A. Otting as already quoted.

ern approach would rather suggest standards testing outcomes (quality), accessibility for all and affordability.

3. The right to (access) health care as being conditioned by human rights instruments

Introduction

International and even national (constitutional) courts increasingly start to test social security norms on their compatibility with fundamental human rights. The latter concern e.g. the respect of private and family life, the prohibition of degrading or inhuman treatment (e.g. due to a sudden, non-motivated stop of benefit payment or in case the benefit was too small to live upon in dignity), the protection of property (e.g. when the beneficiary is confronted with a reduction of his/her benefit or when entitlement conditions have fundamentally changed), the prohibition of discrimination (e.g. when non-nationals were not granted access to a benefit), a right to a fair trial (e.g. with regard to social security proceedings), etc.[53] On an international level, especially the European Court of Human Rights developed some groundbreaking case law in this respect. Hence for the following description, we will mainly focus upon the relation between the European Convention for the Protection of Human Rights for social security in general and social health care (access to health care) in particular. In the following, we will first introduce the case law in general and then try to outline its potential consequences for the access to health care.

Case law of the European Court of Human Rights having consequences for social health care in general

Before embarking upon the case law, it may be interesting to introduce shortly the European Convention for the Protection of Human Rights. The Convention was adopted in 1950 by the member states of the Council of Europe, mainly as a reaction and response to the human rights violations during World War II in Europe. The Convention mainly focuses upon "human rights". Economic or social rights, such as the right to social security, the right to social assistance or the right to access to health care, are strictly speaking not part of it. These rights have already been addressed by a proper instrument of the Council of Europe, viz. the European (Revised) Social Charter (see before). Contrary to the European Social Charter, the European Convention on Human Rights does enjoy direct applicability. Under the Convention complaints can be brought against contracting states either by other contracting states or – in case the accused state has accepted it – by individual applicants to Court specifically installed for this purpose (i.e. European Court of Human Rights, having its seat in Strasbourg). Furthermore, as most of the contracting states have

---

53   See for a more elaborated case law review in this respect: D. Pieters and B. Zaglmayer, *Social Security Cases in Europe: National Courts*, (Antwerpen: Intersentia, 2006), and Kapuy, et al., supra note 35.

incorporated the European Convention in their domestic (constitutional) law, national courts tend to apply the guaranteed rights directly in the case law.

Due to the individual complaint mechanism, and the direct effect of the Convention, individuals started bringing social security cases to the Convention's judicial supervision organs. Although originally the European Court of Human Rights was not inclined to apply the articles of the European Convention on the Protection of Human Rights in these cases, this attitude seems to have been changed fundamentally the last couple of years. [54] A general overview of this case law would bring us too far. Yet especially relevant are the cases which test the compatibility of social security provisions with the prohibition of discrimination (article 14), the protection of property (art. 1, Protocol 1 to the Convention) and the prohibition of an inhuman treatment (article 3).

In the case *Gaygusuz*, a Turkish national was denied entitlement for emergency assistance in Austria after expiration of his right to an unemployment benefit, on the ground that he did not have the Austrian nationality.[55] The Court considered that both article 14 (non-discrimination) and article 1 of the 1st protocol (protection of property rights) had been violated. In somewhat unclear wording, the Court observed that *"without it being necessary to rely solely on the link between entitlement to emergency assistance and the obligation to pay taxes"*. The right to Austrian emergency assistance could be considered as a pecuniary right for the purpose of the application of the first Protocol (protection of property). When the persons concerned fulfilled all relevant conditions, except for nationality, it could be decided that Mr. *Gaygusuz* had been discriminated against. Moreover, in relation to the protection of the property rights, his legitimate expectations to become entitled to the emergency assistance had been infringed upon. Emergency assistance was paid as a follow-up benefit to unemployed persons approaching the retirement age, at the moment their unemployment benefit expired, with the main purpose to bridge the periods until retirement. As *Gaygusuz* had duly paid his contributions, he could thus expect to be entitled to such emergency assistance when his right to unemployment expired.

This judgement has been confirmed in a somewhat more articulated way in the cases *Poirrez* and *Stec*.[56, 57] In these two cases, which dealt with non-contributory social assistance benefits, the Court applied a similar line of reasoning as it had previously developed in the *Gaygusuz*-case. However, the Court made clear that the protection of property rights as being defined under article 1 of the 1st Protocol is not to be confined to contributory benefits only. In *Poirrez*, it clearly stipulated that *"the fact that, in the case Gaygusuz, the applicant had paid contributions and was thus entitled to emergency assistance, does not mean, by converse implication, that a non-contributory social benefit...does not give rise to a pecuniary right for the purpose of Article 1 of the 1st Protocol (protection of property)"*. And in the case *Stec*: *"[g]iven the variety of funding methods, and the*

54   *Ibid.*

55   Judgment of 16 September 1996, *Gaygusuz v. Austria*, Appl. No. 17371/90, § 41.

56   Judgment of 12 April 2006, *Stec and others v. UK*, Appl. No. 65731/01, 65900/01.

57   Judgment of 30 September 2003, *Koua Poirrez v. France*, Appl. No. 40892/98.

interlocking nature of benefits under the most welfare systems, it appears increasingly artificial to hold that only benefits financed by contributions to a specific fund fall within the scope of article 1 of Protocol No. 1. Were an individual has an assertable right under domestic law to a welfare benefit, the importance of that interest should also be reflected by holding Article 1 of Protocol No. 1 to be applicable".

These considerations are of major importance for social benefits stemming from the so-called universal non-contributory schemes, to which social health care systems often belong. When socially covered persons have a subjective right to these benefits, they should be attributed in a non-discriminatory manner, respecting at the same that person's legitimate expectations. This could e.g. mean that when states fundamentally change the health packages covered, they need to do so in a manner respecting the legitimate expectations of their covered citizens. However, it remains questionable whether the European Court will range health care benefits under the scope of Protocol 1. Even though the Court clearly extended the application of the Protocol to rights stemming from non-contributory schemes, the latter still deal with benefits in cash (of a pecuniary nature). So far the Court has not yet made the link to the protection of the right to services, to which e.g. medical care services belong. The Court may consider the protection of pecuniary benefits as something different compared to the safeguarding of a given health care package. Is it after all possible to protect the entitlements to a given health care package, which by essence is subject to constant change?

In the case *Larioshina*, the Court had to verify whether article 3 of the Convention (prohibition of torture and inhuman treatment) had not been infringed upon.[58] That judgement may have some relevance for the right to access to health care as well. In the case, the plaintiff was essentially stating that Mrs. *Larioshina's* pension was too low in order for her to live in dignity. Hence, she considered that the Russian state was treating her in an inhuman and degrading manner. Although the Court stated that the Convention as such does not guarantee social rights, such as the right to free medical assistance or the right to claim financial assistance, a complaint about a wholly insufficient amount of pension or other social benefits may, in principle, raise an issue under article 3 of the Convention. More precisely, when a state pays a person in need such a low benefit that it forces that person in to living conditions below a certain minimum level of severity, such may be considered as violating article 3. However, the person concerned has to prove that his/her living conditions have deteriorated beyond the bare minimum of severity, by showing that he/she is suffering damage to his/her physical or mental health. The Court however did not give concrete indications of this critical minimum level of severity. Consequently, the proof that one suffers such physical and/or mental damage will not be so easy to give.

This might be slightly different when applying this case law on the access to health care. A person, disposing of limited means and suffering from a serious, life threatening disease for which the (expensive) treatment is not covered or for which he or she has to pay a high co-payment, may be in a position to show more easily that he/she is suffering such damage and consequently is

---

58   Judgment of 23 April 2002, *Larioshina v Russia*, Appl. No. 56869/00.

being forced into a living situation beyond the tolerated minimum. A state may then need to indicate justifying reasons (e.g. the experimental character of the treatment, the availability of other treatments that are covered and equally effective, etc.) for not having the treatment covered or for not providing refund of the treatment which the patient underwent abroad.

Similarly, a decision to suddenly stop covering a certain treatment may be considered to be contrary to article 3, especially when the decision is taken on a discretionary basis. An indication for this can e.g. be found in the case *D. v UK*, be it that the case dealt with a rather exceptional and extreme situation. The health treatment of an irregular migrant suffering from AIDS was to be stopped due the decision to expel him from the country.[59] The Court found that implementing the decision to expel would expose the applicant, who was already suffering a very weak health, to a real risk of dying under most distressing circumstances, which would amount to inhuman treatment and hence a violation of article 3. The Court noted that the respondent state had assumed responsibility for treating the applicant's condition and that he had become reliant on the medical and palliative care. However, the Court clearly indicated that the circumstances of this case were very exceptional. Previously, other cases dealing with a person's deprivation of access to a health treatment, were systematically considered not to infringe the human rights invoked (i.e. the prohibition of inhuman or degrading treatment, but also the right to life and the right to respect family life). The cases dealt e.g. with the non-coverage of an alternative treatment for hepatitis B,[60] partial coverage of an expensive treatment (30% own contribution charged for an expensive medicine[61]) and hospital care (of which only the strict necessary procedures and medication were covered[62]). Arguments relating to the fact that the country was already doing the utmost by covering the treatment already to a large extent, or that one cannot expect from a country to fully cover an expensive treatment, taking into account its restricted public finances, were considered to be crucial in the defence *à décharge*. The same is true for the alternative treatment of which the effectiveness was not scientifically proved.

Some preliminary conclusions regarding the impact of the human rights instruments upon the access to health care

Many welcome the growing case law of the European Court of Human Rights in the field of social security. Indeed, it gives a new impulse to the shaping of the social rights, be it from another angle. And although the Court has resisted so far from granting directly any social right on the basis of the Convention on the Protection of Human Rights, it increasingly starts to test the compatibility

---

59 Judgement of 2 May 1997, *D. v UK*, Appl. No. 30240/96.
60 Decision Commission of 1 July 1998, *Scialacqua v. Italy*, Appl. 34151/96; the application for a judgement to the European Court of Human Rights, being declared inadmissible.
61 Decision Commission of 21 March 2002, *Nitecki v. Poland*, Appl. 65653/01; the application for a judgement to the European Court of Human Rights, being declared inadmissible Decision Commission of 4 January 2005, *Pentiocova v Moldova*, Appl. 34151/96; the application for a judgement to the European Court of Human Rights, being declared inadmissible
62 *Ibid.*

of social security rights with the human rights principles laid down in the Convention (such as the non-discrimination principle, the protection of property rights and legitimate expectations, protection against inhuman treatment). Some consider that the case law is finally shaping some concrete fundamental legal principles in the social field, the international social rights instrument for the time being of a too programmatic nature. That these fundamental principles, as enshrined in the Convention, can be invoked directly before a national or even European court, is considered to be positive evolution.

Still some side remarks should be made with regard to this evolution. One should not forget that the Convention is a human rights' instrument protecting in the first place the individual against illicit acting of the state. The approach is thus merely of an individual rights' nature, which does not completely fit the essence of social security (law), including social health care. Social systems do have to protect, next to individual rights, the collective interest (e.g. respecting solidarity). By stressing too much the individual rights (through the human rights' principles laid down in the Convention), one may upset the essential feature of social security systems, viz. redistribution between citizens and hence the collective interest of society as such. Social security systems essentially represent more than the compilation of individual social rights. Those collective aspects are however not clearly defined in a human rights' instrument. It remains to be seen whether the Court will have the necessary discipline to weigh the individual rights against the collective interest of our social systems.

Outlook

If we try to come to terms with the question to what extent international conventions shape the right to access to health care, the following concluding remarks could be made. If one looks at the social rights instruments proclaiming the right to health care, be it as a part of the more general right to social protection, there is a tendency to interpreting this right in a too detailed and technical manner. Especially the Committee that control the application of the conventions, are inclined to develop conditions and rules in relation to the set-up of the social health care system that do not always find a basis in the generally proclaimed right. Consequently, the basic guarantee – accessibility for all – is endangered. Accessibility is not so much safeguarded by developing all kinds of new guidelines with regard to the health care system, but much more by guaranteeing the concrete application of this social right. In practice, this means that this right will take the biggest effect, when it can be applied to the so-called marginal cases, persons who are socially, economically, ethnically or culturally in a weak position. In other words, by ensuring that the essence of the social right is direct applicability, more can be achieved than by developing the concrete contents through all kinds of technicalities which at the end of the day are not enforceable.

When we come to the (minimum) standard instruments, we can ask ourselves whether the existing provisions are still in line with the current health care thinking. They do reflect too much the social security thinking of the 1950s, without concrete yardsticks as to the outcome (effectivity and efficiency) of the health care systems. If we want to maintain the value of these conventions, the major challenge will be to rethink the standard-setting instruments in order to see where direct applicable provisions can go together with more developed standards, measuring concretely: access to health care and health care outcomes.

It would be naïve to believe that by applying human rights' instruments alone, one can address this challenge. The case law developed by the European Court of Human Rights in the field of social security, already indicates that such instruments are developed in a too one-sided manner, stressing mainly the individual rights, without too much interest for the collective interests of society. It is up to the instruments of the next generation to strike this balance between rights and duties, as well as to link individual entitlements and collective interest.

Part Two

Europe: Solidarity and Justice in Health Care

Chapter 2.

The Meaning of 'Justice' and 'Solidarity' in Health Care

Martin Buijsen

Introduction

In the Netherlands - as well as anywhere else - donor organs are scarce. Waiting lists for transplantation surgery are long and patients are dying unnecessary. From time to time resourceful economists and ethicists come up with unconventional ideas to shorten those waiting lists. A few years ago Dutch moral philosopher Govert den Hartogh suggested a new solution to the problem.[1] He devised a so called bonus points scheme. People who have had themselves registered as (post mortem) organ donors receive bonus points once they become patients in need of donor organs themselves. Once allocation of suitable donor organs takes place, these bonus points are taken into account. As a result these patients will not spend that much time on the waiting list. The idea is of course that since it can be in their own interest, more people will be willing to register as post mortem organ donors. According to Den Hartogh the scheme would generate more than sufficient donor organs, enough even to meet the demand of transplantation patients who were not willing to donate their organs after death, of those – other words – who spend relatively more time on the waiting list.

Den Hartogh's plan was not met with great enthusiasm. In fact, the bonus points system was rebuffed quite rapidly. Although the proposal claimed a serious reduction of the number of deaths on the waiting lists for post mortem organ transplantation, it was referred to as 'unjust'. How can concerns of (distributive) justice override concerns of life and death? And secondly, although the plan was new and unconventional in the context of organ allocation, the appeal to self interest as a solution to problems of scarcity is hardly revolutionary. Similar solutions to similar problems are offered quite regularly in other parts of the economy, and not without success. Apparently, the context of organ allocation is characterized by a very specific notion of justice, which is both strong (in that it is adhered to even – as it seems - at the expense of life) and remarkably different from notions of justice prevailing elsewhere.

---

[1]　See G. den Hartogh, *Gift of bijdrage? Over morele aspecten van orgaandonatie* (Den Haag, Rathenau Instituut, 2003).

In the next few paragraphs I will argue that this notion of justice is typical for health care as a whole. By using that concept I will also attempt to interpret some recent developments in Dutch health care. In doing so, I will try to determine the meaning of 'solidarity' in the context of health care.

Justice: an essentially contested concept

Philosophically, justice is an extremely problematic concept. Justice is one of those concepts sometimes referred to as essentially contested concepts. An essentially contested concept is a concept characterized by 1. reference to a practice which is extremely complex because of its many dimensions, 2. relatively open boundaries, in that new and unforeseen situations can be brought within its range, and 3. the apparent habit of expressing a value judgment when used.[2] Now, although justice is a subject studied extensively throughout history, a crude systematic and historical analysis can tell us enough about the notion of justice itself, enough for our purposes.

Traditionally, justice is perceived as a virtue. Aristotle shared the common belief of his days of justice as 'the habit enabling people to act justly'.[3] Furthermore, what interested him was not the so called general or legal justice (*i.e.* the ability to act in accordance with the law), but the justice which is characteristic of excellence of character, which is typical of the habit that enables one to choose the golden mean. One of the types of justice distinguished by Aristotle is the so called distributive justice. This is the one that is of interest to us, not as a virtue, but – more general - as a principle.

Also very familiar is the ancient Roman legal maxim *suum cuique tribuere* ('to each his own'). Thomas Aquinas referred to this adage when he defined Aristotle's notion of justice as 'the unremitting will to give each individual his own'.[4] Now, what is 'giving each his own'? With regard to distributive justice Aristotle thought the word 'merit' very revealing, since 'everybody agrees upon the justice of a distribution when people ultimately get what they merit'.[5] However, he also saw that in the real world 'merit' did not have one single fixed meaning. When speaking about the distribution of a scarce good called political power he noted that 'democrats identify merit with the status of freeman, supporters of the oligarchy equal merit with wealth or birth, et cetera.'[6]

Of course, Aristotle was not the last in trying to determine the meaning of 'justice'. Many have followed him since, with very different outcomes indeed. It is, however, not very difficult to discern to two schools of thought. 'To each according to merit' has been accepted by many. It is, therefore, just to give the only available gold medal to the fastest runner, as it is only just to grant scholarships to the best performing students. And if there is a vacancy, the candidate with the best qualifications should get the job. This concept of justice still

---

2   See W.B. Gallie, "Essentially contested concepts", in Proceedings of the Aristotelian Society 56 (1955), p. 167-198.
3   *Nicomachean Ethics* 1129a7-8.
4   *Summa theologiae* II-II, q.58, a.1.
5   *Nicomachean Ethics* 1131a25.
6   *Ibid.* 1131a26-27.

seems to be tied up with that of virtue, since a merit is nothing more than a quality of a person (or an act) which is valued favourably.

Aristotle also first saw a relationship between the concepts of justice and equality.7 Inequality always seems to be in need of justification. Why, for example, increase already existing inequality by rewarding talent with additional advantages? And where is the injustice in giving a job to a lesser qualified person, who is representative of a group which is seriously discriminated against, and who can do with the extra money?! In other words, should justice not serve equality, especially in the interest of the weak and the needy? And if so, should it not be need rather than merit upon which a just distribution is based? Therefore, to each according to need! This notion of justice was held by Kropotkin and – up to a point – by Rawls.8

History of thought handed down very different notions of justice. And although both reflect intuitive notions of general consciousness, as Raphael noted,9 ultimately they are diametrically opposed. It is, however, too schematic to see the history of thought on the subject as an ongoing battle between those who favour merit as the basis for just distribution and those who argue the case for need. In our post modern age it is accepted, again following Aristotle, that different concepts of justice can and do coexist. Merit and need can be employed at the same time. Nowadays, it is accepted that in sports just distribution is based on other grounds than in education, and that the criteria of just distribution in science are not those employed in health care. There are, as the American philosopher Walzer calls them, many 'spheres of justice'.10 Now, if health care can be seen as a separate sphere, what exactly is the meaning of 'justice'?

Justice as laid down in the rules

Den Hartogh's proposal came to nothing. Some critics referred to human rights law, more specifically to the Additional protocol to the Convention on human rights and biomedicine regarding organ and tissue transplantation (2002). This Protocol, developed by the Council of Europe but never ratified by the Netherlands, is generally seen as the document in which internationally accepted rules and principles regarding organ allocation are laid down. Article 3 of the Protocol puts into words the demands transplantation systems have to meet. According to this article there must be equitable access.11 In the *Explanatory Report*, the authoritative commentary, it is said that 'organs and tissues should be allocated according to *medical criteria*', whereby '[t]his notion should be understood *in its broadest sense* (...) extending to any circumstance capable of influencing the state of the patient's health, the quality of the transplanted ma-

---

7   *Ibidem* 1130b10-1130b14.
8   See P. Kropotkin, *La Conquête du Pain*, (Paris: Tresse and Stock, 1892) and J. Rawls, *A Theory of Justice*, (Cambridge, Mass: Beknup Press, 1971).
9   See D.D. Raphael, *Concepts of Justice*, (Oxford: Oxford Univ Press, 2001), p. 6.
10 See M. Walzer, *Spheres of Justice. A defense of pluralism and equality*, (Oxford: Oxford Univ Press, 1985).
11 *Additional protocol to the convention on human rights and biomedicine concerning transplantation of organs and tissues of human origin*, Strasbourg 24.1.2002, ETS No. 186.

terial or the outcome of the transplant'. With 'circumstances' are meant circumstances such as the compatibility of the organ with the recipient, medical urgency, the time needed for transportation of the organ, the time spent on the waiting list, et cetera. [12] In other words, the text seems to suggest that it is allowed to discriminate between patients but only on medical grounds *sensu stricto* or on grounds reducible thereto. Such discrimination is just, and since the registered willingness to donate organs post mortem by a patient in need of an organ himself cannot be qualified as a circumstance as understood in the *Explanatory Report*, discrimination on that basis must be considered as unjust. Therefore, scarce post mortem donor organs are to be distributed according to need, and need only, *i.e.* objective need, as can be determined according to medical standards.

Although the willingness to donate organs post mortem is regarded as meritorious by many, the justice laid down in the rules regarding organ allocation shows no tolerance for it. It is simply unacceptable as a distributive criterion in this context. Does this intolerance for merit apply to health care as a whole? Article 3 of the Convention on human rights and biomedicine itself also mentions 'equitable access'. 'Parties, taking into account health needs and available resources, shall take appropriate measures with a view to providing, within their jurisdiction, equitable access to health care of appropriate quality.'[13] In the accompanying *Explanatory Report* the authors of the treaty clarify the meaning of 'equitable' with regard to access to health care in general. 'The aim [of article 3] is to ensure equitable access to health care in accordance with the person's medical needs.' And, they add, 'in this context, "equitable" means first and foremost the absence of unjust discrimination. Although *not synonymous* with absolute equality (...).'[14] In other words, article 3 of the Convention on human rights and biomedicine does not prohibit discrimination in health care. Discrimination is perfectly acceptable as long as it is based on differences in need. Unjust discrimination, on other criteria (or not solely on that basis), is not allowed. In health care therefore the adage seems to be: to each according to need.

Equitable access revisited

Since the Convention on human rights and biomedicine is also not ratified by the Netherlands, a reference to article 3 does not constitute a legal argument. Strictly speaking, everything said in the previous paragraph amounts to a moral argument. And even if the Netherlands were party to the treaties mentioned above, one could still argue that a margin of appreciation exists. Parties to human rights treaties take obligations upon themselves, but they are free – in principle - to determine how to go about it. Furthermore, the right (of access) to health care is a so called social right. It is not a 'hard' individual claim right. Usually, health care cannot be claimed (in Dutch courts especially) with

---

[12]   *Explanatory report*, nr. 37.
[13]   *Convention for the protection of human rights and dignity of the human being with regard to the application of biology and medicine*, Oviedo 4.IV.1997, ETS No. 164.
[14]   *Explanatory report*, nrs. 24, 25.

references to international human rights treaties in which the right to health care is included. Parties to those treaties are under the obligation to realize health care for their citizens and whether they succeed is largely dependent upon the means available. As a result individual citizens can usually only claim access to health care once national legislation is in place. It is therefore not uncommon to speak of social human rights as 'soft' rights. But is this true of the social right (of access) to health care?

There are numerous treaties, constitutions and international declarations in which access to health care is presented as a basic human right. However, the wordings differ widely. In the preamble of the WHO constitution the 'highest attainable standard of health' is recognized as a fundamental human right.[15] Article 25 of the Universal Declaration of Human Rights simply mentions a 'right to a standard of living adequate for health and well being', in which not only food, clothing and housing is included, but medical care as well.[16] In article 11 of the European Social Charter the right to protection to health is recognized.[17] A similar concept can be found in the extremely relevant article 12 of the International Covenant on Economic, Social and Cultural Rights (ICESCR), a treaty which has been ratified by the Netherlands.[18]

Human rights are to be respected by governments first and foremost. States party to ICESCR are under the obligation to take care of their citizens' health. This obligation amounts to more than providing for health care. It also includes obligations regarding health and safety at work and obligations regarding the environment. Nevertheless, as recognized by the supervising authority (the Committee on Economic, Social and Cultural Rights – CESCR), the core obligation on the part of governments consists of the provision of health care. In *General Comment no. 14*, the authoritative explanatory document, the right to health care resulting from article 12 is described by CESCR as the right of access to health care, *i.e.* health care which must available, accessible (geographically, financially and as regards information), morally acceptable and of good quality.[19] There is, however, no mention of equity.

Now, some comments given by CESCR, including *General Comment no. 14*, are quite innovative from a legal theoretical point of view. Traditionally, the main difference between individual basic rights and social basic rights is seen as the result of differences between state obligations. Individual rights have to be respected by governments of states party to human rights treaties. Freedom of speech for example may not be violated. Governments have to restrain themselves. All they have to do is keep themselves from doing anything in this respect. Social rights have to be respected by governments as well, of course, but as regards these rights action on their part is required. It is not difficult to see that sometimes action on the part of governments is needed to ensure respect for individual rights. In order to protect people's right to privacy the

---

[15]   *Constitution of the World Health Organization*, New York, June 19th – July 22nd 1947.
[16]   *Universal Declaration of Human Rights*, Paris, December 10th 1948.
[17]   *European Social Charter*, Turin, October 18th 1961.
[18]   *International Convention on Economic, Social and Cultural Rights*, New York, December 19th 1966.
[19]   *General Comment no. 14*, adopted by the Committee on Economic, Social and Cultural Rights on May 11th 2001, nr 12.

Dutch government initiated extensive legislation, creating an extremely observant supervising authority. Likewise, it is conceivable that governments refrain from action in order to respect social rights.

Taking into account these legal nuances CESCR presents a typology of state obligations in *General Comment no. 14*. The different state obligations recognized by CESCR as stemming from article 12 ICESCR are ranked from 'hard' state obligations ('obligations to respect') to 'soft' state obligations ('obligations to facilitate'). Now, although there is no specific mention of equity, the first obligation to respect elaborated on by the Committee is the obligation to abstain from taking measures denying or limiting equal access to health care for all persons. In its motivation CESCR refers to its general non discrimination provision, in which discrimination for reasons of race, sex, religious belief et cetera, is explicitly prohibited.[20] In other words, there is a 'hard' obligation on the part of governments not to discriminate on these grounds, which – again – seems to suggest the permissibility of discrimination on medical grounds only. That is, once a state party to ICESCR has actually realized equal access for everybody.[21] As we shall see, this is not an insignificant thing to point out in view of recent reforms of the Dutch health care system.

The moral nature of health

In health care justice seems to be a remarkably distinct notion. Reflection on appropriate international human rights law (human rights law being the backbone of western legal systems) reveals an uncompromising concept of justice in this sphere. Now, why is that 'justice' has this very specific meaning in the context of health care?

Rules are the product of practical reasoning. The rules concerning health care embody the very special moral demands we place on this type of human activity because of the importance we attach to health itself. Philosophically speaking, health is good in itself.[22] It is intrinsically good: health does not derive its goodness from a higher or more fundamental good. Health can only be intrinsically good, since its goodness cannot be proven logically. The truth of the proposition "health is good" can only be 'proven' by saying that the goodness of health is self-evident (or obvious or 'natural').[23] Health care on the other hand is good, because it serves health. Health care is instrumentally good.

Goods such as health (or life, or friendship), goods which are good in themselves, are points of departure. Moral reasoning, which is practical reasoning, always begins with propositions such as 'health is good', expressly or tacitly. The demands we place on health care can only be explained by pointing

---

20   *General Comment no. 14*, nrs. 18, 34.

21   In addition, there is the obligation to protect (the second level of obligations on states parties) to adopt legislation or to take other measures ensuring equal access to health care. See *General Comment no. 14*, nr. 35.

22   See R. George, *In Defence of Natural Law*, (Oxford: Oxford University Press, 1999).

23   By the way, those who think health serves happiness are gravely mistaken about the nature of happiness.

out the very special nature of health as a moral good. The rules governing health care (legal as well as medical ethical) are as they are because of the goodness of health, which is evident to all of us.[24] Health is a good in itself, and the absence of that good (*i.e.* the need for health care) is in itself justification enough for giving health care. The recognition of the right to health care as a fundamental human right is an expression of that basic truth. Hence, to each according to need.

Justice and health care reform

Justice as understood in health care is remarkably intolerant. The rules as they are on the most fundamental level, *i.e.* that of international human rights law, leave little or no room for merit as a distributive criterion. And yet, introduction of this principle is exactly what characterizes the reform program of the health care system undertaken in the Netherlands during the last few years. Unfortunately, in all of the debates distributive justice was never really perceived as an important issue. The affordability of the system as a whole dominated the debates. Consequently, thoroughgoing philosophical and moral discussions on the acceptability of merit as a distributive principle in health care never really took place.

The reception of Den Hartogh's plans to reduce mortality on the waiting lists for organ transplantation is probably very illustrative. Of course, the proposal was perceived by many as unjust, but only a few were able to argue its injustice. The speedy rejection of the plan was more than likely due to the fact of the bonus points idea being accompanied by a plea for tacit consent organ donorship, which traditionally lacks public support in the Netherlands. In the debates preceding the introduction of *no claim* in the Dutch health care system a similar inability for moral argumentation was displayed.

No claim is not an unfamiliar idea in the 'sphere' of car insurance. It simply means that if you cause no accidents you are entitled to a discount off the price of your car insurance. Such a policy condition makes perfect sense in the car insurance business, but can it be regarded as a just measure for cost containment purposes in health care? That the chronically ill and the handicapped would be unjustly discriminated against, was seen by many, but the fundamental questions (what is just in health care? Can health be seen as meritorious? Can not seeking medical help be seen as such?) were never really raised. All in all, the debates on the subject never outgrew ideology and technicalities.[25]

The *no claim* debate also displayed a worrisome lack of moral sensibility. The ease with which comparisons were made with other parts of the economy

---

24   Most – if not all – features of health care's specific morality can be explained by referring to health's moral nature. As we shall see the way solidarity is understood in the context of health care, can also be linked to this moral nature. See M. Buijsen, "De betekenis van solidariteit in de gezondheidszorg", in Martin Buijsen et al. (eds) *Marktwerking v. Solidariteit. Op zoek naar nieuwe evenwichten in de publieke dienstverlening*, (Nijmegen: Valkhofpers 2007), p.65-98.

25   On January 1st 2008 the rules concerning *no claim* were retracted.

was striking. The inability to see the normative uniqueness of health care became typical of the debates preceding the most fundamental reform of the Dutch health care system ever. Since January 1ˢᵗ 2006 the Dutch health care system is carried out by competing private for profit insurance companies, with competition taking place on the markets of health care insurance and health care contracting. Although every insurer is required by law to offer the same basic health care insurance policy, the logic of the new system demands that he has to make a difference. Better contracts with health care providers will result in a larger share of the health care insurance market. Therefore, it is in the interest of these companies to negotiate priority treatment for their clients. Unfortunately, as we are beginning to see, hospitals especially tend to overcome moral objections when offered adequate financial compensation. Hospitals operating on the basis of such contracts will discriminate unjustly between patients in need of the same basic care. The one with the right contract will be helped sooner, even if other patients have exactly the same need and have spent more time waiting for help. In other words, allocation of health care is made dependent (in part at least) upon merit, *i.e.* patient's virtuosity: his ability to choose the right basic health care insurance policy.

Solidarity in health care

The *no claim* debate also refers to the meaning of 'solidarity' in health care. Solidarity is also very problematic concept in the philosophical sense. Like justice it is essentially contested. However, considering the way 'solidarity' is actually being used nowadays, it is possible to distinguish three levels of meaning.

On the descriptive level 'solidarity' refers to an actual understanding of union and commitment and the subsequent willingness to share the risks inherent to human existence. Whether such solidarity is actually present in a society, is something which can be examined. On the second, analytical level 'solidarity' as a basic notion of sociological theories of human coexistence structures scientific debate. As such the concept is dominantly present in the theories of Marx, Durkheim and Comte. By the way, as an expression 'solidarity' is not older than the 18ᵗʰ century: as a sociological notion it tried to provide answers to questions generated by the Industrial Revolution. And finally, on the normative level 'solidarity' functions as a criterion for judging the quality of human relationships. On this level solidarity is an important ethical concept, socially as well as politically. As such it relates to the institutional organization of society, but not exclusively.[26] It is this normative meaning that is especially of interest to us.

There is no such thing as an abstract of non historical notion of solidarity.[27] Although the expression itself is not that old, the notion is ancient and not in-

---

26   Buijsen, *ibid*, p. 72.
27   See J. Verstraeten, "Solidariteit in de katholieke traditie", in E. de Jong en M. Buijsen (eds) *Solidariteit onder druk? Over de grens tussen individuele en collectieve verantwoordelijkheid*, (Nijmegen: Valkhof Pers, 2005), p. 27.

herent to a particular tradition.[28] The meanings of 'solidarity' in the normative sense are diverse as well. But something of a core meaning is hinted at by the ancient Latin verb 'solidare' ('to fasten' as well as 'to heal') in the way it was used in Roman law. 'In solidum' meant standing surety to another's debts. Now, the normative notion is not to be found solely in law. Some scholars point out that the definition is situated between love on the one hand and justice on the other hand. Where it leans toward love it is called 'caritas' in the Christian tradition, and 'sympatheia' and 'filanthropia' in the Stoic tradition. At the other end of the spectrum the notion refers to justice, as – for example – in the Bible where it refers to the duty to care for orphans, strangers and the poor. This duty is not only a matter of personal and voluntary 'caritas' but also of 'doing justice'. Thus understood solidarity implies a certain degree of force and constraint. And thus understood solidarity leads to ethical and political choices to enforce certain behaviour and to create the institutional and structural conditions for pensions, employment, social security et cetera.[29] And for health care as well.

It makes no sense al all to reflect on the idea of solidarity without taking into consideration the content it has obtained during the period of Enlightenment. As 'fraternité' ('brotherhood') solidarity is part of the famous French revolutionary parole. And as such its meaning becomes secular. Now, in the history of social and political philosophy brotherhood received considerably less attention than the ideas of liberty and equality. By way of explanation it is sometimes said that liberty and equality belong to the same sphere.[30] Liberty and equality are at home in the context of aloof and legally determinable human relationships, while brotherhood is not. Freedom and equality are said to belong to the 'cold part' of the moral spectrum: the domain in which people, emotionally not involved with one another, may have minimal expectations of each other, the area of a minimal morality which can be translated into positive law, and framed in legal expressions, in claim rights.[31]

It is said that the notions of liberty, equality, right and rights are based on the same anthropology, that of the competent and autonomous individual, who lives out his own life plan and squares everything with his own conscience. Brotherhood does not fit the logic of liberty, equality, law and rights because it does not relate to distant relations between independent individuals pursuing their own ends based on self interest. Solidarity relates to people depending on one another, on people who need each other because of their vulnerability, and who have taken responsibility of each others fate. Solidarity is the alliance with others, born from an understanding of the fragility of life, and the corresponding concern for their well being. Solidarity is based on an entirely different anthropology. Unlike liberty and equality solidarity is based on the ideas of human being as essentially social beings. Together with the no-

---

28   *Ibidem.*
29   *Ibid.*, p. 29-30.
30   See K. van der Wal, "Vrijheid, gelijkheid en broederschap?", in K. van der Wal (ed.) *Vrijheid, gelijkheid en broederschap? Betekenis en huidige relevantie van het devies van de Franse Revolutie,* (Budel: Damon, 2004), p. 9-14.
31   *Ibidem.*

tions of love, care, loyalty et cetera it is said to belong to the 'warm part' of the moral spectrum.[32]

Of course, this is not entirely true. As the willingness to take partial responsibility for the risks inherent to the lives of other human beings solidarity has undeniably contributed to current societal relationships. Over the years the 'Rechtstaat' has been transformed into the welfare state, out of the idea that liberty and equality need solidarity. The self realization of individual human beings not only requires civil and political rights, but positive guarantees as well, *i.e.* pensions, education, social security, health care et cetera as well. In other words, in part solidarity does fit the logic of liberty, equality, law and rights, and it does so in as far as it refers to justice.

What is the meaning of 'solidarity' in health care? As we have seen, the notion of solidarity is unmistakably linked with that of justice. As we also have seen, the justice laid down in the rules governing access to health care seems to be 'to each according to (objective) need'. But it is not this notion of justice which makes us see the injustice of no claim in health care. To each according to need is but one part of the story. On consideration health care systems such as the Dutch one comprise not one but two notions of distributive justice. The rules concerning no claim meant that the chronically ill and handicapped never had (part of their) health care insurance premiums reimbursed, since they are always dependent on medical care. Now, saying that it is unjust for them to pay extra for their medical care, saying that they do not deserve to pay extra, is exactly the same as saying that need should not be a criterion for distributing the weight of health care insurance premiums among the participants of the system. In other words, (objective) individual need for health care should not determine (in part) the amount of premium to be paid by that individual. Health care insurance premiums need to be distributed justly as well, and apparently justice in the context of health care - due to health's specific moral nature[33] - also dictates that need, where it is all-determining on the benefits side of the system, plays no part at all on the premium side. The no claim arrangement was unjust because it violated that principle.

On closer consideration, the Dutch health care system consists of two spheres of justice. To each according to (objective) need on one side, and to each NOT according to (objective) need on the other side. For health care systems like the Dutch the latter idea of justice is a necessary condition for equal access as understood by international (human rights) law.[34] Solidarity in such health care systems is at least characterized by a strict separation of the spheres of justice.[35] Reform proposals that violate that separation do not testify of solidarity in the strict sense. A law linking the medical need of individuals with higher premiums is not only discriminatory and unjust but does not tes-

---

32   *Ibidem.*
33   See *supra* note 24.
34   See M. Buijsen, 'De betekenis van solidariteit in de gezondheidszorg', p. 90-91.
35   Equitable access to health care also implies financial accessibility. Solidarity with those in need of health care is what the strict separation of the spheres of justice amounts to. This type of solidarity is not the same as what is often referred to as risk (or chance) solidarity. Solidarity with the those in need of health care probably also requires substantial income solidarity.

tify of solidarity as well. Reversely, a law awarding certain behaviour on the contribution side with certain advantages on the benefits side (see Den Hartogh's bonus point scheme) also violates the separation between the spheres of justice. Such a law is unjust and does not conform to the idea of solidarity as we see to understand it in the context of health care.

Final remarks

The concept of justice and solidarity are essentially contested concepts. By definition 'justice' and 'solidarity' do not have single fixed meanings. Therefore, one should not rule out the possibility of future changes in those meanings, even in health care.

Nevertheless, one should remember that the current concept of justice took decades to develop legally speaking and thousands of years morally speaking. It is, again, an uncompromising notion; uncompromising because of the way we perceive health, absence of health and the need for health care. The recent reforms of the Dutch health care have one thing in common: the introduction of merit (in one form or another) as a distributive criterion. This is something not seen by many. It is unknown whether this phenomenon can be explained by a fundamental change in our perception of health and disease. We simply do not know for the matter was not discussed thoroughly. Here too, philosophical reflection and argument gave way to superficial management speak and economic platitudes. But it seems to me that since there are good reasons for adhering to the present concepts of justice and solidarity, the ones that will prompt us to adopt other notions ought to be even better.

Chapter 3.

Litigating Health Care Access in the Netherlands: Challenging International Treaty Law

André den Exter

In the Netherlands, access to health care has been guaranteed by social health insurance legislation. But since the introduction of the health insurance system in the 1960s, the health insurance system has been in a state of flux. Numerous reforms have changed the system gradually, of which the latest is the introduction of a competitive health insurance scheme for the entire population.

Cutting across the various reforms has, however, been the goal of access to health care services as defined by international treaty law, including European Union law.[1] In particular the leverage of Community law in strengthening the patient's right to health care is remarkable. Since the European Court of Justice (ECJ) has accepted that health care should be considered as a service in terms of the EC Treaty, rights to health care have become inextricably linked with the free movement principles and are no longer restricted to the jurisdiction of the country of origin.

Hereafter, this article examines the consequences of international and European Union law for claiming access to health care in the Netherlands.

Access to Health Care in The Netherlands: The Legal Framework

The Dutch health care system is based on the principle of solidarity. Solidarity means that all members of society in need must have access to health care, regardless of their ability to pay. Solidarity is not a woolly notion about the common good. It has a specific meaning that a health care system is organised and managed on the basis of universal access, without risk selection, based on

---

[1]   E.g., A. P. den Exter and H. E. G. M. Hermans, "The Constitutional Right to Health Care," *European Journal of Health Law* 3 (1998), p. 261-290; A. P. den Exter and H. E. G. M. Hermans, eds., *The Right to Health Care in Several European Countries* (The Hague: Kluwer Law International, 1999); A. P. den Exter, "The Right to Health Care in International Law," in A. P. den Exter and J. Sándor (eds.), *Frontiers of European Health Law* (Rotterdam: Erasmus University Press, 2003), p. 12-26; B. C. A. Toebes, *The Right to Health as a Human Right in International Law* (Antwerp: Intersentia, 1999).

income related premiums and with no significant differences in the benefit package.[2] It is a concept enshrined in Dutch statutory health insurance law and recognised by the decisions of the judiciary, including the European Court of Justice, as described below.

Due to the prohibition of constitutional review by the judiciary, the Dutch legal debate on access to health care starts from a statutory law perspective.[3] More specifically, that debate primarily focuses on health insurance issues (access to the health insurance scheme, the scope and nature of the benefit package, contribution rates, etc.). That does not mean that the constitutional health provision is of no importance, but in terms of health care claims statutory law and international legal standards are decisive.[4]

Generally, the principle of access to health care has been interpreted as a social right, which means that the competent authorities in the Netherlands have quite a broad discretion in determining how and when this social right will be implemented. Based on both the solidarity principle and the equality principle, equal access to health care services has been enshrined in social insurance law (e.g., the new Health Insurance Act, the "*Zorgverzekeringswet*") and formulated into health care entitlements as defined by (secondary) law.[5] The "*Zorgverzekeringswet*," introduced a compulsory health insurance scheme for the entire population, carried out by (non and for-profit) insurance companies. In brief, the new Health Insurance Act provides the insured for essential curative care tested against the criteria of proven efficacy, cost effectiveness, and the need for collective financing.[6] Under the new insurance scheme, the insured may opt for a benefits-in-kind or reimbursement model. Although both models guarantee a standard insurance policy, under the latter model the insured have a free choice of provider. Whereas under the benefits-in-kind variant, the insured may claim the types of care as entitlements provided by contracted health providers. Thus free choice of provider is restricted to contracted providers only. However, in exceptional cases the insured may opt for a non-contracted provider, for instance in case of long waiting times, and will receive a cash benefit (reimbursement model). Due to jurisprudence of the European Court of Justice, the reimbursement rules under the new Health Insurance

---

2   A. den Exter and M. Buijsen, "Keuze voor Solidariteit. Kanttekeningen bij het Voorstel Zorgverzekeringswet," ("In Favour of Solidarity," in Dutch) *TvGR* (*Journal of Dutch Health Law*) 1 (2005), p. 111-117.

3   As an exception to that rule, the courts may review the constitutionality in terms of international and European law.

4   According to Article 22(1) of the Dutch Basic Law the authorities shall take steps to promote public health. This provision has been generally interpreted as a "mere" obligation of the government to be concerned with setting up health facilities and facilitating access to necessary health care. Den Exter and Hermans, *idem*, p. 271.

5   The "Zorgverzekeringswet" (Zvw) came into force on January 1, 2006; (Official Journal of the State 2005): 358. An English summary of the new Health Insurance Act is *available at* http://www.minvws.nl. Next to the *Zvw*, there is a universal scheme covering the whole population, the so-called "AWBZ"-scheme covering exceptional medical expenses. Beyond these compulsory schemes, citizens may opt for an additional private insurance policy.

6   The conditions differ by type of care and include prescription by a general practitioner, quantitative maxima for prescribed pharmaceuticals and prior approval by the insurance fund.

Act had to be amended (this is discussed further below). One of the reasons is the statutory obligation of the insurance fund to guarantee access to medical care under the insurance scheme. This obligation forms the essence of the benefit-in-kind health care system, for which the insurer is accountable and – in case of non compliance – may be held liable. It is therefore a principle of sound management that the benefit-in-kind insurer purchases sufficient care in and/or outside its area of activity. Except for *force majeure*, the insurance fund cannot be released from its obligation to provide for access to health care. The insurance fund cannot defend itself on the basis that it had insufficiently contracted for care or allocated insufficient funds to a hospital facility.[7] It can, however, claim *force majeure* in the case of restrictive residential capacity regulation set by the government as this is viewed as an externality factor beyond the powers of insurers to affect. Nonetheless, given the possibility of contracting health care abroad, such an appeal will be likely be less successful in the future.

International (Social Security) Law

Apart from national health insurance law, the legal framework on social health insurance has been highly influenced by international social security law, as stipulated in several treaties and conventions.[8] These international documents conceptualise the measures that should be undertaken by Member States in order to achieve the full realisation of the right to health care. The formulation used include a certain responsibility upon states with regards to the allocation, finance and provision of health services, but these provisions are generally interpreted as non-enforceable legal entitlements to health care. Therefore, the noble aspirations of universal access to health care must be interpreted within the context of the treaties, meaning a basic level of health care, interpreted in accordance with the formulation, ratio and implementation of legal norms and economic capacities of a given society. In truth, the domestic economic capacities and the non-enforceability of these international treaty provisions temper the actual meaning of the right to health care and thus access to health care services.

In the Netherlands, however, the importance of international treaties on social rights has gradually increased since the concept of "direct effect" or the notion of self-executing treaty provisions. On several occasions, the Dutch judiciary accepted that international treaty law on social rights may have binding effect on all persons ("*erga omnes*" provisions) and certain incorporated rights (on labour issues and social security benefits) have been subject to judicial re-

---

7   Appeal court's Hertogenbosch July 2, 1990 (RZA 1990), p. 127.
8   E.g., International Labour Organisation (ILO) Conventions concerning minimum standards of social security and maternity protection (102 and 103), the International Covenant on Economic, Social, and Cultural Rights (ICESCR), the Council of Europe's Social Charter (ESC) and the European Code on Social Security. In this respect, I refer to the contribution of Paul Schoukens, Chapter 1.

view.9 Particularly the direct effect of norm setting treaties, such as ILO conventions on social security has raised some controversy, both in the legal doctrine, as well as at the courts.10 With respect to health, the highest administrative court, the Central Appeals Tribunal ("*Centrale Raad van Beroep*") ruled that the ILO Convention on social security minimum standards and maternity care include self-executing treaty provisions that can create direct rights to individuals, enforceable by the Court.11 Decisive criteria whether norm setting treaties or treaty provisions are self-executing are their (instructive or imperative) nature, and the (concrete) wording of the specific provision. Therefore, the reliance on the self-executing effect of ILO social security treaties provide Dutch citizens with a limited claim to enforce the social right to health care before national courts. Conversely, the judiciary rejected such reliance repeatedly in case of the International Convention on Economic, Social and Cultural Rights (ICESCR), since the treaty provision are insufficiently precise, and the instructive nature provides States with a broad margin of appreciation to fill in the necessary steps in order to realise these rights.12 So far, the judiciary has continued that line of reasoning and is not willing to incorporate the concept of "progressive realisation" of social rights, as suggested by the treaty Committee in its *General Comments and Concluding Observations* (on health).13

Alternatively, citizens may also rely on the European Human Rights Treaty, the European Convention on Human Rights (ECHR) when claiming access to and/or the reimbursement of a certain medical intervention or medicines. On several occasions, particularly when the medical intervention or medicine was not included in the social health insurance benefit package, the ECHR treaty provisions have been invoked in order to enforce a health care claim on

---

9   E.g., the Railroad strike judgment of the Dutch Supreme Court (Hoge Raad, "Spoorwegstakingarrest" 30 mei 1986, NJ 1986, 688; CRvB January 5, 1988 (RSV 1988): 199; HR May 7, 1993, 440 (NJ 1995), p. 259.

10   In the past courts ruled differently whether or not so-called instructive norm setting treaties are self-executing. See also J. W. A. Fleuren, "*Een ieder verbindende bepalingen van verdragen* (Treaty provisions that are binding on all persons, in Dutch)," (Den Haag: Boom Juridische uitgevers, 2004); CRvB April 10, 1991 (AB 1991), p. 510; CRvB January 24, 2001, AA 9693, CRvB May 29, 1996 (RZA 1996), p. 134.

11   The Central Appeals Tribunal concluded that national regulation that imposed cost sharing in case of maternity assistance was a violation of Article 10 of the ILO Convention 102 setting minimum standards on social security (CRvB May 29, 1996, RSV 1997/9). According to the Tribunal the imperative nature of the treaty obligation (obligation to ensure), and the concrete wording of the treaty provision prohibit the introduction of cost sharing measures. As a consequence of this ruling, the Dutch government annulled the Decree introducing own contributions for hospital admissions. More recently, the Tribunal confirmed its direct effect jurisprudence in case of (parts of) the European Social Security Code 1964, see CRvB 8 September 2006, LJN AY 8221.

12   CRvB December 17, 1991, RSV 1992/164; CRvB March 31, 1995 (RSV 1996), p. 28; HR 28 April 2000 (NJ 2000), p. 430; HR January 30, 2004 (RvdW 2004), p. 26.

13   E.g., In General Comment no. 3 on the nature of States Parties obligations (Art. 2(1) of the ICESCR). UN Doc. E/1991/23, para. 5, the Committee claims that: "any suggestion that the provisions indicated are inherently non self-executing would seem to be difficult to sustain"; General comment no. 14 on health. The right to the highest attainable standard of health. UN Doc. E/C.12/2000/4, para. 30; UN Doc. E/C.12/I/Add.25.

grounds of the private or family life provision (Article 8).[14] For instance, in *Sentges v. the Netherlands*, a teenage boy with multiple handicaps, Nicki Sentges, complained that his request for a robotic arm was denied. He submitted that under Article 8 the authorities were under a positive obligation to provide him with this medical device, arguing that the concept of private life, as interpreted by the Court, encompassed notions pertaining to the quality of life, including personal autonomy, and the right to establish and develop relationships with other human beings.[15] Sentges argued that the constraints on him were unacceptable as he was never able to be alone and his total dependency on others "forced him to establish and develop friendships that he might not chosen had he not been disabled." While the essential object of Article 8 is to protect the individual against arbitrary interference the Court has held that this provision may also include positive obligations inherent in effective respect for private or family life.[16] These obligations may involve the adoption of measures designed to secure respect of private life.[17] But in order for there to be a positive obligation on the state there needs to be a "direct and immediate link" between the measures sought by the applicant and the latter's private life. Regrettably, the Court declined to decide whether such a link had been established. Instead, the Court concluded that particularly in issues that involve the assessment of priorities of limited health care resources, national authorities enjoy a wide margin of appreciation since they "are in a better position to carry out this assessment than an international court." This is also called the "fair balance" test of the competing interests of the individual and the community as a whole, including the costs of health care. In the present case, the Court considered that the provision of a robotic arm fell within the margin of appreciation since the applicant has access to the standard package of health care provided by the former Health Insurance Act, i.e. an electric wheelchair with an adapted joystick. Only in case of manifest unreasonable outcomes will the Court consider intervening. This could occur, for example, if an applicant was denied a life-saving medicine and it is possible for the cost thereof to be met by the State. In the case of life essential treatment or medicines, one may also consider an appeal to the right to life, Article 2 of the Convention.[18]

---

14 *ECrtHR Marzari v. Italy* May 4, 1999, App. No. 36448/97; *Zehnalovà and Zehnal v. the Czech Republic* May 14, 2002, App. No. 38621/97; *Sentges v. Netherlands* July 8, 2003, App. No. 27677/02.

15 *Supra* note 14, Article 8 of the Convention which, in so far as relevant, provides as follows: [...] everyone has the right to respect for his private [...] life; 2. There shall be no interference by a public authority with the exercise of this right except such as is in accordance with the law and is necessary in a democratic society in the interests of national security, public safety or the economic well-being of the country [...].

16 *Lopez Ostra v. Spain*, judgment on December 9, 1994, *Guerra and Others v. Italy*, judgment on February 19, 1998, *Botta v. Italy*, judgment on February 24, 1998, Reports of Judgments and Decisions 1998-I.

17 E.g., *Stubbings and Others v. the United Kingdom*, judgment on October 22, 1996 (Reports 1996-IV): 1505, 62.

18 See, *Nitecki v. Poland*, judgment on March 21, 2002, App. No. 65653/01 §1, where the Court considered that: "it cannot be excluded that the acts of omissions of the authorities in the field of health care policy may in certain circumstances engage their responsibility under Article 2."

Only in exceptional cases, the alternative approach provided by the Human Rights Court may be effective, but given the Court's understandable hesitation to link the health care right with individual rights, *nominatim* life and private life, and its "fair balance" test, makes that it is extremely difficult, if not impossible, to enforce health care claims. Claiming health insurance entitlements based on statutory law provide a more successful remedy to realise one's right to health care. Due to the influence of the European Court of Justice, we will see that these claims are not restricted to the Dutch territory.

European Union law and health care: Public health law

The European Union (previously, the European Community) was established with the ratification of the Treaty of Maastricht (1992). Since Maastricht, the European Union (EU) Treaty has been modernised by the so-called Treaty of Amsterdam (1997), and will be replaced by the Treaty of Lisbon (2009).[19] These Treaties have created a new, distinctive legal order that can be distinguished from traditional international law by its content, instruments and sources of law.[20]

For historical reasons, the EU has no general competence to regulate in the field of health. The original Treaty of Rome establishing the European Communities did not foresee a "European" health system.[21] Health policy, notably the issue of access to health care services and facilities has been regulated by the domestic legal orders of individual Member States. Community competences with respect to health were mainly based on general treaty provisions as far as they concerned the functioning of the common market.[22] It was only in the Treaty of Maastricht that the EU received supranational competence to run a public health policy of disease prevention and health promotion (Article 129 EC Treaty of Maastricht). The conferred public health tasks to the EU were restricted however by the principle of subsidiary, i.e. only if and insofar as the objectives of the proposed action cannot be sufficiently achieved by the Member States.[23] Thus the Treaty constrains EU jurisdiction vis-à-vis health.

The Amsterdam amendment (1997), introduced considerable changes although the lack of legal precision of Article 152(4)(a) still leaves scope for in-

---

[19] The Lisbon Treaty will replace the previous Treaty of the European Union incorporating previous amendments, OJ 2007/C 306. The new Treaty (including the Human Rights Protocol) will replace the EU Constitutional Treaty that was rejected in France and the Netherlands by referendum.

[20] P. J. G. Kapteyn and P. Verloren van Themaat, 3rd ed., *Introduction to the Law of the European Communities* (London: Kluwer Law Int., 1998), p. 77, confirmed by the ECJ's landmark case *Van Gent en Loos* ECR (1963), p. 1.

[21] Treaty establishing the European Community (Amsterdam consolidated version). Official Journal C 325 of December 24, 2002. Hereafter, references to the treaty refer to this version, available at <http://europe.eu.int/eur-lex/lex/en/index.htm>.

[22] Inter alia, articles 94 and 308 EC. Both provisions are aimed at the realisation of the common market. Further restriction of 'intra-communautaire' trade however, can be found in other relevant treaty provisions aimed at the protection of health and life of humans, for instance article 30 EC.

[23] And therefore, by reason of the scale or effects of the proposed action, be better achieved by the Community, Article 5 EC.

terpretation.[24] Article 152 EC of the Treaty of Amsterdam replaced the Maastricht public health provision, Article 129. As a result Union action will no longer be limited to measures or activities, which are preventive in nature.[25] Since "such action shall cover the fight against the major health scourges, by promoting research ... as well as health information and education" (section 1), the Union may also take positive steps in order to improve public health. Further extended Union public health actions include measures, inter alia, setting standards of quality and safety of organs and substances of human origin, blood and blood derivatives and in the fields of veterinary and phytosanitary health.[26]

In the fifth section it is mentioned that Union action in the field of public health "shall fully respect the responsibility of the Member States for the organisation and delivery of health services and medical care." It re-emphasises the reluctance of Member States to hand over their competences in organising and financing their respective national health care system. Consequently, individual claims to access health care services cannot be based on Article 152.

The free movement principles and health care

Although national authorities have in theory exclusive competencies vis-à-vis the organization, financing and delivery of health care services, this jurisdiction is affected by policy decisions made at the European level and by provisions of EU law designed to realise the internal market. According to article 14(2) of the EC Treaty, the internal market "shall comprise an area without internal frontiers in which the free movement of goods, persons, services and capital is ensured in accordance with the provisions of this Treaty." Under certain circumstances, Union citizens may even derive specific rights emanated from the "free movement" provisions. For patients, the most relevant provisions are the free movement of persons, services and goods.[27] The internal market provisions' impact on the health sector is, however, incomplete and differs by provision.

With regard to the free movement of persons, relevant Treaty provisions include the freedom of movement for "workers" (art. 39-42 EC) and the rights of "establishment" (art. 43-44 EC). These provisions have, in turn, been further

---

24   H. D. C. Roscam Abbing, "Public Health in the Treaty of Amsterdam," *European Journal of Health Law* 2 (1998), p. 173.

25   A. P. van der Mei and L. Waddington, "Public Health and the Treaty of Amsterdam," *European Journal of Health Law* 2 (1998): 135.

26   Article 152(4)(a)(b) EC.

27   EC competition rules fall out of the scope of this chapter since these principles are primarily of relevance in the context of competition among health providers and social health insurance funds. See, for instance, T. S. Jost, D. Dawson and A. P. den Exter. "The Role of Competition in Health Care: A Western European Perspective" *Journal of Health Politics, Policy and Law* vol 31, no 3 (2006), pp. 687-703; see also: A.P. den Exter. "Blending Private and Social Health Insurance in the Netherlands: Challenges Posed by the EU" in C.M. Flood, K. Roach and L. Sossin (eds.), *Access to Care Access to Justice. The Legal Debate over Private Health Insurance in Canada*. (Toronto: University of Toronto Press, 2005), p. 257-277.

substantiated by secondary legislation.[28] Free movement for workers shall entail, inter alia, the right to stay in a Member State for the purpose of employment in accordance with the provisions governing the employment of nationals of that State laid down by law, regulation or administrative action.

The free movement provisions are relevant not only to health professionals, but also to patients. Article 22 of co-ordination regulation 1408/71 (Regulation 1408/71) in conjunction with Article 39 EC, entitles cross-border workers to access the health care system in their country of residence; emergency care in case of temporary residence abroad; and pre-authorised care abroad by the patient's insurer or the competent (national) health authority.[29] Since free movement is not restricted to "workers," relatives, tourists and other categories of EU citizens can also make an appeal to benefit from this provision. Although Regulation 1408/71 aims to coordinate the different social security systems in the Member States, free movement of patients remains problematic. A major problem countries face with cross-border health care is how to regulate and finance this varied care. Some Member States fear an influx of patients from those Member States lacking facilities and/or providing lower-quality care. Rulings from the Court of Justice, simplifying patient mobility, have only strengthened this fear.

The ECJ's rulings on patient mobility

The European Court of Justice (ECJ) is entrusted with, inter alia, the provision of preliminary rulings.[30] On references of the parties in the main proceedings before the national court, the ECJ, by means of a preliminary ruling, is exclusively competent to pronounce the interpretation of the Treaty provisions if a question on this subject is raised. As such, the Court is able to promote the uniformity of interpretation of Union law in the Member States.

In quite a number of cases, the Court's jurisdiction has been invoked in national judicial procedures on patient mobility.[31] In a typical case an insured

---

[28] E.g., the mutual recognition directives, which facilitate a general system for the recognition of diplomas of certain health professionals (Directives 89/48/EEC and 92/51/EEC), recently replaced by the new Professional Qualification Directive 2005/36/EC.

[29] Social security co-ordination regulation 1408/71 OJ No. L 149 of July 5, 1971 as amended by Regulation 859/2003 of May 14, 2003 PB No. L 124, 20/5/2003. In the near future Regulation 1408/71 is due to be replaced by Regulation 883/2004 simplifying and modenising the coordination of social security schemes. Article 91 of the new Regulation provides that Regulation 1408/71 will continue to apply until the entry into force of the implementing regulation. The Commission has put forward a proposal for an implementing measure (COM(2006)16).

[30] Art 234 EC.

[31] *Decker v. Caisse de Maladie des Employés Privés* C-120/5 (1998) ECR I-1831 and *Kohll v. Union des Caisses de Maladie* C-158/96 (1998) ECR I-1931. The European Court of Justice overruled the pertinent Luxembourg regulations, which made reimbursement by the social security system of medical services provided in another Member State – respectively orthodontic treatment and the supply of spectacles – conditional on prior authorisation. The *Decker and Kohll* ruling has initiated a number of cases questioning the Dutch health insurance system, e.g., *Geraerts-Smits/Peerbooms* C-157/99 (2001) ECR I-5473 ; *Müller-Fauré/Van Riet* C-385/99, (2003) ECR I-4409; *Van der Duin v Onderlinge Waarborgmaatschappij ANOZ Zorgverzekerin-*

complains that his/her insurance fund has imposed a restrictive condition or denied approval to receive care abroad and thus questions the legitimacy of the Regulation's pre-authorisation requirement in view of the fundamental freedoms. Since the precedent-setting case of *Decker and Kohll*, the ECJ has been confronted with a growing number of cases questioning the conformity of the Dutch social health insurance system with the free movement principles.[32]

In the joined case of *Smits and Peerbooms*, the Dutch social health insurance fund refused Mrs. Smits reimbursement for specific multidisciplinary hospital treatment costs incurred in a German clinic, specialised in Parkinson's disease. Justifying its decision, the social insurance fund said that satisfactory and adequate treatment for Parkinson's disease was available in the Netherlands and that the specific clinical treatment provided in Germany provided no additional advantage. Thus, it was not "medically necessary" that Mrs. Smits undergo treatment at the German clinic.

The second claimant, Mr. Peerbooms fell into a coma following a road accident. He was transferred to a hospital in the Netherlands and then transferred in a vegetative state to the university clinic in Innsbruck in Austria where he received a special intensive therapy using neurostimulation. In the Netherlands, that technique was considered experimental and only used to be used in certain circumstances. Pursuant to guidelines operating in the Netherlands, Peerbooms would not have qualified for such experimental treatment due to his age. Thus the Sickness Fund refused to pay the costs of treatment.

In both cases, the ECJ had to rule on the pre-authorisation rule, and whether such a rule in the circumstances of those particular cases constitutes a barrier to the freedom to provide services. In contrast to the *Decker and Kohll* ruling (dealing with non-hospital care within a reimbursement system), the *Smits/Peerbooms* case concerned access to hospital care services for which the sickness fund had not contracted, and which, within the Netherlands, is provided on a "benefit-in-kind" basis.[33] The Court agreed that sickness funds should not be exposed to the cost of hospital services for which they had not contracted. However, the pre-authorisation condition as applied by the authorities in the Netherlands was criticised for its potentially discriminatory effect. In the Netherlands, the general legal rule under which the costs of medical treatment are covered is where the treatment is found to be "normal in the professional circles concerned."[34] This expression, however, is open to a num-

---

gen and Onderlinge Waarborgmaatschappij ANOZ Zorgverzekeringen v Van Wegberg-van Brederode C-156/01 (2003) ECR I-7045, *Inizan v. Caisse primaire d'assurance maladie des Hauts-de-Seine* C-56/01, (2003) ECR I-12403; *Leichtle* C-8/02 (2004), ECR I-2641, *Keller* C-145/03 (2005), ECR.I-2529; and *Watts* C-372/04.(2006) ECR I-4325.

32 Smits/Peerbooms; Müller-Fauré/Van Riet; Van der Duin, and Wegberg-van Brederode, see note 31.

33 In a benefit-of-kind system, the insured is entitled only to statutory benefits, provided by health providers having an agreement with health insurance funds. This is different from a reimbursement system in which health insurers reimburse the costs of treatment to the insured. In such a model there is no contractual relationship between the health insurer and the health provider.

34 Based on settled case-law of the Central Appeals Tribunal (CRvB) May 23, 1995 (RZA 1995) No. 126.

ber of interpretations, depending in particular on whether what is "normal" is considered as such in Dutch medical circles (this narrow interpretation being favoured by the national court in the Netherlands). In contrast, the ECJ decided that to allow only treatment habitually carried out on national territory and scientific views prevailing in national medical circles to determine what is or is not "normal," will not offer sufficient guarantees to patients that the guidelines in place are objective, non-discriminatory, known in advance and not used arbitrarily. Moreover, such a focus on national conceptions of "normal" will make it likely that Dutch providers will always be preferred in practice.[35] The ECJ found that where treatment is sufficiently tried and tested by international medical science, refusal of the prior authorisation cannot be justified. Further, to satisfy the "normal" criterion, a Member State "must take into consideration all the relevant available information, including, in particular, existing scientific literature and studies, the authorised opinions of specialists and the fact that the proposed treatment is covered or not covered by the sickness insurance system of the Member State in which the treatment is provided."[36]

From this case, it became clear that Member States must apply the pre-authorisation procedure consistently and that patients cannot be denied health care abroad arbitrarily (i.e., there have to non-discriminatory, transparent procedures, and appeal mechanisms). For patients entitled to benefit-in-kind services, such as provided in the Dutch system, the ruling means that it should be just as easy to receive medical treatment from a foreign non-contracted provider as it is to obtain from a non-contracted provider in the country of insurance. As such, the ECJ's interpretation of communal pre-authorisation conditions creates new opportunities for extended access to health care abroad.[37]

Subsequent to the *Smits/Peerbooms* case, the ECJ had to rule on two more or less identical situations in the Dutch mixed case of *Müller-Fauré/Van Riet*.[38] Here, the Court consolidated and clarified its previous reasoning on prior authorisation, at least concerning inpatient hospital care. However, the Court also confirmed that there are several reasons that may justify requiring prior authorisation where social health insurance funds cover benefits provided in another Member State. These reasons include: the protection of public health in as much as the system of agreements is intended to ensure that there is a high-quality, balanced medical and hospital service open to all; to guarantee the financial balance of the social security system; and, finally, to enable managing authorities to control expenditures for and the planning of health services. The Court noted that concerns regarding undermining the financial balance of the social security system particularly valid vis-à-vis hospital care. In the case of hospital services, according to the Court, it is well known that to ensure sufficient access to a wide range of hospital services and in order to contain costs, that careful planning is required regarding the number of hospi-

---

35 Smits/Peerbooms, at para 96.
36 *Ibid*, at para 98.
37 H. A. G. Temmink, "Kroniek van het Europees recht (European law column, in Dutch)," *Nederlands Juristenblad* 31 (2001), 1502.
38 Müller-Fauré, *ibid*.

tals, their geographical distribution, the mode of their organisation and the equipment with which they are provided.39 Nonetheless, the conditions attached to the grant of authorisation must be justified and satisfy the requirement of proportionality, and such a prior authorisation scheme must likewise be based on a procedural system which is easily accessible and capable of being challenged in judicial or quasi-judicial proceedings.40

However, with respect to outpatient (non-hospital) health care, as is the case in Müller-Fauré (i.e. dental care), the Court was not convinced that abolishing prior authorisation will have a system-undermining effect. According to the Court, "there was no evidence that indicated that the removal of the prior authorisation requirement for that type of care would give rise to patients travelling to other countries in such large numbers, despite linguistic barriers, geographic distance, the cost of staying abroad and lack of information about the kind of care provided there, and that the financial balance of the social security system would be seriously upset."41 Therefore, in case of non-hospital services, there was no justification for requiring prior authorisation when one applies the free movement principle.

Although the Müller-Fauré/Van Riet case was considered the latest in a line of cross-border rulings, new Court rulings on hospital-related expenditures in another Member State (the Leichtle case), as well as the reimbursement of hospital services in non-EU countries, have further extended the notion of patient mobility (the Keller case), and its relevance to national health system funded systems (Watts).42 Although the cases question the German (Leichtle), Spanish (Keller), and the UK (Watts) legal norms on cross-border care, the outcome is relevance to all Member States, including the Netherlands.

In the Leichtle case, the question raised did not concern so much the approval and reimbursement of the expenditures of the health care facility abroad (i.e., health spa), but the rules concerning the reimbursement of other expenditures related to the treatment abroad (travel, lodging, etc.). Since the conditions for reimbursement of this kind of costs were set for out-of-country treatment only (i.e., increased prospects of success, and the report written by a medical officer), Germany could deter the insured from approaching health care providers abroad, ergo, hindering free movement. Expenditures related to board and lodging can be considered as an integral part of the health care itself. After all, just as hospital treatment may involve a stay in hospital, a health care services administered for therapeutic purposes may well, by its nature, in-

---

39   Müller-Fauré, para 77.
40   *Ibid*, para 85. Under the proportionality test, if a less invasive alternative measure or arrangement could perform an assigned task under the same conditions as the arrangement being challenged, the less invasive alternative should be chosen.
41   *Ibid*, para 95.
42   *Ludwig Leichtle v. Bundesanstalt für Arbeit* Case C-8/02 (2004), ECR I-2641, and the Keller case, *Keller v. Instituto Nacional de Gestión Sanitaria* (Ingesa), formerly Instituto Nacional de la Salud (Insalud) being discussed by the author in: A. P. den Exter, "Patient Mobility in the European Union: Health Spas in Italy," *Croatian Medical Journal* 46, no. 2 (2005): 197-200; A. P. den Exter, "The European Court of Justice and the Keller case: A Bridge too Far?" *Medicine and Law* (2005), and *Watts* being discussed by Chris Newdick in his contribution *"Solidarity, Rights and Social Welfare in the NHS – Resisting the Tide of Bioethics?" (Chapter 4).*

volve admission at a spa. Although travel costs and visitor's tax are not medical in character, they are, according to the Court, "inextricably linked to the cure itself since the patient is required to travel and stay at the spa in Italy."[43] Consequently, the conditions for these expenditures have to be tested according to the previously accepted reason for justification. Additionally, this means that the measure taken should be necessary and that its objective cannot be reached by an alternative, less invasive measure under the same conditions (proportionality test).

The German authorities claimed that the absence of the disputed conditions would seriously harm the financial equilibrium of the German social security system if it is not accompanied by an analysis of the appropriateness and proportionality of the restrictive measure. Since they could not support that claim with well-founded arguments, the Court did not accept the general-interest reason as justification for restricting the free movement of patients. Therefore, Mr Leichtle was compensated for the additional expenditures of the health spa abroad. A contrario, in case a Member State can show there is no less intrusive alternative equally effective as the suggested measure, or make a reasonable case for the financial instability of the system in case many people would access health spas abroad, the outcome of this case may have been different.

What has become clear from the *Leichtle* case is that national rules that restrict contracting to health institutions in the Member State exclusively are forbidden. However, the condition that a treatment should be provided by an institution listed in a so-called "Registration of Health Spas" does not necessarily hinder access to spa services in another Member State, since the rationale of such a measure is to ensure that the health insurance fund can check the "seriousness" of services provided by health spas, in and outside the country.[44] Nonetheless, the registration requirement may still have a potential hindering effect, which depends on the objectivity of the conditions for registration. Finally, the definition of the health plan entitlements, as well as the amount of reimbursement granted, remains the prerogative of the member states themselves. This is caused by the absence of harmonizing competences at Community level in the field of social security.

In the *Keller* case, the Court was confronted with the question whether EU citizens, may ask for (the reimbursement of) medical treatment outside the European Union based on European social security rules. More specific, the Court was being asked whether the granted authorisation, provided by the Spanish health authorities (Insalud) to undergo a medical treatment in a Member State (Germany), should be interpreted as an approval for a surgical operation that, in view of its extreme delicate nature and the special expertise required, could only be performed in a non-Member State private clinic (Switzerland). In other words, whether the Insalud is bound by the diagnosis and choice of treatment of the doctors authorised by the German medical bodies, and thus whether consequently there is an obligation to reimburse the costs of Keller's hospital treatment the Swiss clinic.

---

43   Leichtle, para. 35.
44   Conclusion A-G Ruiz-Jarabo Colomer, Case C-8/02. ECR (2004), supra note 42, para 34.

The Court refers to the objective of the applicable social security provision, and its function, i.e., helping to facilitate the free movement of persons covered by social insurance, and to the same extent, the provision of cross-border medical services between Member States based on Article 22 of regulation 1408/71. The achievement of the objective pursued is based on a sharing of responsibilities between the competent institution (Insalud) and the institution of the Member State of stay (Germany). Whereas the Insalud is responsible for granting authorisation for receiving health care abroad, it is for the German physicians to provide those services in accordance with the applicable German law. It follows from that rule of shared responsibilities, in correlation with the Union measures relating to the mutual recognition of diplomas of the formal qualifications of practitioners of medicine, that the Insalud is bound by the hands of the German physicians, and that it is obliged to accept and recognise the findings and choices of treatment made by those doctors.45 In this particular case, Insalud gave permission to undergo a medical surgery in Germany. Accordingly, when it has agreed to receive a medical treatment outside Spain, it is bound by the findings relating to the need for urgent vital treatment made by the authorised doctors. Similarly, Insalud is bound by the choice of treatment made by these doctors given the circumstances that the urgent treatment could only be provided outside the EU.

Under these circumstances, Ms Keller cannot be required to return to the competent authority, the Insalud to undergo a medical examination there, when doctors in Germany considered that her state of health required urgent treatment. Moreover, asking prior approval of the Insalud would disregard the rule of shared responsibilities underlying European social security law and the principle of mutual recognition of doctors' professional skills.46

With respect to the conditions for reimbursement of the costs linked to medical treatment in a non-Member State, the Court refers to its previous rulings in which it concluded that, in principle, the insured enjoy the benefits-in-kind provided by the health services of the Member State of stay, on behalf of the competent authority.47 In this particular case, it means that the costs of treatment borne by (the heirs of) Keller have to be reimbursed by the Insalud, in accordance with German reimbursement rules. By doing so, the Spanish insured are treated under the same conditions as insured citizens within Germany. Furthermore, it should be clear that the treatment received is among the benefits provided by the legislation of the competent member state, i.e., Spain.

The *Keller* case can be added to a series of rulings from the European Court of Justice on health care abroad. The difference with other rulings is that Keller asked for (reimbursement of) medical treatment outside the European Union, whereas previous rulings concerned in and out patient health care in another Member State. What makes this case interesting is the interpretation given by the Court on European social security law, more specific the meaning of Regulation 1408/71 on the coordination of social security. Although the ter-

---

45   Keller, note 42, para. 50.
46   *Ibidem*, para. 57.
47   Vanbraekel C-368/98, ECR (2001) I-5363, para 32.

ritorial scope of Union law is restricted to its Member States that does not exclude its applicability when it concerns services provided outside the European Union. Essentially, this is what the Court of Justice has made clear. The Spanish government disputed such an extensive interpretation of Community law by claiming that since the medical treatment provided outside the European Union, the outcome of the proceeding does not therefore depend on the interpretation of Union law, but is a matter exclusively for national law.[48] The Court parried that argument by stating that the decisive criterion for the applicability of the regulation is that the insured is affiliated to a social security scheme of a Member State. Since Ms Keller was affiliated under the Spanish Insalud, the applicability of Union law was therefore beyond doubt.

Furthermore, the Court based its decision on the rule of shared responsibilities between the home Member State and the Member State of stay. Secondly, due to the system of mutual recognition of diplomas, one may assume that German doctors are qualified and authorised to make a diagnosis and choice of treatment. Given that competence, the fact that the state to which the patient has been transferred is not a member of the European Union, is of no importance.

Finally, in the *Watts* case, the Court confirmed the interpretation on 'undue delay' as pointed out in the *Smits-Peerbooms* and *Müller-Fauré* rulings. In order to determine whether treatment can be obtained without undue delay in de Member State of residence (UK), the competent institution is required to have regard to all the circumstances of each case, including the patient medical condition, the degree of pain or the nature of the patient's disability, but also his medical history. Furthermore, the competent institution cannot base its decision exclusively on the existence of waiting lists on that territory without taking into account of the specific circumstances of the patient's medical condition. Only if the waiting time arising from the general planning objectives does not exceed a medically acceptable waiting time, the competent institution is allowed to refuse to grant authorization. In the situation opposite, the competent institution will grant authorization to receive hospital treatment abroad at the expense of the system of the state of residence.

Consequences for the Dutch Health Insurance Scheme

One may question whether the Court's case law, and in particular the recent ruling in Keller, has not opened a Pandora's box. Will the result be that patients, now empowered to search for the best health care services abroad, begin the eventual demise and dismantlement of the social health insurance system? The answer is, in short, no; but the implications for the Dutch – and other – health care schemes are considerable.

First, it is now clear that medical activities fall within the scope of the EC treaty provision on free movement of services, even hospital services. Consequently, national social security rules cannot be used to exclude application of the free movement provision.[49] This applies to insurance schemes, such as in

---

48   Keller, para. 37.
49   Smits/Peerbooms, para. 54.

the Netherlands, providing benefits-in-kind services, but also to hospital services provided by a National Health Service such as exists in the UK (*Watts*). The UK government unsuccessfully attempted to exempt NHS services from the ambit of article 50 of the EC since it provides services directly rather than reimbursing the cost of services received. The ECJ noted "that a medical service does not cease to be a provision of services because it is paid for by a national health services or by a system providing benefits-in-kind."[50]

Second, the Court has also, on occasion, made it clear that EU law does not undermine the power of the Member States to organise their respective social security systems.[51] In the absence of harmonisation at EU level, each Member State may pass legislation pursuant to which citizens have first a right or duty to be insured with a social security scheme, and, second, the conditions for entitlement to benefits.[52] Moreover, it is not incompatible with EU law for a Member State to establish, with a view toward achieving its aim of limiting costs, a negative list excluding certain products from reimbursement.[53] It follows that EU law cannot, in principle, have the effect of requiring a Member State to extend the list of medical services paid for by its social insurance system.[54] Nonetheless, in exercising its powers, the Member State must not disregard EU law.[55] Essentially, this means that the list of insured medical treatments must be drawn up in accordance with objective criteria, which are known in advance, and without reference to the origin of the service (non-discrimination). In the Netherlands, the health insurance system is not based on a pre-established list of types of treatment for which payment will be guaranteed; rather the Health Insurance Act has chosen a 'functional description' of the care covered by the insurance package (e.g., medical, dental and pharmaceutical care). Whereas the law sets the legal requirements for what entitlements include, it is up to the provider and insurance fund who provides the care and where. Furthermore, the legislature has enacted a general rule providing that the care provided will also be determined by "the state of medical science and practice"[56] This new criterion replaces the "normal criterion", used under the former Health Insurance Act. Even under the new insurance regime, it is largely up to the discretion of the health insurance funds to decide which types of treatment satisfy that condition; however, in applying that crite-

---

50   Müller-Fauré, para. 103, Watts, para. 89.
51   Duphar and Others C-238/82 (1984) ECR I-523 para. 16 and Case C-158/96; Kohll, para. 17.
52   E.g., Kohll para. 18. In the Dutch situation, the nature and scope of entitlements are being set by the main social insurance scheme, the new Health Insurance Act (arts. 10 and 11 Zvw).
53   Duphar and Others, para. 16.
54   Smits/Peerbooms, para. 87.
55   This means, for instance, that they should respect basic community principles, including the non-discrimination principle. *Ferlini v. Centre hospitalier de Luxembourg* C-411/98 (2000), ECR I-8081. In this case, the Court ruled that the application, on a unilateral basis, by a group of health care providers to EU officials of scales of fees for medical and hospital maternity care that are higher than those applicable to residents affiliated to the national social security scheme constitutes discrimination on the ground of nationality prohibited under Article 12(1) EC, in the absence of objective justification.
56   The state of medical science and practice-criterion follows the principles of evidence based medicine (EBM). Besluit Zorgverzekeringswet artikel 2.1 sub 2, 28 June 2005.

rion, these funds must now interpret the criterion on the basis of what is sufficiently tried and tested by international medical science.[57] This could mean
that where a certain treatment has sufficiently been tried and tested by international science, authorisation by the insurance fund could not be refused on the
grounds that it is not presently provided in the Netherlands. The only justifi-
able reason to refuse approval is where, given the need to maintain an adequate supply of hospital care and to ensure the financial stability of the health
insurance system, the "same or equally effective treatment can be obtained
without undue delay" at a contracted provider.[58] It should be noted that in determining whether "the same or equally effective treatment can be obtained
without undue delay," the mere fact that a person is on a waiting list does not
necessarily mean that the treatment is unavailable.[59] "Undue delay" should be
determined as the period within which medical treatment is necessary with respect to the patient's medical condition and history. Moreover, those Member
States, like the Netherlands, that use the "normal criterion" in determining entitlements to coverage will not be required to allow their citizens to obtain
treatment in any hospital in any EU country unless that treatment is both accepted in international medical circles and is not sufficiently available in the
home country (medical necessity criterion).[60]

Third, patients are now entitled to search for non-hospital services abroad
that are not available in their home country or, if available, are not available in
a timely fashion (*Müller-Fauré/Van Riet*). One should keep in mind, however,
that without prior authorisation, social health insurance funds are still fully entitled to reimburse only costs up to the maximum amount that is applicable in
the country of residence. For that reason, the Court did not consider the removal of the administrative prior authorisation condition to be a serious threat
to the financial balance of the social security system, since it had to bear the
cost of treatment when received in the patient's home country anyway. Patients seeking non-hospital care in other EU nations without prior authorization must bear any additional costs above and beyond the relevant tariff that
provided for in the relevant tariff in their own country.

Fourth, as mentioned above, the larger public interest in maintaining a
sustainable social insurance system may be accepted as justifying barriers to
freedom to provide medical services in the context of hospital infrastructure.[61]
Member States need to determine whether their respective national rules can
be legitimately justified in the light of such overriding reasons. In accordance
with settled case law, it is necessary to ensure that they do not exceed what is

---

57 This means, for instance, to include evidence from clinical randomized controlled trails (stage III studies).
58 Smits/Peerbooms, para. 103.
59 Here, the Central Appeals Tribunal refers to standards, so-called "Treek-normen," defining the maximum acceptable waiting time for a specific medical intervention. The underlying idea is that hospitals, for planning and efficiency reasons, need a certain waiting time, CRvB June 18, 2004, para. 92. Also, CRvB June 18, 2004, USZ 2004/277, 11 month waiting time for a hip replacement is not considered as "timely."
60 CRvB 5 November 2003, USZ 2004/17; CRvB July 20, 2004 identical treatment timely available.
61 Kohll, para. 41; Müller-Fauré/Van Riet, para. 72.

objectively necessary for the given purpose and that the same result cannot be achieved by less restrictive rules. As determined in *Müller-Fauré/Van Riet* and *Watts*, these requirements apply regardless of the type or nature of the health care system (e.g., whether a social insurance system as in the Netherlands or a national health service as in the U.K.).[62]

Fifth, the various ECJ rulings leave some unsettled questions particularly given that the difference between hospital (inpatient) and non-hospital (outpatient) care is not always that clear.[63] For example, some surgical services may be provided in a hospital or in an outpatient clinic. Moreover, certain types of care are only partly hospital-based, e.g., hospital treatment combined with admission to an outpatient clinic. Disagreement about the nature of the provided care concerned may give rise to legal uncertainty among the insured and cause an increase in litigation. Patients need to be particularly aware of whether or not the provided services will be classified as a hospital service. In such a case if a patient has not obtained prior authorization before receiving treatment in another Member State, then he or she may be denied reimbursement.[64] In a previous ruling, the ECJ confirmed the nexus between the need for prior authorization and hospitalization finding that where the "multidisciplinary treatment of pain which the claimant envisages [...] involves her hospitalization, then this necessitated the patient obtaining prior authorisation."[65] In contrast, the District Court in Maastricht concluded that a special type of physiotherapy, which requires hospital admission, should not be considered to be hospital care, since it is generally qualified as non-hospital care.[66]

These contrasting cases demonstrate that the difficult question of what constitutes hospital or non-hospital care is decisive for determining whether prior authorisation is required and thus whether patients will be reimbursed for the costs of treatment received in other Member States. However, in some cases there may be no *communis opinio* among medical professionals about whether or not hospitalization is necessary. In that case, patients searching for alternative treatment options in other Member States without prior authorisation take a considerable financial risk. Arguably at least, hospitalization should be interpreted in the patient's favour (as opposed to the national authorities'), meaning that the place of actual treatment should be decisive in interpreting whether hospitalization is required.[67] Any other interpretation may create a

---

62 Müller-Fauré and Watts.

63 As a rule, the Health Care Insurance Board (CVZ) decided that hospital care requires at least one day admission in an hospital institution. Letter no 03/35, June 25, 2003.

64 Also suggested by Advocate General Colomer in his opinion on Smits/Peerbooms, para. 61. The risk of denial of reimbursement is also present in case a non-hospital treatment still requires hospital admission, for instance due to medical complications. In such a case, since prior authorisation is absent, the costs of hospital admission and treatment will not be reimbursed.

65 *Inizan v. Caisse Primaire d' Assurance Maladie des Hauts-de-Seine* C-56/01(2003) E.C.R. I-12403 at para. 55.

66 Maastricht District Court, September 26, 2003, AL 3183, the Netherlands.

67 See also G. Davies, "Health and Efficiency: Community Law and National Health Systems in the Light of Müller-Fauré," *Modern Law Review* 67, no. 1 (2004), p. 103.

perverse incentive for social insurance funds to organise outpatient care in a hospital sphere for merely opportunistic reasons.[68]

Sixth and finally, based on the Court's extensive interpretation of the patient mobility provision in the Keller ruling, in exceptional cases, health insurance funds can be forced to reimburse the costs of planned treatment in a country outside of the EU. However, as a rule, the treatment provided, should be recognised by the Member State of stays' national law.

In sum, there is no doubt that the Court's jurisprudence on patient mobility has significantly contributed to the development of a corpus of rights to access health care, although one may question whether the Court has gone too far at the battlefield of cross-border care. In contrast to Field Marshal Montgomery's experience with World War II's most tragic blunder, Operation Market Garden at the bridge of Arnhem, the Court has succeeded to force a break in the Dutch and other Member States' line of defence on social security.[69] Starting with the *Decker and Kohll* ruling, further case law has extended the patient's options to receive health care abroad and simplified the necessary conditions, and simultaneously, taking into account the public interest. In this respect, the *Watts* case was definitely not the last battle in this area. By strengthening the rights of patients, there is no bridge too far. The importance of the Court's role in patient mobility issues has been confirmed by the latest Commission's proposal on regulating patient mobility in a framework Directive. However, due to internal disagreement within the Commission and heavy criticism from some MEP's, the controversial proposal was shelved. In terms of content, the framework Directive was expected to set out clear rules on which institution is responsible for covering the costs and securing quality of cross-border treatment.

International legal concerns

Although the *"Zorgverzekeringswet"* has – to a certain extent - been inspired by both international and European law, critics have questioned the law's conformity with treaty law.[70] So far, that debate was primarily focussing on the new role of health insurance entities when introducing a dose of competition in health insurance in relation to EU law.

---

68 A similar interpretation – mutatis mutandis – was used by the Court in the *Vanbraekel* case, note 47, when ruling that the level of reimbursement for foreign hospital services should have been the same, had the same services been received in the home country.

69 Operation Market Garden was aimed at crossing the bridge of Arnhem, near the German borders, in order to march on to Berlin. Unfortunately, British paratroops were dropped behind enemy lines, whereas allied forces could not release them since the German army occupied the bridge over the river Rhine. This historic battle inspired Hollywood filmmakers to shoot a film titled "A bridge too far."

70 E.g., A. P. den Exter, "De Europese kwetsbaarheid van de Zorgverzekeringswet (EU legal implications of the new Health Insurance Act)," *NJB, Dutch Law Journal* 2 (2005), p. 87-93; see also, A. P. den Exter (ed.), *Competitive Social Health Insurance; Yearbook 2004* (Rotterdam: Erasmus University Press, 2005); and: "De Zorgverzekeringswet en GATS: een controverse?" In E. Ten Napel en A. Hendriks (eds.), *De veellagige rechtsorde* (The Haque: Kluwer Law International, 2007), p. 95-106.

However, little attention has been paid to the international legal consequences of the introduction of cost-sharing measures, such as the (withdrawn) no-claim refund and compulsory co-payments. Although cost-sharing measures may be successfully to achieve the goal of cost-reduction, there may be serious consequences for certain categories of patients (e.g., chronically ill, low income patients). As a rule, cost-sharing should be so designed as to avoid hardship, but considering the amount of co-payments, in combination with the introduced fixed premium, there is a serious risk that the total costs will exceed the specified percentages as set in the (revised) European Social Security Code and therefore violate the Treaty hardship-clause.[71] In a way, history may repeat itself given the Central Appeals Tribunal's ruling prohibiting co-payments for maternity care.[72]

The hardship-clause can be considered the Code's equivalent of the "standstill" provision, as it is known in international treaty law. In the International Covenant on Economic, Social and Cultural Rights (ICESCR), the standstill clause has been defined as "[a]ny deliberately retrogressive measure would require the most careful consideration and would need to be fully justified by reference to the totality of the rights provided by the Covenant and in the context of the full use of the maximum available resources."[73] Although the standstill-clause is not absolute, "there is a strong presumption of impermissibility of any retrogressive measure," explained by the State party.[74] Also in that respect, a retrogressive measure such as the co-payment arrangement, is highly questionable, and can only be justified by means of the 'health care allowances' to be introduced simultaneously with the "*Zorgverzekeringswet*".[75] But in case such a grant appears insufficient, and the financial burden hinders the effectiveness of medical protection to (high-risk) persons, the impermissibility of the cost-sharing measure revives, causing a violation of the Treaty's core obligation.[76] Whether or not the judiciary would accept such a hardship or stand-

---

[71]   Under the hardship-clause, cost sharing measures are limited to a certain level. In this respect, see the Resolutions from the Council of Ministers of the Council of Europe, in which cost-sharing measures were considered incompatible with the European Code (Part IV): CSS(86)10, February 17, 1986; resolution CSS (87) 10, March 12, 1987, and resolution CSS (90) 11, February 21, 1990.

[72]   See also, M. W. Wetters-Bronsgeest. "Eigen bijdragen aan een zijden draadje? (Own payments by a threat, in Dutch)," *Rechtspraak Zorgverzekering, RZA* (2004), p. 979-980. The European Code corresponds to ILO Convention 102, but foresees in (maximized) co-payments but avoiding hardship. In this respect, see also note 11, the CRvB ruling of 8 September 2006. Although it concerned the ILO Convention 102 (already withdrawn by the Dutch government), it ruled that co-payments were a violation of the European Code (Part VI).

[73]   UN Committee on Economic, Social and Cultural Rights (CESCR), General Comment no. 3, at 9. The nature of State parties obligations, Art. 2(1) UN Doc. E/1991/23 Fifth session, 1990.

[74]   General Comment no. 14. The right to the highest attainable standard of health (Art. 12, par. 1), UN Doc. E/C12/2000/4 (Twenty second session, 2000): at 32.

[75]   Under the new regime, the insured pay a nominal insurance premium to their health insurer. To keep the health insurance system financially affordable for all, a "health care allowance" was introduced. But that allowance will not compensate premium cost entirely.

[76]   Concluding Observations Iraq UN Doc. E/1998/22, at 253, in which the UN Committee concluded that economic sanctions imposed by the UN on Iraq do not justify retrogressive

---

still argument remains to be seen. First of all, it requires hard evidence of the retrogressive effects of the new law.

Final Remarks

It is clear that international law, including European Union law, has had a significant influence on guaranteeing access to health care in the Netherlands. International legal norms conceptualise the content of the health care right, whereas the judiciary confirmed the enforceability of such a right in terms of benefit entitlements. Moreover, the European Court of Justice, with its rulings on patient mobility has extended the meaning of such a right, in the Netherlands and abroad.

There are, however, also reasons for concern. Generally interpreted as a social security right in the Netherlands, access to health care is based on the concept of solidarity and equality. With the new Health Insurance Act, introducing cost-sharing measures that may affect high-risk persons disproportionally, a change towards a more restricted notion of solidarity is emerging. Although the government claims that the new Health Insurance Law does not alter the nature of the social health insurance scheme, the competitive and for-profit nature of the insurance and providers market, or the increased elements of capitalisation (e.g., co-payments, medical care saving accounts considerations, etc.), the evidence is otherwise. It reflects a gradual shift from social towards more direct insurance that seems difficult to match with the solidarity notion, at least in terms of European and international law. The development of liberalizing the health (insurance) market challenges the country's autonomy to define the entitlements, as well as setting conditions restricting access to health care. A simple referral to the financial sustainability clause will not be sufficient to convince the judiciary of the importance of access' restrictive measures. As such, international treaty law challenges the future sustainability of the system and thus, ironically, may result in retrenchment in the entitlements as seen in the Netherlands.

---

measures towards Iraq's treaty obligation to guarantee food and pharmaceuticals. Although the standstill clause is not absolute, see: M. M. Sepúlveda Carmona, "The Obligations of the State under the International Covenant on Economic, Social and Cultural Rights." (*Utrecht University* diss., 2002), p. 348-349.

Chapter 4.

Solidarity, Rights and Social Welfare in the NHS – Resisting the Tide of Bioethics?

Christopher Newdick

Health care provides a good opportunity to discuss solidarity. We know it has something to do with promoting collective interests,[1] but how does the concept affect our *individual* rights to welfare? A number of factors combine to make sustained discussion of solidarity difficult. First, modern legal theory tends to highlight the rights of the individual, rather than the needs of community. Rawls, Nozick and Dworkin all emphasise individual autonomy *against* the state so that, as HLA Hart has said, we have moved away from a belief in *public* interests to a new faith that "the truth must lie with a doctrine of basic human rights, protecting specific basic liberties and interests of individuals."[2] Second, when cases come before the courts, the very process of litigation is likely to incline judges to respond to individual needs. The visibility and intensity of individual claims will understandably stir judicial sympathies more forcibly than more recondite claims based on *community* interests.[3] This concern has arisen especially in recent jurisprudence of the European Court of Justice, which we return to in the conclusion.

Also, the "politics" of health care (certainly in the NHS) often speaks of patients as "consumers" with individual rights to choose where and when they will be admitted to hospital.[4] In an environment that encourages patients to

---

[1]   Education and the environment are also important in this respect. See generally, T.H Marshall, *Citizenship and Social* Class (Cambridge University Press, 1950), and, in health care, *Choices in Health Care* (Government Committee on Choices in Health Care, Zoetermeer, The Netherlands, 1992) and *Priorities in Health Care* (Final Report of the Swedish Parliamentary Priorities Commission, 1995).

[2]   H.L.A. Hart, "Between Utility and Rights", in A. Ryan (ed), *The Idea of Freedom* (Oxford: Oxford University Press, 1979), p. 77, quoted in M. Sandel, *Liberalism and its Critics* (New York: New York University Press, 1992), p. 4-5.

[3]   See eg R (Watts) v Bedfordshire PCT Case (2006) ECJ, C-372/04 (discussed below), *Minister of Health v Treatment Action Campaign* (No 2) 2002 (5) SA 721 (South Africa), *Chaoulli v AG of Quebec and AG of Canada* (2005) SCC 35 (Canada), *R v Secretary of State for the Home Department, ex p Limbuela* [2005] UKHL 66 (England, an asylum seeker case).

[4]   Successive Secretaries of State have made demands which the NHS could not sustain. See the critical comments of Professor Sir Ian Kennedy in his *Learning from Bristol: The Report of the Public Inquiry into Children's Heart Surgery at the Bristol Royal Infirmary, 1984-95* (Cm. 5207, 2001) p. 57, at para. 31.

think of health and consumer rights as much the same, it is not surprising that we find it difficult to articulate concepts of community, citizenship and social trust. Yet it is important that we do so. Finite public resources impose constraints that make a wholly *individualistic* view of health care rights untenable. Talk of rights as "trumps,"[5] which "even the welfare of society as a whole cannot override,"[6] is implausible in respect of socio-economic rights such as public health care. It fails to recognise the polycentric nature of claims in which paying for Peter's right to care may be achieved only at the expense of diverting it from Paula. As Pellegrino has said:

> Rights language focuses too often on the negative rights of freedom from coercion and not enough on obligation and duties. Given the vulnerable and dependant state of sick persons, it is not intrusion they fear, but abandonment to their fates by their fellow humans. As a result there is a growing interest in communitarian and common good conceptions of justice.[7]

All social welfare systems give rise to a community of interests in which a wholly individualistic response is inappropriate. This is the problem of solidarity. How should "rights" in this environment be understood?

Although, at a theoretical level, Rawls imagined individuals coming together to make a social contract behind a "veil of ignorance,"[8] without some understanding of "community", it is difficult to visualise how negotiations would proceed. Individuals might contemplate a minimalist "night watchman" state to preserve themselves from lives otherwise hedonistic, nasty, brutish and short,[9] but to suggest that individualists behind such a veil could discuss a system of social welfare is fanciful.[10] Many of the liberal rights we take for granted are meaningful only in the context of society. More plausible are the observations of, for example, Sandel[11] and Etzioni[12] who emphasise the need to locate the discussion of rights in the context of public values and to think of individuals in terms of communitarian ethics. As they say, autonomy and the idea of rights *against* the state provide an incomplete analysis of rights in society; community is integral to our character, individuality and capacity to flourish. Family, history, language, race, religion, nationality, education and employment all influence our perception of ourselves. Concepts of autonomy that fail to accommodate these forces present a distorted and artificial view of people in society. As Sir John Laws has said, to define autonomy in terms of rights alone is a serious mistake. To do so

---

5   See R. Dworkin, *Taking Rights Seriously* (London: Duckworth, 1978), ch. 4 and 364.
6   See J. Rawls, A Theory of Justice (Oxford: Oxford University Press, 1971), p. 3.
7   E. Pellegrino, "The Commodification of Medical and Health Care: The Moral Consequences of a Paradigm Shift from Professional to a Market Ethics," (1999) 24 *J Medicine and Philosophy* 243, p. 258.
8   See Rawls, *ibid., p.* 136-42.
9   See R. Nozick, *Anarchy, State and Utopia* (Oxford: Blackwell, 1994).
10 See the cogent critique of M. Sandel, *Liberalism and the Limits of Justice* (Cambridge University Press, 2nd ed, 1998), p. 24-28.
11 See above and M. Sandel, *Liberalism and its Critics* (New York University Press, 1984).
12 See A Etzioni, *The New Golden Rule – Community and Morality in a Democratic Society* (New York: Profile Books, 1997).

would be to deny men's shared morality. If it becomes the systematic feature of a prevailing social philosophy, it would tend to give rise to a community of selfish individuals, and therefore to no community. A society whose values are defined by reference to individual rights is by that very fact already impoverished. Its culture says nothing of individual duty... and therefore nothing of community.[13]

Equally, although Etzioni, Sandel and others develop an attractive picture of communitarian *values*, it is difficult to see them as practicable and persuasive ethical *principles*. This presents another difficulty for the concept of solidarity. Since Kant, we have focused individual rights in society and the appeal of such a concept is easy to grasp. Freedom, autonomy and the right to self-determination are powerful and persuasive concepts. History too, gives ample warning of the risks of coercive and over-arching states which undermine the individual; or societies that simply neglect, or marginalise minority groups.[14] By contrast, "solidarity" is a chameleon concept with different meanings.[15] Its imprecise nature presents another obstacle. How can civic and republican interests also protect the individual and minority groups from oppression, or neglect? Isaiah Berlin has warned of "communal" concepts of liberty being used to undermine the individual.[16] How can we recognise the status of the individual without ignoring our need for society?

The following balances individual and communitarian values and argues that an uncritical application of individualistic "bioethics" in health care dilutes public values we take for granted. Calls for courts to become more actively involved in the substantive allocation of finite public resources should be resisted.[17] Given my experience, the discussion tends to be NHS-centric, but I hope the analysis applies more generally. It puts the concept of solidarity into a framework of rights by discussing (A) the distinction between individual and community rights and (B) the extent to which the distinction is recognised in the laws regulating the NHS.

Distinguishing Individual and Community Rights

How can "rights" be claimed and enforced in ways that recognise both individual and community interests? The following unravels the nature of "rights" to health care to illuminate the different promises they can make and the considerations to be borne in mind enforcing them. We distinguish (1) the nature of rights and (2) the enforcement of rights.

---

13   Sir John Laws, "The Constitution: Morals and Rights", *Public Law*, (1996), p. 622, 624.
14   See W. Kymlicka, *Liberalism, Community and Culture* (Oxford University Press, 1991).
15   S. Stjerno, *Solidarity in Europe: The History of an Idea* (Cambridge University Press, 2005).
16   See I. Berlin, *Four Essays on Liberty* (Oxford: Oxford University Press, 1979). Dworkin's distinction between *principle* and public *policy* is a similar reaction against utilitarianism to promote public interests. See Dworkin, above, at p. 90.
17   For the case in favour, see eg G. Van Bueren, "Including the Excluded: The Case for An Economic, Social and Cultural Rights Act," *Public Law* (2002), p. 456 and N. Jheelan, "The Enforceability of Socio-Economic Rights," 2 *EHRLR* (2007), p. 146.

1. Nature of Rights

Let us distinguish three features which demonstrate the tensions between individualist and communitarian values inherent in the concept of rights. These distinctions are seldom water-tight and provoke disagreement. I use them, however, as paradigms to highlight different *emphases* in the concepts of individual and community rights, rather than as black-and-white ideas. I distinguish (a) private and public rights, (b) negative and positive rights, and (c) rights which promote freedom, or equality and build upon each to demonstrate that "rights" should be perceived on a spectrum, some of which focus on individuals, others on communities.

(a) Private, or Public Rights?

The distinction between private and public rights addresses the issue of the origin of the right. Private rights are generated between individuals (including private, corporate institutions). For example, private individuals may make themselves subject to whichever contractual obligations they choose (subject to their being lawful) and may enforce their rights for their own benefit without reference to public interests. Public rights arise against and between public authorities by virtue of entitlements created by the state to promote community interests by means of welfare and other benefits. Public authorities are often subject to specific statutory duties, including a duty not to exceed finite budgets, yet have little freedom to increase revenue. Accordingly, the rights claimed against public bodies are different to those arising within private agreements and may require hard choices between competing needs. Of course, rights to some statutory benefits may be quantified according to precise scales (eg unemployment benefit or statutory pensions), but such an exact calculation is seldom possible in respect of health care. In the National Health Service (NHS), for example, the Secretary of State must "continue the promotion... of a comprehensive health service,"[18] a duty delegated to local health authorities to perform,[19] and which, in turn, are duty-bound not to exceed their annual financial allocations.[20] Thus, within this framework, the NHS creates *public* rights which arise by virtue of a statutory commitment to retain funds for the purpose. The nature and extent of the difference between *private* and *public* rights becomes clearer as we analyse the consequences of this distinction.

(b) Negative, or Positive Rights?

Public/private rights give rise to another distinction between negative and positive rights. Negative rights are essentially concerned to protect individuals

---

[18] S 1, National Health Service Act 2006. The new Act re-enacts a statutory duty first introduced in 1948.

[19] Currently called Primary Care Trusts (PCTs), although they are also responsible for commissioning *secondary* care.

[20] S 229, National Health Service Act 2006 and *R v NW Lancashire HA v A, D & G*, 53 BMLR (2000), p. 148.

from interference. Positive rights impose a duty to provide goods or services. Each may arise within private, or public context.[21]

For example, in the *private* context, many commercial agreements involve duties to provide goods and services to another and may be characterised as *private-positive* rights. Contracts of private health insurance are an example, in which patients may seek to obtain as much as they can from insurers (subject to the terms of the agreement), without concern for others who might be adversely by their claim. By contrast, an agreement to have sole trading rights without competition from another, or by a landlord to give a tenant quiet enjoyment of the premises, may involve *private-negative* rights. Because parties are entitled to enforce contracts according to their terms without regard to public interests, the positive/negative distinction attracts little attention in private law. However, in respect of *public authorities* the distinctions are crucial. *Negative- public* rights impose on public authorities a duty "to let alone."[22] So, for example, many of the rights contained in the European Convention on Human Rights fall into this category; eg the right to free speech and religion, freedom of assembly, and to private and family life all require public authorities to *refrain* from interfering with the individual[23] and are often referred to as civil and political rights.

Compare rights of this nature to *positive*-public rights to receive social welfare benefits, education, or health care. Although the distinction is far from black and white,[24] there is a clear conceptual difference between rights to be let alone, and rights to economic benefit from another party and each may be enforced in different ways. Leaving aside the issue of their enforcement, my rights to freedom from degrading and inhuman treatment, or to have the lawfulness of my detention reviewed by a court is not dependant on the resources available to government.[25] But my right of access to NHS treatment is profoundly influenced by issues of NHS funding, the extent of which depends on

---

[21]   The distinction is disputed. Some argue that positive rights are inherently "political" and beyond the competence of judges, others that the distinction is untenable in practice. Compare eg C. Fried, *Right and Wrong* (Cambridge Mass: Harvard University Press, 1978) with R. Plant, "Citizenship and Rights," in D. Milligan and W. Watts Miller (eds), *Liberalism, Citizenship and Autonomy* (Avebury: Aldershot, 1992). I argue that positive rights may be enforceable, but by means of "procedural" rather than substantive claims, see below.

[22]   Of course, by definition, all rights-based systems presuppose litigation and the need for resources to manage it. Indeed, negative rights may impose positive duties on government to protect individuals whose rights are threatened. See *Venables and Thompson v News Group Newspapers* (2001) 1 All ER 908.

[23]   Eg See *Pretty v United Kingdom* 35 EHRR 1, para 50.

[24]   See R. Plant, *Modern Political Thought* (Oxford: Blackwell, 1991), p. 269 and S. Fredman, "Human Rights Transformed: Positive Duties and Positive Rights," *Public Law*, (2006), p. 498.

[25]   Eg the substantive rights of mental health patients to review by an independent tribunal are enforceable (largely) irrespective of the resources made available by government. See *R (on the application of KB) v MHRT and Secretary of State for Health* [2002] EWHC 639.

a variety of economic and political factors which culminate in executive policies subject to scrutiny by Parliament.[26]

(c) Liberty, or Equality?

Let us now ask: What is the objective of the right we seek to achieve? Liberty promotes rights which may not enhance equality. But equality may require limitations which discourage differences between individuals. Both are valuable objectives. How should we incorporate each into a conception of rights? My liberty to make a fortune in business and for my income to far exceed yours is protected by my *private* rights (positive, or negative) to make money. Equality is not a dominant consideration. Arguably, the same is the case with respect to *public-negative* rights. My right to freedom of speech and religion does not depend on others expressing their rights equally with me (although others require equal access to do so). There is no limit to these freedoms measured according to the equal interests of others.

By contrast, *public-positive* rights give rise to different considerations. *Equality* of access lies at the heart of my right to public health care, social welfare and education. Although the objective is often difficult to achieve, rights to public welfare presuppose that the service will *tend* to reduce inequality. In the UK, for example, there is concern that standards of health vary from region to region. Accordingly, the formula by which funds are allocated allocates more to some regions than others. (Of course, the question is not simple. What "equality" is required in this context; of "inputs" (ie funding per person), or of "outputs" (ie that individuals achieve similar standards of health)? And the problem is further complicated by the contribution education and housing also make to standards of public health).

This enables us to consider the difference between individualistic and communitarian concepts of rights. By contrast to traditional notions of negative rights, the concern of a publicly funded health care system is to promote *public-positive* rights in which an important objective is the reduction of health inequality in the system.

2. Enforcement of Rights

Now let us turn to the manner in which rights may be enforced, again distinguishing between individualistic and communitarian concerns.

(a) Substantive, or Procedural Rights?

Rights may confer *substantive,* or *procedural* benefits. Substantive benefits give individuals the right to claim access to the right itself. *Private* rights will often confer substantive benefits on parties, say, arising from a commercial contract, for example, the right to obtain the goods, or services agreed (or compensation

---

26   See Laws, *ibid,* p. 622, 629: "...there will always be hard choices... This is the area in which constitutional responsibility rests on the shoulders of our elected politicians. It is not the domain of judges...In relation to positive rights, Parliament is necessarily supreme."

in case of failure). They are also significant with respect to *public-negative* rights. Many of the rights arising under the European Convention on Human Rights impose a duty on public authorities to respect the *substantive* rights of individuals and these rights may be enforced by the courts.[27]

To what extent does this approach to rights apply to *public-positive* rights – rights conferring social welfare benefits? In respect of health care, specific statutory entitlements are unusual. Instead, patients' rights are often described in more generic terms, such as a right to "comprehensive," "normal," or "non-experimental" care. Add to this the finite resources within which health care systems operate and the emphasis given to achieving *equality* in the allocation of scarce resources and it becomes clear that courts are ill-equipped to assess the impact of financial constraint on general decision-making. Given the focus of their attention on the rights of *individual* claimants, they are ignorant of the needs of those not before the court, or the impact that a decision in favour of one person will have on another, ie the "opportunity costs" of diverting finite resources from A to B.

For this reason, use of substantive rights in respect of public-positive rights is often inappropriate. The danger is that they tend to focus resources on those who happen to litigate – which is often the product of private circumstances rather than public strategy. As a result, using substantive rights to allocate scarce resources could distort the fair and consistent allocation of health care benefits and undermine public policy. The better alternative is the use of *procedural rights*. Here, the right is contained in access to a procedure by which a tribunal determines the merits of a claim. Such a tribunal should be subject to judicial review by the courts, to ensure that it has acted properly, but the review should be limited to scrutinising the manner in which its decision was made, that it considered all the relevant factors, excluded irrelevant factors, weighed the evidence fairly and came to a reasonable conclusion within the confines of its statutory obligations.[28]

Of course, there is a danger of procedural rights being a sham; of their being so feeble and casual that they enable decision-makers to avoid any real scrutiny. "Hard-look" procedural rights are essential for the notion of procedural "rights" to be meaningful. They demand that the individual's needs are not lost within a crude utilitarian calculus which focuses only on the needs of the greatest number. This is why concepts such as the Quality Adjusted Life Year (QALY) are helpful in this debate at the macro-level, but they cannot be decisive. They risk dazzling decision-makers with "public" benefits, but blinding them to individual needs.[29] To that extent, QALYs need to be assessed alongside other measures of need. Thus, in addition, English courts have insisted that judicial review satisfy itself, not only that the tribunal came to a reasonable decision at the "macro" level, but that it also considers any special, "exceptional" needs of the individual at the "micro" level. The duty of public

---

27 Including, if needs be, a positive duty to take steps to insulate citizens from systematic infringements of the liberties by others. Supra note 22 and 23.

28 See *ex p A, D & G* (above) and discussed below.

29 In other words, QALYs should not discourage doctors from acting as patient advocates because the "hard decisions" should be the responsibility of others.

authorities is to consider all the relevant factors, including the particular needs and circumstances of the individual. This is clearly a relevant factor and must be considered for the decision to satisfy the test of reasonableness.

(b) Absolute, or Relative Rights?

This brings us to a final distinction helpful to our discussion of individual and communitarian rights, that between *absolute* and *relative* rights. Absolute rights are enforceable irrespective of the interests of others. Relative rights depend on a prior consideration of the rights of others and may vary from time to time. Few rights can be exercised in ways that wholly disregard those of others. My freedom of speech is limited by laws that respect others (eg, defamation and rights to private and family life), freedom of association does not include a right to threatening, dangerous, or immoral behaviour, and rights to private and family life do not entitle me to abuse my children.[30]

Nevertheless, the willingness of courts to circumscribe some categories of rights may be more pronounced than in others. Freedom of speech and religion should require compelling grounds to justify their restriction. On the other hand, with respect to claims to health and social welfare, there may be a presumption in the opposite direction. Comparing my claim to health care to that of others is not simple. How can different treatments be compared, or the claims of adults be compared to those of children? What factors should be weighed and considered; economic, clinical, social, political? Given the unsuitability of the courts to adjudicate in matters of this nature, the question should normally be delegated to specialist tribunals with expertise to balance the competing demands, acting transparently, always conscious of the fact that investment in one category of care, or patient, may mean *disinvestment* from another.

Thus, rights, and the way they are enforced, serve a variety of different roles. They can be understood on a matrix emphasising on one axis, private-public rights and, on another, negative-positive rights which demonstrates the different values and objectives at work in rights-based claims.[31]

	NEGATIVE		
	Liberty	Equality	
PRIVATE			PUBLIC
	Substantive	Procedural	
	POSITIVE		

---

30 Even basic civil and political rights such as the right to vote and own property have been modified in the interests of the preservation of aboriginal communities. See Kymlicka, *ibid*.

31 See my discussion of the matrix, C. Newdick, "The Positive Side of Health Care Rights," in S.A.M. McLean (ed), *First Do No Harm – Law, Ethics and Health Care* (Ashgate: Aldershot 2006) ch. 36.

Solidarity in the NHS

How does this apply to the NHS? Health care resource allocation is performed by (currently, 152) health authorities in England. Each operates within a relatively wide margin of discretion and (at least in theory) they may differ from one another in the priorities they identify.[32] Until relatively recently, although the law of medical negligence permitted patients to pursue their private rights against the NHS, judicial review failed to articulate any meaningful notion of patients' *public* NHS rights. A series of cases dismissed applications for judicial review on the ground that decisions concerning the allocation of scarce resources were normally beyond the competence of the courts. But in reality, the standard of review was so weak, so inadequate, that patients were subject to adverse decisions without any explanation of reasons or how they were justified in the public interest. In *Collier,* a case that shamed the Court of Appeal in 1988, the judges refused to scrutinise the denial of surgery for a four-year old to repair a hole in the heart. He subsequently died from the condition. Other than being told that the hospital had a shortage of paediatric intensive care nurses, no-one explained why the boy could not have been transferred to another hospital to receive his treatment and the court refused to enquire why.[33]

However, in 1995, this passive, deferential response to complainants changed. Judges began to demand of decision-makers reasonableness in decision-making. Whilst conceding that hard choices between deserving patients were endemic to the NHS, a framework of analysis was recommended, in which the particular needs of the individual applicant were consciously weighed and balanced.[34] The clearest demonstration of this approach is contained in *R v North Lancashire Health Authority, ex p A, D & G.*[35] Applicants for transsexual surgery were refused access to surgery. The health authority explained that it had to make difficult choices with scarce resources. It argued that, although such surgery was available from responsible doctors, there were no reliable randomised controlled trials (RCTs) to demonstrate whether it was effective or not. Therefore, although it provided *psychotherapy* and counselling, it refused to fund surgery.

Their application for judicial review was successful. The following principles arise from the case: First, when a treatment has the support of reasonable doctors, it is not legitimate for a health authority to refuse treatment without persuasive reasons. Here, the absence of RCTs was explained by the small numbers of patients who had undergone transsexual surgery. To demand RCTs when none can be expected to be available is unreasonable. In this case, the authority had to examine the clinical evidence to determine whether the doctors themselves provided sufficiently robust "anecdotal" clinical evidence to

---

32 Although legal theory gives PCT's liberty to pursue their own priorities, in practice central government policies take the lion's share of PCT resources and differences occur at the margins only.

33 *R v Central Birmingham HA, ex p Collier* (Court of Appeal, unreported, 1988).

34 For the evolution of law in this area, see generally, C. Newdick, *Who Should We Treat? – Rights, Rationing and Resources in the NHS* (Oxford: Oxford University Press, 2005).

35 *R v NW Lancashire HA v A, D & G* BMLR (2000) 53, p. 148.

justify treatment, even if only to a limited category of such patients. In other words, all the relevant evidence must be weighed and considered.

Second, the manner in which such a review is conducted must treat patients fairly, equally and consistently. Decisions should be made according to a reliable ethical framework in which health authorities should balance, for example, the nature and seriousness of the patient's need, the effectiveness of the treatment, the reliability of the clinical evidence, the absolute cost of treatment, and its cost and benefits relative to other suitable treatments. Inevitably, some treatments will not normally be made available, but all the relevant factors should have been considered before such a decision is made.

Third, QALYs cannot dictate this analysis. "Blanket bans" are highly likely to be unlawful precisely because they ignore the interests of the individual. This is not just rhetoric. The guarantee that special circumstances will be considered is contained in the need to establish "exceptional case review committees." For example, say an authority creates a generic "Ethical Framework" and introduces a policy which assigns low priority to treatment X on grounds of the limited evidence of effectiveness, its cost, or the marginal nature of the health "need." Now, an individual patient may seek exceptional case review of their clinical need for that treatment. The patient may seek to persuade the authority that his/her particular capacity to benefit from it is so exceptional that it ought to be funded *exceptionally* in their case.[36] For example, although cosmetic surgery may be excluded within the generic ethical framework, applications for post-operative cosmetic surgery may be approved on an exceptional basis.

Fourth, the remedy is *procedural.* The application, if successful is remitted back to the health authority to be reconsidered in the light of the court's guidance and observations. In this way, decision-making in the NHS has a template against which to weigh *public-positive* rights to treatment in a way that balances community and individual need and which favours equality of access to care. The health authority has the right to confirm its original decision, provided it considers the factors highlighted by the court and comes to a reasonable conclusion which is within its statutory power.[37]

Conclusion

Theories based on rights "as trumps" emphasise *negative,* civil and political rights. In respect of *public-positive,* economic and social rights, however, they fail to accommodate the competing interests of others. There is a danger to fairness and equality of applying substantive, individualistic notions to "public" rights. The danger is illuminated by the case of *Watts v Bedfordshire PCT* in

---

36 See generally, C. Newdick, "Exceptional Circumstances – Access to Low Priority Treatments After the *Herceptin* Case," 1 *Clinical Ethics* (2006), p. 205, and *R (Ann Marie Rogers) v Swindon Primary Care Trust and the Secretary of State* [2006] Lloyds Rep Med 364 and *R (Linda Gordon) v Bromley NHS Primary Care Trust* [2006] EWHC 2462 (both of which concerned exceptional access to treatment for cancer).

37 Although, under the pressure from the courts, the media and patients, PCTs that lose in judicial review tend to concede defeat by diverting funds to those claiming access to them.

which the European Court of Justice (ECJ) insisted that local health care systems must permit EU patients to obtain "normal" treatment elsewhere in the EU if it is not available without "undue delay" at home.[38] To return to the analysis of rights outlined above, such rights of access exist in the *public-positive* corner of the matrix, and should normally be *procedural* in nature. The ECJ considers them to be individualistic and substantive.

The consequences of this policy are obvious. First, it favours those who are strong, fit and willing to travel. Very ill, elderly or disabled patients will not be able to do so. Second, since EU law imposes a public *duty* to fund such treatment abroad, those able to travel take automatic priority to finite PCT funds. "Home" PCTs are duty-bound to accommodate the costs incurred thereby, irrespective of the severity of the needs of others. Inevitably, those that remain at home will find access to care more difficult to obtain. Their rights (to the resources now depleted by those who have obtained health care elsewhere in the EU) will remain *procedural*. In practice, the groups subject to this disadvantage are consistently the same; they are inarticulate, poorly represented and "unpopular" patients who are typically elderly and disabled (and especially mentally ill and disabled). For these categories of patient, the ECJ's intervention is likely to erect a further obstacle to access to care.

Compare this to the approach of the European Court of Human Rights. In *Sentges v Netherlands*, the applicant suffered from Duchenne Muscular Dystrophy. His health insurance fund refused to pay for a robotic arm to attach to his wheel chair to improve his autonomy. The application to the Luxembourg Court was held to be inadmissible. The Court said:

> ... regard must be had to the fair balance that has to be struck between the competing interests of the individual and of the community as a whole and to the wide margin of appreciation enjoyed by States in this respect in determining the steps to be taken to ensure compliance with the Convention... This margin of appreciation is even wider when, as in the present case, the issues involve an assessment of the priorities in the context of the allocation of limited State resources. In view of their familiarity with the demands made on the health care system as well as with the funds available to meet those demands, the national authorities are in a better position to carry out this assessment than an international court.[39]

This is a vastly preferable. Any health care system which ignores the fact that investment in some patients may mean disinvestment from others deserves to be condemned.[40] To treat public health care like the right to buy a refrigerator

---

[38]   Case C-372/04, R (Watts) v Bedfordshire PCT (2006, ECJ). The application was made under the freedom of movement provisions of Art 49, notwithstanding Art 152(5), which states that "Community action in the field of public health shall fully respect the responsibilities of Member States for the organization and delivery of health services and medical care."

[39]   (2005) App no 27667/02.

[40]   C. Newdick, "Citizenship, Free Movement and Health Care: Cementing Individual Rights by Corroding Social Solidarity," *Common Market Law Review*, (2006) 43, p. 1645. Although the ECJ recognises the need for financial stability in social welfare systems, it has created *substantive* health care rights that fail to take account of the opportunity costs of health care "tourism."

is a profound error. Instead, we need an approach that consciously recognises and balances the needs of others. Health care rights provide an ideal setting to discuss the more intractable problems which arise in this sector. I have suggested that those rights are best recognised by distinguishing *procedural* from *substantive* rights and, in so doing, promoting *equality between* people, rather than the *liberty* of individuals. These are the notions which underpin social solidarity; it is based on a *system* which promotes equal treatment rights commensurate with the needs of others. To some extent, solidarity is about the institutional ethics required to promote social cohesion. Work has commenced explaining the need for fair and reasonable resource allocation procedures,[41] but we need greater understanding, both of the *theory* of "rights" on which such a system is based, and of its *practice* in a modern health care system. In the Thames Valley, for example, building on the notions discussed above, we have established an Ethical Framework within which access to scarce NHS resources should be assessed, and under which there are (currently) 108 policies guiding clinicians as to when and how specific treatments should be implemented.[42]

Solidarity in health care cannot just be about courts awarding substantive rights to particular patients. Rather, it is about a robust system of institutional ethics capable of reassuring the community that it recognises the need for hard choices between competing demands, will have proper regard for the needs of individuals, and which promises to respond to the difficulties of resource allocation in ways that treat patients fairly, equally and consistently.

---

[41]   See N. Daniels and J. Sabin *Setting Limits fairly – Can we Learn to Share Medical Resources?* (Oxford: Oxford University Press, 2002).

[42]   See C. Newdick, "Accountability for Rationing – Theory into Practice" (2005) 33 *Law, Medicine and Ethics* (2005) 33, p. 660 and the Thames Valley Ethical Framework and its application by the Berkshire Priorities Committee, www.berkshire.nhs.uk/priorities/tools/policy-display.asp.

Part Three

Health Care Access in North and South America

Chapter 5.

Health Care Rights in Canada: The Chaoulli Legacy

Colleen Flood and Sujith Xavier

Introduction: The Chaoulli Legacy

The 2005 Supreme Court decision of *Chaoulli v. Quebec (A.G.)*[1] is the most significant Canadian case vis-à-vis health care rights in the last decade. This decision went to the very heart of Canadian Medicare by challenging the principle that health care should be allocated on the basis of need and not ability to pay. *Chaoulli* has generated policy responses and a wave of related litigation, which we examine below.

At issue in *Chaoulli* was the constitutional validity of Quebec legislation. This legislation (which is similar to legislation that exists in five other Canadian provinces)[2] prohibits private insurance for publicly-insured physician and hospital services. This regulation, in conjunction with others, aims at inhibiting the flourishing of a private insurance sector for medically necessary care. In *Chaoulli* the two litigants were Dr. Chaoulli, a physician originally from France who was frustrated with governmental limits on his ability to practice privately, and George Zeliotis, a sixty-seven-year-old patient with hip and heart conditions who had to wait nine months for a hip operation. Mr. Zeliotis thought that if he were permitted to purchase private insurance then he could have financed his hip operation in the private sector. Chaoulli and Zeliotis were unsuccessful at both the trial and appeal levels but struck controversial success before the Supreme Court of Canada.

In this decision, the Supreme Court ruled that Quebec laws preventing the purchase of private insurance, in the face of long wait lists for public treatment, violated guarantees within the *Quebec Charter of Human Rights and Freedoms.* Justice Deschamps, writing for a slim majority (it was a 4-3 decision), dismissed the Quebec government's claim that the law prohibiting private health insurance was needed to protect the public health care system.[3] But because the majority decision only pertained to the *Quebec Charter* and not the

---

[1]   *Chaoulli v. Quebec (Attorney General)*, [2005] 1 S.C.R. 791, 2005 SCC 35.
[2]   C. Flood and T. Archibald, "The Illegality of Private Health Care in Canada", *Canadian. Medical Association Journal* 825 (2001), lbu (6).
[3]   C. M. Flood, "Chaoulli's Legacy for the Future of Canadian Health Care Policy", *Osgoode Hall Law Journal*, 273-310 (2006) 2, p. 273-310.

Canadian Charter of Rights and Freedoms the Court's decision does not directly overturn equivalent or similar laws in other provinces. This means, for example, that laws in other provinces, like Alberta or Ontario, preventing the purchase of private health insurance are still legitimate because the *Chaoulli* decision only has direct application in Quebec. This resulted from Justice Deschamps' decision not to rule on the *Canadian Charter* challenge which would have applied across all Canadian provinces. Her stance was that her findings vis-à-vis the *Quebec Charter* disposed of the case. Notwithstanding, the other majority judges (Chief Justice McLachlin and Justice Major, writing for themselves and Justice Bastarache) concurred with Justice Deschamps with respect to the Quebec Charter but also found for the applicants in terms of the *Canadian Charter* challenge. These three judges concluded that the law was "arbitrary" and thus in breach of section 7 of the *Canadian Charter* and could not be saved by section 1. The three minority judges found Quebec's law prohibiting private insurance did not breach either the *Quebec Charter* or the *Canadian Charter*.

The end result was that on the critical issue of the *Canadian Charter* (and thus the constitutionality of similar laws in other provinces), the court was split, three in favour and three against. This tie means that those wanting to challenge similar laws in other provinces must launch their own challenge to the relevant legislation. Uncertainty prevails. It is unclear what the Supreme Court will decide if and when a similar challenge is brought before it again, particularly as a number of members of the *Chaoulli* court have retired and that only seven members, rather than the usual nine, heard the *Chaoulli* challenge.[4]

In this paper, we first set out the rationale for the majority's decision in *Chaoulli* and critique four assumptions/conclusions inherent in this reasoning. We then discuss the Quebec government's politically astute response to this controversial decision, in the form of a White Paper and Bill 33. *Prima facie* the Quebec government seemed to respond to *Chaoulli* by liberalizing the law relating to private health insurance. But it did so only for three specific interventions and it also significantly reduced any incentive to buy private health insurance by putting in place measures in the public health care system to cap waiting times in those three specific areas. This nimble policy response balanced the need to respond to the Supreme Court's decision with the need to protect the publicly-funded health care system. However, as we discuss, this adroit response may be in jeopardy due to changing political circumstances, in particular the election of the *Action démocratique du Québec* (ADQ), the new official opposition in Quebec. Finally, we explore how, across Canada, *Chaoulli* has inspired a range of different claims to health care based on *Charter* rights. We discuss three types of cases: first, Charter cases that have sprung up post *Chaoulli* arguing for greater access to *publicly*-funded care; second, *Charter* cases that (similar to *Chaoulli*) seek to liberalize present regulations and open up the system to further private financing; and third, challenges based in private law, for example tort law, to limitations in publicly-funded care.

---

4   J. Major has retired and has been replaced by Mr. Justice M. Rothstein and more recently J.
     Bastarache has retired; *Chaoulli v. Quebec (A.G.)*, SCC 35, [2005] 1 S.C.R. 791.

The Chaoulli Rationales

McLachlin C.J. and Major J. (Bastarache J. concurring) found that the law prohibiting private health insurance created a virtual monopoly.[6] In their words,
"[t]he state has effectively limited access to private health care except for the
very rich, who can afford private care without need of insurance". "This virtual
monopoly, on the evidence, results in delays in treatment that adversely affect
the citizen's security of person".[7] Therefore, "by imposing exclusivity and then
failing to provide public health care of a reasonable standard within a reasonable time, the government creates circumstances that trigger the application of
the *Charter*."[8]

Implicit in the reasoning of the judges that found the law prohibiting private health insurance unconstitutional are assumptions or conclusions about
the dynamics between public and private financing and how different health
care systems function. We examine and rebut four of these assump-
tions/conclusions below.

False Conclusion 1: The Public Insurance "Monopoly" Causes Waiting Lists
The majority's pejorative use of the word "monopoly" to describe Canada's approach to financing health care implies that there is something beneficial or
profit-making about this approach. The goal, in fact, is the very antithesis of
profit-making or monopoly creation, namely to ensure access for all Canadians
to medically necessary care on the basis of need and not ability to pay. In any
event it is clear from a review of waiting times in other countries that the presence or absence of a Canadian "monopoly" on health insurance for medically
necessary care does not correlate with the existence of wait lists or long waiting
times. Other countries do not have a monopoly on health insurance and yet
many of them have significant problems with wait times, often far worse than
those experienced in the Canadian system. Indeed, countries that allow parallel or duplicate private health insurance such as sought by the appellants in
Chaoulli (like New Zealand, Australia, Ireland, the U.K.) have all historically
had chronic wait list problems. There is no evidence to support the majority's
assumption that the public sector's monopoly on health insurance for medically
necessary care is causative of wait lists.

False Conclusion 2: Freedom to Purchase Private Insurance will Reduce Wait
Times in the Public System

---

5   The analysis of the *Chaoulli* decision is largely taken from earlier work by one of the authors:
     see C. M. Flood, *ibid.*, p. 273-310. See also C. M. Flood et al (ed), *Access to Care, Access to Jus-
     tice: The Legal Debate over Private Health Insurance in Canada* (Toronto: University of Toronto
     Press, 2005).
6   The reader should recall that in *Chaoulli*, C.J. McLachlin and J. Major (J. Bastarache concur-
     ring) concur with J. Dechamps on the Quebec Charter making the Deschamps judgment the
     majority judgment. However, C.J. McLachlin and J. Major (J. Bastarache concurring) also
     find for the appellants with respect to the *Canadian Charter* claims.
7   *Chaoulli*, [2005] 1 S.C.R. 791 at 66.
8   *Ibid.*

An assumption implicit in the reasoning of the majority is that allowing medically necessary services to be privately insured would result in a decrease of wait times in the public system. The intuition behind this assumption is that some of the demand on the public system would ease as it would be transferred to a duplicate/parallel private market. The problem is that health care markets do not work this way because, in economic terms, there is inelastic supply. It takes a long time and a lot of public dollars to train doctors, nurses and other medical professionals and those trained can only work so many hours in a day. The time a doctor spends working in the private sector is time that cannot be spent in the public system. In the absence of a significant increase in the number of medical professionals in Canada (which would require significant investment of public spending) or a significant increase in the overall hours worked, the emergence of a flourishing duplicate or parallel private tier must mean less time overall will be spent by medical professionals in the public system treating public patients.9

The other problem is that the majority seems to assume that medical needs are fixed whereas in fact "needs" expand in a private system (thus if a portion of those fixed needs are treated in the private sector there will be reduced demands upon the public sector). What was previously thought of as more of a luxury treatment or not really necessary, becomes a "need" in the private sector. The result is that issues that would not have received priority in the public system will now be treated in the private sector by personnel who could have been treating more needy patients in the public system. Of course, it is reasonable to question why we should prevent a person from buying medical treatment if that is what they wish. After all even if a treatment is very expensive and of small benefit shouldn't an individual be free to spend her money as she chooses? And, of course, to a certain extent the Canadian system allows this by deeming certain treatments not "medically necessary" (e.g. IVF treatments, cosmetic surgery, etc). But the primary justification for preventing a duplicate private tier for *medically necessary* care is that it must be staffed by a limited resource – our publicly-trained surgeons, specialists, family doctors, nurses and other health professionals – and they will not then be providing care to public patients.

False Conclusion 3: The Canadian System is an Outlier

The majority judges characterize Canada as an outlier from the rest of the world in prohibiting private health insurance for essential hospital and physician services. But they do not acknowledge that the private insurance sector already plays a very significant role: Canada is tied for third place in the OECD with respect to the extent to which private insurance plays a role in funding the

---

9   We acknowledge that there may be some increase in productivity if in fact specialists/surgeons are presently not able to work at 100% capacity because of a lack of theatre time, hospital beds etc. The extent of this effect is simply not known.

health care system.[10] Where Canada differs (and then only in six provinces including Quebec prior to *Chaoulli*) is in explicitly prohibiting private health insurance for "medically necessary" hospital and physician services. But one cannot write off the Canadian health care system on this basis alone as akin to those in Cuba or North Korea.[11] The Canadian system has a relatively large role – already – for private financing and for private delivery.

Where Canada does not differ from other countries is in trying to suppress through regulation a flourishing private sector for essential care. As a result of the majority failing to acknowledge the prevalence of this policy objective across countries, the consequences of *Chaoulli* are much worse than originally anticipated. In particular the McLachlin/Major judgment implies there is no justification for regulation protecting the public system from a private insurance tier and this may provide the basis for some provincial governments to consider removing other important regulations, such as the prohibition against doctors working at the same time in both the public and private sectors. In our view, this latter regulation performs a much more important role in protecting the public system than the laws banning private health insurance which were the subject of the *Chaoulli* decision. Indeed, the latter is almost a red herring as evidenced by the fact that some provinces (New Brunswick, Newfoundland, Nova Scotia and Saskatchewan) do not ban private insurance and yet still have no flourishing two-tier system. Why is this? In our view it is because other regulation limits the extent to which physicians can or are willing to work in the private sector by requiring them to be fully in or fully out of the publicly-funded payment system. Obviously, unless a significant number of doctors work at least part of their time in the private sector then there are no private services to insure making the question of private health insurance moot.[12]

McLachlin C.J. and Major J., in their analysis of s. 7 of the *Canadian Charter*, fail to mention that other provinces and a number of European countries also take measures (short of prohibiting private health insurance) to limit the scope of a duplicate private insurance tier. By ignoring this fact McLachlin C.J. and Major J. are much more readily able to dismiss the Quebec government's claim that it is a legitimate policy objective to protect public Medicare from the emergence of a duplicate private tier. They do so by characterizing Canada's aspirations in this regard as odd compared to other countries. If they had ac-

---

[10]   Organization for Economic Cooperation and Development (OECD), *Health Data 2005* (Paris: OECD, 2005). Figures show that in both Canada and France private health insurance accounts for 12.7% of total health spending. Health care financed by private insurance is highest in the United States, at 36.7%, which reflects the fact that private insurance is the dominant form of coverage in this country. The Netherlands, where private insurance is the primary payer for more than 30% of the population, reports the second highest level of financing at 17.2%. According to OECD statistics for 2003, private insurance accounts for less than 10% of total health expenditure in all remaining OECD countries supplying such information.

[11]   The comparison seems to originate from the following opinion piece: David Gratzer, Wanted: Credible Health Care Analysis (1998) 7(2) Fraser Institute Canadian Student Review, http://oldfraser.lexi.net/publications/csr/1998/september/health_care_analysis.html.

[12]   Flood and Archibald, *ibid.*

knowledged that a number of other countries take legal and policy measures to protect their public systems from a duplicate private tier, it would have been much more difficult to describe Quebec's law prohibiting private health insurance as "arbitrary." [13]

False Conclusion 4: Portraying Canadian Medicare as Inferior

McLachlin C.J. and Major J. (Bastarache J. concurring) reach the damning conclusion that other jurisdictions that "do not impose a monopoly" have "delivered to their citizens medical services that are superior to and more affordable than the services that are presently available in Canada."[14] For health policy analysts this is a breathtaking conclusion as the intractability of comparing different health systems is well documented.[15]

First, with regard to "affordability," presumably the judges are not speaking from an individual perspective as further privatization must surely result in more direct costs to individuals either through private insurance premiums or out-of-pocket payments and thus decreased affordability. We assume therefore they are referring to the overall affordability of the system as measured by total spending as a percentage of GDP. Here it is true that Canada is clustered in the top ten of the OECD in terms of total health care spending[16] but it is not out of line with other countries of comparable wealth. As the wealth of a country increases so does the total percentage of its wealth devoted to health care – in this regard Canada is exactly where it should be in terms of total health care spending. Indeed, from a cross-national perspective Canada seems to have done relatively well from the perspective of overall cost control. In 1970, Canada spent 7.0% of GDP on health care while in 2000, it spent 9.2%. In contrast in the same time period, spending as a percentage doubled in some other countries (the U.S. 7.0% to 15.2%; France 5.3% to 10.4%).[17]

The fact that Canada spends more on health care than some other countries does not necessarily reveal much about efficiency. It is important to know that, setting aside drug spending, a great proportion of total health care spending is for the remuneration paid to health professionals. Canada pays its skilled professionals higher rates than some other jurisdictions. Indeed many feel that we do not pay these professionals enough! Thus the fact that we

---

13   Chief Justice McLachlin and Justice Major further discount governmental arguments (and the evidence of expert witnesses) about the detrimental effect of a private tier on a public system and seem to accept that there is no downside to allowing a private tier.

14   *Chaoulli*, [2005] 1 S.C.R. 791 at 78.

15   For example, a recent *prima facie* poor ranking for Canada by the World Health Organization has been roundly criticized and can be largely explained because a discount was factored in for educational attainment; in other words, because Canadians are more highly educated than for example the citizens of France our otherwise excellent performance on health care outcomes like infant mortality and life expectancy was severely discounted – see R. Deber, "Why Did the World Health Organization Rate Canada's Health System as 30th? Some Thoughts on League Tables", 2:1 *Longwoods Review* 2 (2003).

16   Organization for Economic Cooperation and Development (OECD), *Health Data* (2005); In 2003, Canada tied Greece for 7th place in the OECD in terms of total health care spending measured as a percentage of GDP.

17   OECD, *Health Data* (2006).

spend more on health in Canada than, for example, the UK or New Zealand, does not itself mean that the money is wasted (or at least no more than in any other system).[18] All it means is that we remunerate our health professionals at rates consistent with our total level of wealth. McLachlin C.J. and Major J. also failed to note that countries with higher rates of private spending (and, as pointed out previously, Canada already records high rates of private spending compared to many other countries) record higher levels of overall spending (public and private combined).[19] For example, the US government already pays more *public* funds per capita (that is government dollars per person) than is paid in Canada despite leaving over 14% of the U.S. population with no insurance and many more uninsured.[20] Allowing more private financing of the system, particularly private health insurance, will increase, and not reduce, overall spending or "affordability."

McLachlin C.J. and Major J. boldly state that other countries deliver "superior" medical services than those presently delivered in Canada. Again it is hard to know what they really mean by this. One assumes that they do not mean the quality of individual services delivered to patients by clinicians and hospitals because there is no evidence to support this. One must assume that in the context of the facts of *Chaoulli* they are referring to the problem of wait times and that the "superiority" of other jurisdictions relates to the dubious assumption that either there is no waiting or their wait times are lower than those recorded in Canada. But in support of this conclusion they make *no reference at all to empirical data of wait times in other countries.* Had they had done so, they would have found that Canada is far from alone in its struggle with waiting times and that many other countries also struggle with this problem -- particularly those that allow duplicate or parallel private health insurance that provides coverage for care that is meant to be provided in the public system.

The Quebec Governments Response:

The Supreme Court's decision in *Chaoulli* gave the Quebec provincial government a specific time within which to alleviate the violation of the *Quebec Charter of Rights and Freedoms.*[21] In this section, we provide an overview of Quebec's response (in terms of a White Paper and then subsequent legislation in the form of Bill 33) and examine the implications of recent changes in political power (particularly the election of ADQ as the official opposition) that likely will have an impact on the future of Quebec's health care system.

---

18   See A. Maynard, "How to Defend a Public Health Care System: Lessons From Abroad" in C. M. Flood et al (eds.), *Access to Care, supra* note 5.

19   F. Colombo and N. Tapay, *Private Health Insurance in OECD Countries: The Benefits and Costs for Individuals and Health Systems,* (2004), p. 15 OECD Health Working Papers, para. 20, http://www.oecd.org/dataoecd/34/56/33698043.pdf.

20   Canadian Institute for Health Information, Research Reports, *Exploring the 70/30 Split: How Canada's Health Care System is Financed* (2005).

21   *Chaoulli,* [2005] 1 S.C.R. 791.

White Paper and Bill 33

In response to the Supreme Court's decision in *Chaoulli*, the Quebec legislature first produced a White Paper[22] and then subsequently passed Bill 33: *an Act to Amend the Act respecting health services and social services and other legislative provisions.*[23] Bill 33, largely based upon the White Paper, modifies provisions of a number of different legislative instruments dealing with health care.[24] The White Paper called for the creation of wait time guarantees (discussed below). Bill 33 does not, however, set out explicit wait time guarantees and thus Quebec patients do not have legal rights to timely treatment in the public system. But Bill 33 does provide for measures to achieve wait time goals and, in particular, carves out a greater role for the private delivery (as opposed to private financing) of health care. It also, however, provides for limited liberalization of the prohibition on the sale and purchase of private health insurance for three specific areas.

i. Wait Time Guarantees

The White Paper (a discussion paper) that preceded Bill 33 spoke of two types of guarantees:
- A wait time guarantee of 3 months for radio-oncology services, cancer surgery, and advanced cardiac care. The White Paper provides that a patient who has to wait longer than 3 months should then be able to access treatment at a private clinic or outside of Quebec and the cost thereof will be paid for publicly.
- A wait time guarantee of 6 months for hip, knee and cataract surgeries. The White Paper provides that if a patient waits for more than 6 months then the government will pay for treatment in a private clinic. If the patient waits for more than 9 months, then the patient may receive care outside of Quebec at public expense. [25]

Although the White Paper speaks of wait time "guarantees", Bill 33 does not explicitly provide for them. It seems that the Quebec government plans to follow the approach of the UK and not provide for wait time guarantees in law but rather set wait time goals as administrative targets for hospitals and other actors within the public health care system to reach. Consequently, Quebeckers still have no specific legal right to timely treatment in the public health care system.

---

22   Ministère de la Santé et des Services Sociaux (Quebec), *Guaranteeing Access: Meeting the Challenges of Equity, Efficiency and Quality* (Quebec City: Government of Quebec), http://publications.msss.gouv.qc.ca/.

23   An Act to amend the Act respecting health services and social services and other legislative provisions, R.S.Q., ch.43 (2006).

24   Hospital Insurance Act, R.S.Q. c. A-28, Health Insurance Act, R.S.Q. c. A-29, Medical Act, R.S.Q. c. M-9 and Health services and social services, An Act respecting, R.S.Q. c. S-4.2.

25   Library of Parliament, Parliament Information and Research Services, Economics Division, *Duplicate Private Health Care Insurance: Potential Implications for Quebec and Canada* (2006), http://www.parl.gc.ca/information/library/.

Although there are no explicit legal rights to timely treatment provided for in Bill 33 it does provides for a range of measures to try to achieve wait time targets. Section 7 and section 8 of Bill 33 create a centralized mechanism for the management of wait lists by hospitals for specialized and super-specialized services. The Director of Professional Services is responsible for ensuring that each clinical department manages its wait times accordingly.[26] Additionally, the Executive director of each hospital must report on the efficacy of the mechanism to the relevant Board of Directors.[27] If there are long wait times for specific specialized medical services in a region, Bill 33 also empowers the Health Minister to take measures to implement alternative procedures to alleviate the strain and ensure reasonable standards are maintained.[28]

ii. Limited Liberalization of Law Preventing Sale and Purchase of Private Health Insurance

The *Chaoulli* ruling suggests that there is no justification for prohibiting private health insurance for medically necessary care. The Quebec government was clearly not persuaded by the majority's view and whilst Bill 33 lifts the ban on private health insurance it did so only for three specific types of services (hip, knee and cataract). If the Quebec government is successful in meeting the wait time goals set out in the White Paper with respect to hip, knee and cataract services then it seems unlikely that a significant market will develop for private insurance to cover treatment for these services. Why buy private health insurance if timely treatment is assured in the public health care system?

The Quebec government could, given the tenor of the majority judgment, have responded to the *Chaoulli* decision by putting in place wait time guarantees for a few services and allowed private health insurance for all the rest or they could have responded by simply liberalizing the law relating to the sale and purchase of private health insurance without taking any steps to improve wait times for those left in the public health care system. It chose not to do this and liberalized the law regarding private health insurance but *only* for services for which there are now wait time targets (hips, knees, and cataracts). It thus responded to the majority in *Chaoulli* in terms of *prima facie* allowing a greater role for private health insurance but cleverly cut-off the possibility of real and significant growth in a parallel/duplicate private insurance tier (as if the Quebec government is successful in meeting the wait time goals for hip, knee and cataract services then a significant market for private health insurance will not develop). The Quebec government's policy response clearly demonstrates a disagreement with the majority's view in *Chaoulli* that private health insurance would be the cure for the problems of wait times in the public health care system. Its response was instead a balanced one; looking to respond to the prob-

---

26   An Act to amend the Act respecting health services § 7 & 8.
27   M.-C. Premont, *Wait Time Guarantee for Health Services: An Analysis of Quebec's Approach* (Translation by Bob Chodos and Susan Joanis) Vol. 47 (3) *Les Cahiers de Droit*, 539 (2006) [on file with the authors].
28   An Act to amend the Act respecting health services § 17 (1).

lems of long wait times but seeking to do so primarily in the context of improving efficiency within the public health care system.

Bill 33 also aims to ensure that the provision of privately-insured services is not cross-subsidized by the public insurance system and to make sure that there is a sufficient supply of physicians to work in the public health care system. Thus all services related to privately-financed surgeries or treatments must be provided in a specialized medical centre where only physicians who do not participate in the public health insurance plan practice (i.e. "opted out" physicians) may practice.[29] Further, any duplicate private insurance "must cover all preoperative, postoperative, rehabilitation, and home-care support services, subject to any applicable deductibles."[30]

iii. A Greater Role for Private Clinics within the Public Sector

Bill 33 envisages a larger role for private clinics in terms of the *delivery* of services in two senses: first, to provide additional capacity to the public health insurance system and, secondly, to permit a slight widening of a pre-existing narrow window for the operation of a parallel private tier.[31]

In the first sense, providing additional capacity to the public health insurance system, if a wait time target for hip, knee or cataract surgery are not able to be met, a hospital may have to enter into arrangements with a private clinic (in Bill 33 the terminology is "Associated Medical Clinic") to have the treatment performed. These clinics must be majority-owned by Quebec doctors and cannot have any shares held by a producer or distributor of health-related goods or services that could be required by a clinic's patients at any point. Private clinics that are paid from the public purse cannot also receive private payment for medically necessary services and cannot charge higher fees than the patient would have paid in a public hospital for the same service.[32]

In addition to the Associated Medical Clinics (private clinics that serve as extensions of public hospitals and are paid by public funds) there is also now legal recognition of other private clinics in which opted-out physicians work and which may be paid by private funds (either out-of-pocket or private health insurance for hip, knee or cataract surgeries). These private clinics are already in existence in Quebec; the only major difference here is their recognition in law and the fact that they may also receive some limited funding from private health insurance. But as discussed earlier, if the government realizes the wait time guarantees for hip, knee and cataract surgery its unlikely that there will significant growth in the private health insurance market and thus, in turn, unlikely to be significant growth in the role for privately-financed clinics.

---

29   An Act to amend the Act respecting health services ∫ 7 & 8.

30   M. Giguere, *Mercer Human Resource Consulting Communiqué : Québec Improves Specialized Access and Provides Limited Private Health Insurance Access*, (2007), http://www.mercerhr.com/

31   For a full discussion see Premont, *supra* note 27.

32   Giguere, *Ibid.*

Somewhat surprisingly in Canada the prospect of a greater role for private *delivery* has generated as much if not more concern than the prospect of a greater role for private financing.[33] If private clinics are fully-publicly funded then this should raise no equity concerns. There is still much debate about the relative effects of public, private-not-for-profit and private for-profit delivery on the safety and quality of care delivered but it is far from conclusive that careful contracting out to private clinics etc in the Canadian context will adversely affect the quality of care provided. Although it is not usually explicitly stated, much of the concern about private clinics is likely to do with the effect on the wages and conditions of those who work within them and the resulting effect on the bargaining power of those left remaining to work within public hospitals.

It is very important to note that the Quebec government to date has stipulated that physicians who work for the public plan must be 100% employed in the public plan and cannot also provide medically necessary services in the private sector. If a physician wishes to provide privately-financed treatments (whether paid for by private insurance or out-of-pocket) then he or she must opt out of the public plan and work solely within the privately-financed sector. This is important as it relates back to the earlier point that health care markets are characterized by limited capacity (as it is expensive and takes many years to train a health care professional). Requiring doctors to work solely for the public sector or opt out to practice privately, effectively makes it more difficult for private clinics to find cheap (publicly-subsidized) manpower to provide private services and this in turn ensures that existing manpower (whose cost of training is one mainly borne by the public sector) is primarily devoted to the public system.

Action démocratique du Québec (ADQ) Platform

The 2007 Quebec provincial elections witnessed the rise of the ADQ as official opposition to a minority Liberal government. During the run up to the election, health care issues, especially wait time concerns, were a central component of the political manifesto of the three major parties. The Bloc Quebecois and ADQ used the *Chaoulli* decision as their window of opportunity to attack the Liberal's approach to health care policy. As a minority government, the Liberals must now negotiate with at least one of the other two parties in order to achieve its policies.[34]

ADQ in its official party manifesto claims that "[a]fter the Supreme Court ruled that our current health care system undermines the dignity of citizens, the Health Minister choose to maintain the system as it now stands, without

---

33   See, for example, M.-C. Prémont, "Crunch Time for Public Health Care in Quebec", *The Toronto Star*, Friday, November 17, 2007, at A21.

34   The official results from the Quebec provincial election are as follows: Québec Liberal Party: 48 seats, Action démocratique du Québec: 41 seats and Parti québécois: 36 seats; Members, National Assembly of Quebec, http://www.assnat.qc.ca/eng/Membres/index.html.

grasping the opportunity for change offered by the *Chaoulli* ruling".35 The platform also trots out the fallacy that Canada is comparable to Cuba and North
Korea in terms of its health insurance monopoly (neglecting to note that Canada is tied third in the world with respect to the importance of private insurance for the financing of its system!).36 With reference to its commitments, the
ADQ lists a number of key promises that include treatment within a reasonable time period, giving priority to the development of a truly mixed health system and, of most concern, allowing doctors to practice in both the private and
public sector.37 These policies reflect either the ADQ's lack or limited understanding of the complexities of the health care systems (specifically the dynamics of the public and private funding and delivery of care), or, what is worse,
the party's support for distributing health care more generously to the wealthy
as opposed to those with highest needs.

Certainly in the Quebec government's response to *Chaoulli* there are the
seeds that would allow the eventual growth of a parallel private tier. As Marie-
Claude Premont has noted, it would be easy enough for the government to expand the number of services covered by private health insurance. She also
fears that public-funding of Associated Medical Clinics and formal legal recognition of privately-financed clinics is the slippery-slope down which Quebec
will travel to a fully-fledged two-tier system.38

On May 25, 2007, the Quebec government appointed a working group to
examine the alternatives to the public financing of the province's health system. The Commission was headed by Claude Castonguay, a former Liberal
Minister. The two other members of the Commission were Ms. Joanne Mar-
cotte, representing the ADQ, and Michel Venne, for the Parti Québécois. The
Castonguay Commission recently emerged with much stronger recommendations for private financing and delivery39 and has recommended, as per the
ADQ policy manifesto, that doctors be allowed to work for the public system
and top-up by working privately. Castonguay, once considered the father of
Medicare in Quebec, has had a change of heart and is now known as an advocate of more private financing and delivery. Given the leadership role he has
played in Quebec politics, combined with a political desire to come up with
suggestions palatable for the ADQ, one may have thought the Commission
would have a powerful impact on public policy. The Liberal government however, has largely rejected the Castonguay report, particularly the recommenda-
tion to allow doctors to be paid in the public system and to practice privately as
well. The Minister of Health and Social Services Philippe Couillard has gone

---

35   Action démocratique du Québec, *Au Québec on passe a l'action* (Party Platform, 2007),
      http://www.adq.qc.ca/accueil.
36   OECD, *Health Data*, (2005).
37   Action démocratique du Québec, *Au Québec on passe a l'action* (Party Platform, 2007),
      http://www.adq.qc.ca/accueil.
38   Premont, *supra* note 27 at 23.
39   Task Force on the Funding of Health System, *"Getting our Money's Worth"* (Quebec City:
      Government of Quebec, 2007), available at http://www.financementsante.gouv.qc.ca/en
      /groupe/index.asp; Hébert, *"Quebec set to pry lid off medicare"*, The Toronto Star, June 04,
      2007, available at http://www.thestar.com/printArticle/221191.

so far as to state that "[t]elle que présentée, nous considérons cette mesure difficilement applicable et même critiquable…".⁴⁰

Rights to Health Care?

Canadians often believe that they have rights to publicly funded health care and the *Canada Health Act* is the source of these rights. They are mistaken. Federal legislation, the *Canadian Health Act* (*CHA*), establishes the criteria and conditions upon which federal funds will flow to provinces in support of their respective health insurance plans. Effectively, the *CHA* requires provinces to provide first-dollar coverage of all "medically necessary" hospital and physician services; but this does not provide free-standing rights to Canadians to public treatment. It is largely at the federal government's discretion whether or not to enforce the terms of the *CHA*.

Some provinces provide for "rights" to health care in their legislation but usually such rights lack any real substance as they are rights to "insured services" or "medically necessary" services, leaving to the discretion of governmental agencies to determine what is insured or medically necessary.⁴¹ If there are no specific rights to timely health care in legislation, then of course such rights may nonetheless be sourced in the Constitution. However, although many scholars think there is scope within section 7 of the *Charter* to source rights to publicly-funded health care (i.e. positive rights),⁴² the Supreme Court has been unwilling to find such rights, even, for example, in the case of life-saving drugs.⁴³ Where, however, a government has undertaken to provide some form of publicly funded care, a government may be required pursuant to section 15 of the *Charter* to provide it without discrimination.⁴⁴ Thus, for example, in the case of *Eldridge*,⁴⁵ the Supreme Court found that it was discriminatory and contrary to section 15 of the *Charter* for the government of British Columbia to refuse to fund translation services for the hearing impaired

---

40 "As presented (the report), we consider the measure difficult to apply and even deserving of criticism…" [Translated by Authors]; R. Dutrisac, "*Couillard did non!*", Le Devoir, February 20, 2008, available at http://www.ledevoir.com/2008/02/20/176941.html.

41 For example, s. 5, 6 and 13 of the Act Respecting Health Services & Social Services in Quebec clearly states that everyone has the right to medically necessary insured services – but all turns on the definition of "medically necessary" and the process by which services are deemed to be publicly insured. See generally C. M. Flood (ed.), *Just Medicare: What's In, What's Out, How We Decide* (Toronto: University of Toronto Press, 2006).

42 M. Jackman, *The Implications of Section 7 of the Charter for Health Care Spending in Canada*, Commission on the Future of Health Care in Canada, Discussion paper 31 (2002).

43 *Brown v. British Columbia (Minister of Health)*, (1990) 42 B.C.L.R. (2d) 294.

44 Section 15: (1) Every individual is equal before and under the law and has the right to the equal protection and equal benefit of the law without discrimination and, in particular, without discrimination based on race, national or ethnic origin, colour, religion, sex, age or mental or physical disability. (2) (2) Subsection (1) does not preclude any law, program or activity that has as its object the amelioration of conditions of disadvantaged individuals or groups including those that are disadvantaged because of race, national or ethnic origin, colour, religion, sex, age or mental or physical disability; Part 1 of the Constitution Act, 1982, Schedule B to the Canada Act 1982, c. 11 (U.K.).

45 *Eldridge v. British Columbia (Attorney General)*, [1997] 3 S.C.R. 624.

within hospitals. The reasoning was that in order to be able to access the same medically necessary hospital care that persons with hearing could access at government expense, that interpretation services were required.[46] However, success with respect to section 15 claims in health care is limited. For example, in *Auton*[47] the parents of autistic children had their claim for funding of Lovas therapy rejected by the Supreme Court and in *Cameron*,[48] an infertile couple was unsuccessful in their claim for funding of *in vitro* treatment.

Chaoulli was a challenge based in section 7 of the *Charter* which provided for rights to life, liberty and security of the person. The applicants did not attempt to argue for a *positive* right to timely treatment in the public health care system that would have benefited all Canadians. Rather the applicants argued that given long waiting times, governments could not prevent individuals buying private health insurance. The applicants claim was in effect for a negative right; the right not to be interfered with by government policy. *Chaoulli* was the first time since the case of *Morgentaler* (a case involving governmental limitations and barriers to abortion) that a section 7 challenge with respect to health care has been successful before the Supreme Court of Canada. The *Chaoulli* decision has spurred a number of further Charter challenges which we discuss below.

Litigating Health As a Right: A Cross Country Tour

In what remains, we briefly examine three types of recent challenges to the Canadian health care system: *Charter* claims for greater access to publicly-funded care; *Charter* claims for greater access to private treatment; and claims in private law, particularly a class action in tort, which may have a greater chance of improving the overall performance of the health care system for all Canadians than any claim in constitutional law given the Supreme Court's present approach to positive rights under s.7.

Charter Claims for Better Public Access

A number of challenges spurred by the *Chaoulli* case have been for positive rights and greater access to publicly-financed care. It is ironic that the *Chaoulli* decision, a case that lauds private health insurance, has inspired claims for better *public* coverage. We discuss one case here, *Flora* v. *Ontario Health Insurance Plan*.[49]

Adolfo A. Flora, a high school teacher in Toronto was diagnosed with liver cancer in 1999. After consulting with Ontario physicians, Mr. Flora was deemed unsuitable for a liver transplant and he was given six months to live. Mr. Flora, unwilling to accept the prognosis, commenced exploring alterna-

---

46   *Cameron v. Nova Scotia (Attorney General)*, (1999) D.L.R. (4th) 6 (C.A.); *Brown v. British Columbia (Minister of Health)*, (1990) 42 B.C.L.R. (2d) 294; *Auton (Guardian ad litem of) v. British Columbia (Attorney General)*, (2004) SCC 8.
47   *Auton*, (2004) SCC 8.
48   *Cameron*, (1999) D.L.R. (4th) 6 (C.A.); *Brown*, (1990) 42 B.C.L.R. (2d) 294.
49   *Flora v. Ontario Health Insurance Plan*, (2007) CanLII 339 (ON S.C.D.C.).

tives. He found the Cromwell Hospital in London, England in March of 2000 and one month before his 51st birthday he underwent both chemoembolization and a living-related liver transplant, incurring a cost of $450,000. The treatment involved removing a portion of a living donor's liver.

Subsequently, Mr. Flora sought to have his costs of treatment in England reimbursed by the Ontario Health Insurance Plan (OHIP) t.[50] This request was denied by OHIP on the basis that the treatment was not, as required by the regulations, generally accepted in Ontario as appropriate for a person in the same medical circumstances.[51] Subsequently Mr. Flora sought to have the decision reviewed by the Health Services Appeal and Review Board (the Board). In November 2002, the Board upheld the OHIP decision and rejected his claim. Flora in turn appealed the Board's decision to the Ontario Superior Court. The parts of his claim relevant to our discussion pertain to whether the relevant regulation should be struck down as inconsistent with the *Charter*.[52] Section 7 of the *Charter* provides that "[e]veryone has the right to life, liberty and security of the person and the right not to be deprived thereof except in accordance with the principles of fundamental justice". Epstein J., relying on *Gosselin v. Quebec (Attorney General)*,[53] sets out the three elements required: 1) the regulation must affect one of the protected interests (i.e. life, liberty or security of the person), 2) that the regulation amounted to a deprivation by the state and 3) if there is such a deprivation, then it must *not* be in accordance with the principles of fundamental justice.

Mr. Flora's claim faltered on the second part of the test for s. 7, the demonstration of deprivation by the state. Mr. Flora argued that the Ontario government, in passing a 1993 amendment to the relevant regulation, narrowed the circumstances in which an out-of-country treatment can be considered an insured service and thus able to attract public funding. He claimed that this effectively amounted to a restriction on a benefit that would have been available prior to the amendment resulting in a violation of section 7. Epstein J. rejected this claim and distinguished the facts from that of *Chaoulli*, noting that the latter dealt with a governmental prohibition on private health insurance which allegedly deprived an individual of the opportunity to avoid life-threatening delay in obtaining treatment. In this instance however, the government has not taken such measures, as the regulation in question did not in any way restrict an individual from securing his or her own health care or arranging his own treatment in private markets.[54]

Although the *Chaoulli* decision deals with the right to be free from government interference when purchasing private insurance (a negative right), it

---

[50]   Pursuant to s. 28.4(2) of Ontario Regulation 552 of the *Health Insurance Act*, R.S.O., c. H.6 (1990) ("HIA").

[51]   Mr Flora was found to satisfy the Milan Criteria. The Milan Criteria are used to determine the eligibility for cadaveric liver transplant and are also used by Ontario physicians for a Living-Related Liver Transplant. The criteria are as follows: 1. A solitary tumour less than 5 cm in diameter, or 2. Multiple tumours, three or fewer in number, with a maximum diameter of 3 cm; and 3. No evidence of vascular invasion or evidence of spread outside the liver.

[52]   *Flora*, 22 CanLII 339, (ON S.C.D.C.) (2007).

[53]   *Gosselin v. Quebec (Attorney General)*, (2002) 4 S.C.R. 429.

[54]   *Flora*, 174 (2007) CanLII 339, (ON S.C.D.C.).

establishes the connection between deprivations of the basic necessities of life and fundamental rights. Lorne Sossin has argued it is possible that although *Chaoulli* itself seems regressive in protecting only the rights of those who qualify for and can afford to buy private insurance, it may nonetheless serve as a catalyst for progressive change.[55] *Flora* suggests that *Chaoulli* is not having the effect hoped for by Sossin and others – at least not yet – and we must wait for another more compelling case to see whether s. 7 will ever evolve to embrace rights to *publicly*-funded treatment.

Claims for Greater Access to Private Care:

In addition to claims for public funding of treatment, there are several actions pending that, similar to the *Chaoulli* decision, seek to challenge restrictions on private insurance and more problematically, other laws that protect the public health care system from the ill-effects of a parallel-private tier such as the law restricting doctors who are reimbursed by Medicare from also billing privately for medically necessary care. These claims have a much higher chance of success than a claim like *Flora* for public funding as they more directly rely upon the precedent from *Chaoulli vis-à-vis* rights to access private insurance markets. If successful these challenges will have profound implications for the future of Canadian health policy. We discuss two claims presently working their way through the courts in Alberta and Ontario.

i. William Murray et. al. v. The Queen et. al.

This emerging challenge in Alberta centres on William Murray, a 57-year-old who was diagnosed with severe osteoarthritis in his left hip requiring either replacement or resurfacing. Mr. Murray requested a resurfacing procedure using the Birmingham prosthesis (the Birmingham Procedure) as this was less evasive and included removal of much less bone than the traditional hip replacement procedure. His request was denied because of an alleged policy decision by the Calgary Health Region (CHR) which limited access to the Birmingham procedure to patients below the age of 55. According to the statement of claim, Mr. Murray then sought to have the surgery through a private surgical facility (Health Resource Centre). Allegedly the facility had accepted to perform the surgery but subsequently cancelled the surgery because of pressures from the CHR. After further complications, Mr. Murray finally then travelled to Quebec to have the Birmingham Procedure, incurring costs of over $22,000.

The statement of claim articulates two strands of arguments, the first of which, similar to *Chaoulli*, seeks to gain greater access to private treatments and the second of which, similar to *Eldridge, Auton*, etc., seeks to ensure greater fairness *within* the delivery of the public health care system.

The first line of argument is that the *Alberta Health Care Insurance Act*[56] prohibits the provision of commercial insurance for basic health services to

---

55   C. M. Flood et al, *Access to Care, supra* note 5.
56   Alberta Health Care Insurance Act, R.S.A. 2000 c. A-20.

residents of Alberta for which there is public coverage. The claim is this that effectively prevents residents from accessing health care outside the government-run system. It is alleged that the lack of coverage and the refusal of service delivery (the Birmingham Procedure) by the CHR, amounts to a breach of section 7 of the *Canadian Charter of Rights and Freedoms* in so far as depriving Mr. Murray of his right to life, liberty and security of the person and in a manner inconsistent with the principles of fundamental justice. The statement of claim, however, not only challenges the specific law prohibiting private health insurance but also seeks a declaration that *all* provisions of the Act which create a "virtual monopoly" be declared unconstitutional and of no force and effect.

The second line of argument is grounded more in fairness *within* the public health care system and particularly fairness of the decision to limit access to the Birmingham procedure on the grounds of age. In this regard, the arguments will rest on section 15 of the *Charter* (equal protection and equal benefit of the law without discrimination based on age) and the claim that such rights have been breached by the establishment of an age limit in the delivery of the Birmingham Procedure within the public health care system.

This case is particularly interesting as although the claimants portray the age cut-off for the Birmingham procedure as criteria developed by the Health Authority it in fact appears to be a criterion developed by Alberta orthopaedic surgeons as a clinical guideline, and that is why it was not possible for Mr. Murray to obtain the procedure in a private clinic. Clinical guidelines apply whether treatment is provided within a public *or* a private facility. If it were a decision by the government or governmental agency that the Birmingham hip procedure was not an insured service for those over the age of 55 (i.e. not medically necessary) then there would be no reason in the Canadian model why it could not be provided in the private sector. In other words, it may be tougher sledding for the applicants if it is proven that the age cut-off was generated as a clinical criterion and not a resource allocation decision. The Murray challenge is also interesting in that the plaintiff's initial claim for a declaration overturning all provisions that create a "virtual monopoly" be declared unconstitutional is a very broad one indeed. We will have to wait to see as the claim develops whether or not the applicants will specifically challenge the law preventing doctors from working in both the public and private sectors at the same time which, as we argued earlier, is a critical piece of regulation protecting the integrity of the public system.

ii. McCreith & Holmes v. Government of Ontario

A similar case pending in Ontario is that of Mr. McCreith and Ms. Holmes who plan to challenge the framework regulating access to private health care in Ontario, which is alleged to have almost endangered their lives.

The statement of claim was filed in the Ontario Superior Court of Justice on September 5th 2007 and is being argued as a public interest issue. The statement claims that on January 2, 2006, Mr McCreith experienced an onset of seizures and was diagnosed with a brain tumour. The attending specialist diagnosed the tumour as benign based on a CT-scan and refused to order an

MRI. The family physician requested an MRI but Mr. McCreith was told he would have to wait for four months. In light of the long wait times, the family enlisted the services of Timely Medical Alternatives Inc., a Vancouver-based company whose primary purpose is to assist patients in obtaining private medical services. The Timely Medical Alternatives Inc. arranged for an MRI in Buffalo, New York. The MRI confirmed that brain tumour was in fact malignant and the family physician referred Mr. McCreith to another specialist who confirmed the diagnosis obtained in Buffalo. This specialist then referred Mr. McCreith to a neurosurgeon, but the neurosurgeon was not available for another three months. Using his own savings, Mr. McCreith, went back to Buffalo to have the malignant tumour (diagnosed as cancerous grade II astrocytoma) removed.

With respect to Ms. Holmes, the statement of claim alleges that she has a history of endocrine problems and began to experience headaches and vision impairment in March of 2005. Her family physician tried to refer her to a neurologist and an endocrinologist. Ms. Holmes, similar to Mr. McCreith faced significant wait times for an assessment: over four months for a consultation with a neurologist and over six months for a consultation with an endocrinologist. She was able to have an MRI on May 6th 2005, which showed an 8-9 mm tumour located between the optic chiasm and the pituitary glad. The visual field testing conducted by the optometrist indicated a significant loss of vision in both her eyes. Despite these symptoms, Ms. Holmes was not able to consult any of the required specialists and subsequently began to look outside of the Canadian health care system for treatment. She was able to have her symptoms assessed at the Mayo Clinic in Arizona where she was informed by the specialists that her symptoms were being caused by the pressure exerted on the optic chiasm by a Rathke's cleft cyst (a fluid filled sac that grows near the pituitary glad) rather than a tumour. She then returned to Ontario with this diagnosis and was told that she would have to undergo further testing and consultation with a neurologist. Confronted with the risk of losing her sight and possibly dying, Ms. Holmes decided to return to Arizona to have the cyst removed on August 1st, 2005.

The Ontario Health Insurance Plan (OHIP) has, to date, refused Mr. McCreith's request to be reimbursed for the cost of the treatment on the grounds that he did not, as the regulations require, acquire pre-approval before undergoing the treatment. OHIP has also refused Ms. Holmes' request for reimbursement for the out-of-country services because an Ontario neurosurgeon did not recommend the treatment prior to the surgery.

In a sweeping challenge to public medicare, Mr. McCreith and Ms. Holmes claim that sections 14(1), 14(2), 15 (1), 15 (2), 15.1 (1) and 15.1(2) of the *Health Insurance Act (HIA)*[57], sections 10(1) and 10(3) of the *Commitment to the Future of Medicare Act, 2004*[58] and sections 3 (3) and (3.1) of the *Independent Health Facilities Act*[59] violate the right to life and security of the person as guaranteed by

---

[57]   Health Insurance Act, R.S.O. 1990, c. H.6.
[58]   Commitment to the Future of Medicare Act, S.O 2004, c. 5.
[59]   Independent Health Facilities, R.S.O. 1990 c.H.6

section 7 of the *Charter*. Section 14(1) and 14 (2) of the *HIA* prohibit purchasing private insurance for any services that are insured by OHIP, while section 15.1 requires physicians to bill OHIP directly for any insured services.[60] Section 10 (1) of *Commitment to the Future of Medicare Act* prohibits physicians from charging or accepting payment or other benefits for more than an amount prescribed by OHIP. Section 10 (3) of the Act requires that physicians can only accept payment for an insured service from OHIP, a public hospital or as prescribed by regulation in "the prescribed circumstances and on the prescribed conditions".[61]

The claimants will argue that the prohibition on direct billing, extra billing, private health insurance and MRI facilities are inconsistent with section 7 of the *Charter* and furthermore cannot legitimately be justified under section 1 of the *Charter*. In essence the claim argues that there is no rational connection between the prohibition and the policy objective, rendering these regulations arbitrary and contrary to principles of fundamental justice. Mr. McCreith and Ms. Holmes plans to argue that these provisions deny Ontario residents access to essential medical services in a timely manner, inflict unnecessary physical and psychological suffering and increase the risk of complications, permanent impairment and death.

There are many issues raised in this claim. The facts as reported in the media so far raise the question of whether or not claims in private law (medical malpractice) may not be possible against the specialist who determined initially that Mr. McCreith was not deserving of priority in treatment and whether or not he should have been referred to a surgeon with a shorter waiting list or bumped up the queue of the neurosurgeon he was referred to given the nature of his condition. Similarly, given the imminent likelihood of loss of eye-sight, one has to query the decision of Ms. Holmes' neurosurgeon not to prioritize her care. If such private actions were launched a further question that arises is whether or not the physicians involved would be able to argue in response a defence of limited resources. The other issue of interest is the challenge to the law in Ontario – a recent amendment – that prohibits most doctors from providing medically necessary services in the private sector (s. 10 (3) of the Commitment to the Future of Medicare Act). This goes further than laws in other provinces that require doctors be either in or out of the public system; the law in Ontario effectively conscripts physicians to the public service. Other provinces simply make it less lucrative by foreclosing the possibility of the sale and purchase of private health insurance for medically necessary care. The Ontario government may have a more difficult time defending this challenge as, just as in the ban on private health insurance it will not be possible to go to court and point out that other countries adopt the same measure. Given this the Ontario government will have to provide compelling evidence that this provision is necessary to protect the public health care system.

---

60   Health Insurance Act, R.S.O. 1990, c. H.6.
61   Commitment to the Future of Medicare Act, S.O 2004, c. 5.

Litigation to Improve the Public Health Care System

Claims to improved health care (access, quality, and timeliness) grounded in the Charter have largely been unsuccessful and if successful are generally in the context of s. 15 claims for equal treatment with respect to existing governmental programs (for example, the claim in *Eldridge* that translation services should be provided to the deaf so they could access the same hospital and physician services available to those without hearing disabilities). The *Charter* jurisprudence has not evolved to provide any free-standing right to publicly-funded health care. In the context of the Quebec *Charter*, *Chaoulli* provides for a right to buy private health insurance but does nothing to help those who cannot afford or are not able to purchase private health insurance. Moreover, if more people "exit" to the private sector there will be fewer voices remaining to keep the standards of the public health care high. Thus decisions like *Chaoulli* will, in the longer run, further result in deterioration of standards in the public health care system.

In the absence of the *Charter* being used as a tool to improve overall accountability in the public health care system, what other options are there in terms of legal claims? One of us has earlier argued that a greater role for administrative law would help to improve the overall accountability of the public health care system.[62] For example, in the Quebec case of *Stein* v. *Quebec (Regie de l'Assurance-maladie)*[63] the court found that it should be very deferential to resource allocation decisions in health care made by public administrators but nonetheless found that the Quebec insurance authority had been "patently unreasonable" in not compensating Mr. Stein for cancer treatment in New York, given the severity of his condition and the wait for treatment in Quebec. But in addition to claims in public law, whether grounded in the *Charter* or in administrative law, there is also the possibility of actions in private law, particularly mass tort claims, sparking the prospect of overall improvements in the public health care system.

One example of such claim is that of *Cilinger*,[64] a case presently working its way through the Quebec courts. Anahit Cilinger was diagnosed with breast cancer in October 1999 and was still awaiting the appropriate treatment in January 2000. Frustrated with this wait, Ms. Cilinger obtained treatment in Turkey, her native homeland for an approximate cost of US $12,000.[65] She then initiated a class action on behalf of herself and other women with breast cancer who were unable to receive the requisite radiation therapy within eight weeks of surgery.[66] The claimants argue that the twelve Quebec hospitals are in breach of their statutory obligations and therefore liable for "leaving their

---

[62] See Colleen M. Flood, "Just Medicare: The Role of Canadian Courts in Determining Health Care Rights and Access". *J. of Law, Medicine & Ethics*, (2005) 4, p. 669–680.

[63] *Stein* v. *Quebec (Regie de l'Assurance-maladie)*, (1999) R.J.Q. 2416 (Sup. Ct.).

[64] *Cilinger v. Centre hospitalier de Chicoutimi*, (2004) R.J.Q. 3083.

[65] M. King and A. Hanes, "*Quebec breast cancer patients suing hospitals: Class-action lawsuit takes aim at delays in radiation treatments*", National Post,11 March 2004, available at http://www.charterhealth.ca/news/2004mar11.html.

[66] L. Hardcastle, "Case Comment: Cilinger c Centre Hospitalier de Chicoutimi", *Health Law Review* (2006) 3, p. 44.

patients waiting beyond what is medically recommended".[67] The Quebec Superior Court has already ruled on whether this class action claim will be able to proceed under article 1003 of the *Quebec Civil Code*.[68] In his ruling, John Bishop, S.C.J accepted that the necessary components are present within the claim to be deemed a class action. Interestingly, however, whilst the judge in this case was prepared to certify the class action to proceed against the twelve public hospitals he was not willing to accede to the petitioners' request to join the Government of Quebec as a party. This latter decision was appealed to the Quebec Court of Appeal where it was upheld.

If the *Cilinger* claim is successful against the hospitals it will likely spur timely treatment in the case of cancer services not just for the individuals involved but for all future patients in the public health care system. The mere fact of the litigation itself may spur improvements regardless of the outcome of the case. Moreover, although the Quebec government was not joined to the class action it seems the adverse media coverage surrounding this case and that of the *Stein* decision has resulted in the Quebec government putting in place wait time targets for cancer services – a result that benefits all Quebeckers and not just those rich enough or well enough to buy private health insurance.[69]

Conclusion

Health care resources are limited; there are only so many services that can be provided and distributed amongst the population given existing capacity (the numbers of doctors, nurses, hospitals, etc.). Historically Canadians have been committed to the concept of division of health resources on the basis of need and not ability to pay. Over the course of the last decade the Canadian system has seen the advent of lengthening wait times and the commitment to the principle of redistribution from the healthy to the sick and from the wealthy to the poor has started to fray. The Supreme Court's decision in *Chaoulli* reflects growing concern, particularly amongst the middle-class and wealthy, that the public system will not be there when they require it nor will it deliver care in a timely way. It also reflects a renewal of the long-held resistance on the part of physicians to restrictions on their ability to extra-bill patients or bill privately (Dr. Chaoulli it should be remembered was a physician not a patient). Organized medicine opposed the advent of universal Medicare in Canada; in recent years their voices in opposition to one-tier medicine have been muted because of the strong public support for universal, one-tier Medicare. Embolded by *Chaoulli*, organized medicine is now more frequently speaking out in favour of greater privatization. Indeed the Canadian Medical Association was an intervener in the *Chaoulli* case and has recently released a vision paper, stating that physicians should be able to work in the public health care system and be paid for the delivery of medically necessary care in a private system as well.[70] This

---

[67]   *Ibid.*
[68]   Civil Code of Québec, R.S.Q., chapter C-1994.
[69]   *Stein* v. *Quebec (Regie de l'Assurance-maladie)*, (1999) R.J.Q. 2416 (Sup. Ct.).
[70]   Canadian Medical Association, *Medicare Plus*, (2007).

proposal should be fiercely resisted; it would clearly result in a cross-subsidization of the supply of private services by the public sector and unless carefully regulated would see the number of contract hours worked in the public system by physicians fall.

Post-*Chaoulli*, advocates of greater privatization are turning their attention to challenging other laws that better protect the public health care system than the law banning private health insurance. In particular, they now have their sights set on the law preventing doctors who bill the public health care system from also billing privately for medically necessary care. Advocates of privatization now recognize that this is a far more important law in terms of preventing the flourishing of a parallel-private tier than the ban on private health insurance. So far the Quebec government has held fast on this front and whilst liberalizing the law vis-à-vis private health insurance for three specific conditions has not liberalized the law with respect to the requirement that doctors either opt into or out of the public health system. Moreover, though Quebec liberalized the law banning private health insurance it did so only with respect to three specific conditions and for those three conditions put in place wait time targets, which should dampen incentives to purchase private health insurance. This adroit policy response, however, stands on a knife-edge since the election of the ADQ as official opposition. The appointment of Claude Castonquay to head a commission looking at the future funding of Medicare and the commission's recommendations is a signal that further inroads to privatization are possible in Quebec.

Optimists hoped that *Chaoulli* would not be as regressive as it first seemed and would in fact inspire rights to timely treatment in the public system as a *Charter* right for all Canadians and not just those who qualify for and are able to pay for private health insurance. Early indications from the *Flora* case suggest that this will not be the path that Canadian courts will take. Instead, cases such as those pending in Alberta and in Ontario that challenge laws protecting the public health care system from the development of a parallel private tier seem more likely to succeed than cases like *Flora* grounded in claims for public funding. Whilst there seems faint hope that claims for constitutional rights to health care will improve publicly-funded Medicare there are other legal avenues. One path is to rely to a greater extent on administrative law, seeking to improve the accountability of those who make resource allocation decisions within the public health care system. Another hope is the prospect of actions in private law, particularly class actions in tort. These claims against public institutions may provide the spur for overall improvements in the timeliness of treatment for all Canadians and not just those who qualify for or who are able to afford private health insurance.

Chapter 6.

Health Care Access in the United States. Conflicting Concepts of Justice and Little Solidarity

Timothy Stoltzfus Jost

The concept of solidarity, on which most European public health insurance systems have been built, is rarely mentioned in popular health policy debate in the United States. Most Americans believe that access to health care should not depend entirely on wealth, and many believe that the government has a legitimate role in assuring access to health care.[1] But although proposals for universal health coverage have been discussed in the United States for nearly a century, they have never become a reality.

Access to health care financing in the United States

Americans obtain access to health care through four routes. First, most Americans, (about 62.9 percent of those under age 65 in 2005), receive health insurance through their place of employment.[2] Employers are not legally required to offer insurance in the United States, and many do not. On the other hand, money that employers pay toward health insurance premiums (and, often money that employees pay as well) is free from federal and state income and payroll taxes, and most large and many small employers do offer insurance, which usually covers the employee's family as well as the employee.

Second, some Americans (about 5.4 percent of those under 65) purchase individual or family health insurance policies in the nongroup market.[3] These policies are usually risk-rated and subject to high marketing and underwriting costs. They are comparatively costly and often unavailable to those who most

---

[1]   A recent poll found that 56% of Americans favour a government-run program to finance health insurance for all Americans, but the number shrinks to 35% if universal health insurance would mean higher premiums or more taxes, and to 18% if it meant that some treatments now covered would be no longer covered. ABC News/Kaiser Family Foundation/USA Today, Health Care in America 2006 Survey, http://www.kff.org/kaiserpolls/ 14, Oct. 2006.

[2]   J. Holahan. and A. Cook, 2006, Why Did the Number of Uninsured Continue to Increase in 2005? (Washington, D.C.: Kaiser Family Foundation 2006), p. 3. Virtually all Americans over the age of 65 are covered by the public Medicare program, although many also have supplemental private group retiree or nongroup policies.

[3]   *Ibid.*

need insurance. On the other hand, they are reasonably affordable to healthy persons, and are the only route to insured coverage for many persons who are self-employed, early retirees, or employees of firms that do not offer health insurance.

Third, many Americans are publicly insured. The United States has two large public insurance programs that together cover about 13.8 percent of the nonelderly population, and virtually all of the elderly.4 Medicare is a social insurance program that covers persons over the age of 65 and the long-term disabled. Medicaid is a means-tested program that covers the elderly and disabled, families, and pregnant women whose resources and income are low enough to meet eligibility requirements (which vary by category and by state within the country). Other public programs also exist, for veterans, native Americans, and low-income children not poor enough for Medicaid, for example, but Medicare and Medicaid are the biggest programs.

Fourth, many Americans, about 45 million or about 17.5 percent of the population at any one time, are uninsured, that is to say self-insured. They may have access to "safety net" health care services, in public hospitals or free clinics, but in general they have to pay for health care out of pocket. This number has grown significantly over the past half-decade, as employer-sponsored coverage has declined dramatically and public coverage has not expanded quickly enough to fill the void.5

The problems of the uninsured and insured Americans

A simple snapshot of the number of uninsured at any one time does not fully capture the problem that uninsurance and underinsurance poses for access to health care in the United States. If one examines the phenomenon of uninsurance over time, one sees that many more people - almost 82 million, or one-third of all non-elderly Americans were uninsured at some point during 2002 and 2003.6 One also sees a very dynamic picture - people moving from private to public insurance, from public to private insurance, or among private insurers; people lacking insurance for long periods; and people uninsured for a single short period, or for repeated short periods.7 Most of those uninsured at any one time have been uninsured for a year or more.

Although health policy discussions commonly draw a bright line between the insured and the uninsured, the ultimate issue here is access to health care, not insurance. The degree of difficulty experienced in gaining access to health care varies tremendously among both the insured and the uninsured. Just because a person is uninsured does not mean that he has no access to health care. But neither does the mere fact that one is insured mean that one can gain access to health care without difficulty or undue expense.

---

4   *Ibid.*
5   *Ibid.* at 9 - 13.
6   Families USA. One in Three Non-Elderly Americans without Health Insurance, 2002–2003, 3. (New York: Families USA, 2004).
7   P. F. Short and D. Graefe, "Battery-Powered Health Insurance? Stability in Coverage of the Uninsured", *Health Affairs*, (2003) 6 , p. 244, 247-49.

Almost 85 percent of uninsured Americans are either employed or in the household of someone who is employed.[8] Although, as noted earlier, most American employers offer health insurance, most of the employed uninsured do not have health insurance available from their place of employment. Many are low-wage, part-time or seasonal employees or work for very small businesses.[9] Other uninsured people are in fact eligible for health benefits at their place of employment, but decline the offer rather than pay the employee's share of premiums.

Many uninsured Americans are otherwise disadvantaged. The uninsured tend disproportionately to be drawn from minority groups - especially Hispanics. Uninsured adults are also more likely than the insured to report fair or poor health.[10] Most uninsured persons have very low incomes: 25 percent are from households with incomes below the poverty level, and 54 percent from households with incomes below 200 percent of the poverty level. The picture is complicated, however. Over eighteen percent of America's uninsured are from households that earn $75,000 a year or more.[11] As an increasing number of Americans have become independent contractors, consultants, contingent or temporary employees, and as whole industries have moved away from a traditional full-time employment model, many of the uninsured are middle- or upper-class Americans who simply do not have access to traditional employment-related insurance.[12] Yet others are reasonably well off but temporarily between jobs.

Many of the uninsured are young people who have not yet entered the employment market or who are working at low-wage jobs. During the period from 1996 to 2000, two-thirds of young adults aged nineteen to twenty-three went without insurance coverage at some point, and almost a quarter were uninsured for more than two years.[13] A significant proportion of older Americans are also uninsured. More than half of adults aged fifty to sixty-four in households earning less than $25,000 have been uninsured at some time since turning fifty.[14]

Many of the uninsured (particularly children) are eligible for Medicaid or for their state's State Children's Health Insurance Program, but are not enrolled. Bureaucratic barriers, including burdensome application procedures, frequent and onerous redeterminations, and lack of enrolment education ef-

---

8   Cover the Uninsured Week, Uninsured Workers, http://covertheuninsured.org/factsheets (2007).

9   Institute of Medicine, *Coverage Matters: Insurance and Health Care*, (Washington: National Academy Press, 2001), p. 60-62, p. 67-70; P. Fronstin, Workers' Health Insurance: Trends, Issues, and Options to Expand Coverage, (New York: Commonwealth Fund, 2006), p. 3-4.

10   J. A. Graves and S. K. Long, *Why Do People Lack Health Insurance?*, (Washington: Urban Institute, 2006), p. 3.

11   C. DeNavas-Walt, B. D. Proctor, and C. H. Lee, *Income, Poverty, and Health Insurance Status in 2005*, (Washington, D.C.: U.S. Census Bureau, 2006), p. 22.

12   K. Swartz, *Reinsuring Health: Why More Middle-Class People Are Insured and What Government Can Do*, (New York: Russell Sage Foundation, 2006), p. 18-28.

13   S. R. Collins, et al. *Rite of Passage? Why Young Adults Become Uninsured and How New Policies Can Help*, (New York: Commonwealth Fund, 2006), p. 4.

14   S. R. Collins, et al., *Health Coverage for Aging Baby Boomers: Findings from the Commonwealth Fund Survey of Older Adults*, (New York: Commonwealth Fund, 2006), p. vii.

forts on the part of the states discourage enrolment. In some states, moreover, certain categories of persons potentially eligible for Medicaid are not covered unless they are desperately poor.[15]

The experience of being uninsured varies. Healthy middle-age executives who are temporarily between jobs may also get by without any ill effects. But even higher-income uninsured Americans suffer. They are significantly less likely than insured Americans to receive recommended medical services[16] and - more likely - to run into financial trouble.[17] The "insured," on the other hand, are also far from monolithic. At the one extreme, employees of large employers still covered by collective bargaining agreements may have broad first-dollar medical coverage. At the other extreme, individuals and families insured in the nongroup (individual) market may have deductibles as high as $10,000, co-insurance as high as 50 percent, co-payments of $200 a day for hospital coverage, exclusions for pre-existing conditions, and no coverage for mental health, maternity, or pre-natal care.[18] Adults in the nongroup market are at much higher risk for high financial burden than those with group coverage or public insurance.[19] The access difficulties experienced by low-income, privately insured persons are quite similar to those experienced by Medicaid recipients.

In between these extremes are many people insured through managed care organizations with limited networks of available providers, significant gaps in coverage, and high cost-sharing obligations. Deductibles and co-payments have increased dramatically in recent years.[20] Recent research has demonstrated that a significant number of Americans experience serious financial problems because of health care expenses, but that most of these Americans in fact have health insurance. Nearly two-fifths of Americans report serious problems with paperwork or bills relating to health care or insurance, while half of Americans earning less than $50,000 a year had serious problems paying for care in the past two years.[21] One-third of working-age adults are either paying off accrued medical debt or have had medical bill problems in the previous year. Three-fifths of these Americans with financial problems were insured.[22] Many Americans have credit card debt attributable to medical expenses. Some lose their homes when they cannot pay off home equity loans they have taken out to cover their medical debt, or find themselves unable to rent apartments

---

15 Kaiser Family Foundation, *Medicaid: A Primer*, (Washington: Kaiser Family Foundation, 2007), p. 6.

16 J. S. Ross, et al., "Use of Health Care Services by Lower-Income and Higher-Income Uninsured Adults", *Journal of the American Medical Association* (2006), p. 2027, 2032-33.

17 S. Collins, et al. *Gaps in Health Insurance: An All-American Problem*, (New York: Commonwealth Fund, 2006), p. viii-ix.

18 America's Health Insurance Plans. *Individual Health Insurance: A Comprehensive Survey of Affordability, Access, and Benefits*, (Washington: America's Health Insurance Plans, 2005), p. 11, 13, 17, 21, 26.

19 Y. Yu-Chu Shen and J. McFeeters, "Out-of-Pocket Health Spending Between Low- and Higher-Income Populations", *Medical Care*, (2006), no. 3, 200, p. 207-8.

20 Kaiser Family Foundation / *Health Research and Educational Trust. Employer Health Benefits: 2005 Annual Survey.* (Washington: Kaiser Family Foundation, 2006), p. 1-2.

21 C. Schoen, et al, *Public Views on Shaping the Future of the U.S. Health System*, (New York: Commonwealth Fund, 2006), p. 6-7.

22 S. Collins, supra note 17, at viii.

because their credit rating has been ruined by medical debt. About half of all bankruptcies have some medical cause.[23]

Even though the "underinsured" suffer financial problems in getting access to health care, the uninsured face worse difficulties. In general the uninsured get less health care than the insured, and get it later, when it is often less effective. Because of the Emergency Medical Treatment and Active Labor Act (EMTALA), it is possible even for the uninsured to gain access to emergency care in the United States without health insurance.[24] Care provided under EMTALA is not free, however, and some choose to forgo it rather than incur further medical debt. It is much more difficult, moreover, for the uninsured to gain access to preventive or primary care or care for chronic conditions than it is to get emergency care. Over one quarter of uninsured adults with chronic medical conditions reported no visits to health professionals in the twelve months preceding a recent survey.[25] One-quarter of Americans with below-average incomes have to wait six days or more to see a doctor when sick, compared to only 13 percent of Americans with above-average income.[26] Among uninsured Americans of working age, 60 percent report not filling a prescription, not seeing a specialist when needed, skipping a medical test or treatment, or not seeing a doctor for medical problems because of lack of insurance.[27] Americans with medical debt are also much less likely to get needed medical care than those who do not have problems with medical debt.[28] Not surprisingly, the uninsured suffer higher morbidity and mortality. An estimated eighteen thousand adults die prematurely every year from lack of insurance.[29] Even those who are insured for part of the year receive much worse care than those continuously insured in terms of delayed care, unmet medical needs, and unfilled prescriptions.

The uninsured also suffer even more financially than Americans with insurance. More than half of those adults who have been uninsured at any time in the preceding year report medical debt problems, and 40 percent of those currently uninsured with medical debt problems have difficulty paying for basic necessities because of medical bill problems. Half have used up all their savings, 11 percent have taken out a mortgage or loan to pay for medical debt, and almost a quarter have taken on credit card medical debt.[30] Hospitals in communities with high rates of noninsurance offer fewer services to vulner-

---

23 D. Himmelstein, et al, "Illness and Injury as Contributors to Bankruptcy", *Health Affairs* (2005) Web Exclusive, February, W5-63–W5-73.
24 42 U.S.C. s. 1395dd.
25 Urban Institute / University of Maryland. *Uninsured Americans with Chronic Health Conditions*, (Princeton: Robert Wood Johnson Foundation Urban Institute / University of Maryland, 2005), p. 4.
26 P. T. Huynh, et al., *The U.S. Health Care Divide: Disparities in Primary Care Experiences by Income*, (New York: Commonwealth Fund, 2006), p. 7.
27 Collins, et al. supra note 17, at 9.
28 M. M. Doty, et al., *Seeing Red: Americans Driven into Debt by Medical Bills*, (New York: Commonwealth Fund, 2005), p. 5-6.
29 Institute of Medicine, *Insuring America's Health: Principles and Recommendations*, (Washington: National Academy Press., 2004), p. 8.
30 Collins, et al., supra note 17, at 7.

able populations and have worse financial margins.[31] Even higher-income residents of areas with high levels of noninsurance suffer from overcrowded emergency rooms or deterioration of the health care infrastructure.[32] Indeed, the entire country loses because of the diminished productivity of those whose diseases and disabilities go untreated for lack of health insurance.

Possible approaches to expanding access to health care

Obviously, we need to find some way to provide a more reliable route to health care for the uninsured. One route to this end would be to expand our national health insurance programs, Medicare and Medicaid. These programs have been expanded somewhat in recent years. Medicare, which long covered only institutional and professional care, was extended in 2003 to cover outpatient prescription pharmaceuticals, as well as additional preventive services.[33] Prescription drug coverage has been provided though a managed competition program that has high cost sharing, that requires Medicare beneficiaries to enrol in a private plan, and that obligates all but the poorest beneficiaries to pay a premium.[34] Only about half of Medicare beneficiaries have enrolled in this program, but in fact almost 90 percent of beneficiaries have some drug coverage, since many are covered through their retiree benefits or through other government programs.[35] Most low-income children in the United States are now eligible for Medicaid, and the State Children's Health Insurance Program (created in 1996), though many are not enrolled because of bureaucratic barriers or parental inaction.[36] There is no national political consensus, however, to expand public coverage beyond poor children, elderly people, and the disabled. Some states are pushing ahead with programs intended to expand health insurance coverage. Massachusetts, for example, created a program in 2006 that it hopes will cover most its uninsured. This program expands Medicaid coverage, offers subsidies to make private insurance affordable for individuals and families whose income is below 300 percent of the federal poverty level, organizes the insurance market through a purchasing alliance to make insurance more affordable, requires employers to at least allow their employees to purchase health care with after-tax income, and obligates individuals who are not otherwise insured to purchase health insurance if it is "affordable."[37]

---

[31]   D. M. Wolman and W. Miller, "The Consequences of Uninsurance for Individuals, Families, Communities and the Nation", *Journal of Law, Medicine, and Ethics* (2004), p. 401-03.

[32]   Institute of Medicine, *A Shared Destiny: Community Effects of Uninsurance*, (Washington: National Academy Press, 2003), p. 82-119.

[33]   This was done through the Medicare Prescription Drug, Improvement, and Modernization Act, *Pub. Law* No. 108-173, 117 Stat. 2066 (2003).

[34]   Kaiser Family Foundation, Fact Sheet: The Medicare Prescription Drug Program, http://www.kff.org/medicare/upload/7044-05.pdf (2006).

[35]   See Center for Medicare and Medicaid Services, Medicare Drug Plans Strong and Growing, available at www.cms.hhs.gov/apps/media/press_releases.asp.

[36]   See Kaiser Commission on Medicaid and the Uninsured, A Decade of SCHIP Experience and Issues for Reauthorization, http://www.kff.org/medicaid/upload/7574-2.pdf (2007).

[37]   See Kaiser Family Foundation, Massachusetts Health Care Reform Plan, http://www.kff.org/uninsured/upload/7494.pdf (2006).

Vermont also launched a voluntary program in 2006 to make health insurance more affordable to the uninsured, while Maine is in the process of implementing a program for making subsidized health insurance available to the uninsured, which was enacted in 2003, and is to be fully implemented by 2009.[38] Illinois and Pennsylvania have created programs to cover all uninsured children, while a number of other states have expanded their Medicaid or SCHIP programs through federal waivers to cover poor adults, or have created programs to encourage small employers to offer health insurance to their employees. Finally, thirty-three states currently have high risk insurance pools that make health insurance available (if not affordable) to persons whose health condition makes them otherwise uninsurable.[39]

Many Americans, however, do not support expansion of public programs to cover the uninsured. Indeed, an influential group of health policy advocates argue that the primary health policy problem in the United States is not underinsurance, but rather overinsurance.[40] These advocates of "consumer-driven health care" believe that health care costs are so high and growing so fast in the United States primarily because of moral hazard. Health insurance greatly reduces the price of health care services to the consumer—indeed makes it free if there are no cost-sharing obligations. Insured health care consumers, therefore, purchase health care products and services with little value because they do not have to pay, or to pay much, for them. Consumers also do not go to the trouble of shopping around for lower cost services, indeed they may not even shop for quality given the low price they are paying for services. Insurers, however, must pay for services that consumers use at full price, and prices become ever more expensive without the discipline of competitive markets.

The solution to this problem, "consumer-driven health care" advocates believe, is to impose greater cost-sharing obligations on health care consumers through higher deductibles, coinsurance, and copayments. Insurance should only, these advocates claim, cover catastrophic events for which consumers would otherwise have to do without care. Other health care products and services should be purchased with out-of-pocket funds, so that consumers will have to decide whether to spend money on health care or to spend it on other products and services.

"Consumer-driven health care advocates" also advocate special savings accounts for health care costs, so that consumers will have money to pay for health care when they need it, and for tax subsidies to encourage saving in these accounts. These "health savings accounts" are to be structured so that the funds in them will ultimately (when the consumer turns 65 under current

38   See National Council of State Legislatures, 2007 Bills on Universal Health Care Coverage, Legislatures Fill in the Gaps, http://www.ncsl.org/programs/health/universalhealth2007. htm (2007).

39   BlueCross BlueShield Association, State Legislative Health Care and Insurance Issues, 2006 Survey of Plans, (Washington, BC-BS Association, 2007), p. 62.

40   See, representing the consumer-driven health care movement, J. C. Goodman and G. L. Musgrave, "Patient Power: Solving America's Health Care Crisis" (1992); M. F. Cannon, M.D. Tanner, *Healthy Competition* (Washington: Cato Institute, 2005), p. 46-54. See, analyzing the consumer-driven health care movement, T. S. Jost, *Health Care At Risk: A Critique of the Consumer-Driven Movement* (Durham, N.C.: Duke University Press, 2007).

U.S. law) be available to the consumer for other purposes. The consumer will, therefore, it is contended, shepherd these funds carefully, only consuming products and services worth their cost and shopping around for the best value. This will in turn bring down health care costs, and thus make health care more accessible.

Congress adopted national legislation in 2003 providing tax subsidies for health savings accounts coupled with high-deductible health policies (policies with deductibles of at least $1100 for individuals, $2200 for families in 2007).[41] Since then, enrolment in these accounts has grown rapidly, with at least 4.5 million Americans now covered by HSA eligible high-deductible health plans.[42]

It is an open question, however, whether consumer-driven health plans will improve or worsen the problem of access to health care. Clearly consumer-driven plans are a good deal for relatively wealthy Americans, who in fact constitute a considerable number of the uninsured. These plans do offer a very attractive tax benefit for this population.[43] It seems that in fact wealthier Americans disproportionately purchase these plans.[44] HSA-qualified high-deductible plans also offer relatively low premiums that might be affordable to some Americans or small businesses who cannot currently afford health insurance.

On the other hand, once a person insured by one of these high-deductible plans becomes ill, they face considerable expenses. A $5000 deductible may be affordable for someone earning $100,000 a year, particularly if his or her employer has been regularly paying into a health savings account. The same expense poses, however, a crushing burden for a person earning $20,000 a year, receiving no employer contribution (as is true with 30 percent of persons with HSAs),[45] and with little discretionary income to invest in an HSA and no tax benefits of doing so (since the person may owe no income tax in any event). Such a consumer may simply have to go without health care, even urgently needed care, or to try to get it some how on credit and then declare bankruptcy.[46]

---

41   26 U.S.C. s. 223
42   See America's Health Insurance Plans, January 2007 Census Shows 4.5 Million People Covered by HSA/High Deductible Health Plans, Washington: AHIP (2007).
43   All contributions to these accounts and the return on the money invested in the accounts are tax free if they are used for health services or kept in the account until age 65) for this population. 26 U.S.C. s 223(f).
44   See, E. Park and R. Greenstein, GAO Study Confirms Health Savings Accounts Primarily Benefit High-Income Individuals (Ctr. on Budget Pol'y Priorities, Washington, D.C.), Sept. 20, 200, at 1, available at http://www.cbpp.org/9-20-06health.pdf.
45   KFF/HRET Survey, supra note 20, at 5.
46   See K. Davis, et al., How High is Too High? Implications of High-Deductible Health Plans (Commonwealth Fund, 2005).

Different visions of Justice

Ultimately, the United States seems in a state of policy paralysis at the moment, caught between sharply conflicting visions of justice.47 For many Americans, justice means that each person pays his or her own way in life. No one has the right to demand the resources of others. "Just" health insurance means actuarially fair insurance–everyone pays a premium based on his or her own risk profile. Those who believe in this vision of justice, which underlies much of the consumer-driven movement, have been in the political ascendancy for the past decade.

For other Americans, however, justice looks very much like solidarity - the healthy help those in poor health, the wealthy help those who lack wealth. Everyone should receive at least a basic minimum of health care, which should be publicly funded if necessary. This group may be moving toward the political ascendancy. Many of the candidates running for the presidency for 2008 have proposed some form of universal coverage with a strong public insurance component (though most would retain a strong role for private health insurance).

In the mean time, if estimates of our Institute of Medicine are accurate, 18,000 Americans die prematurely each year because they lack health insurance.48 It is hard to see how these Americans have received justice.

---

47   See D. A. Stone, "The Struggle for the Soul of Health Insurance", *J. Health Pol., Pol'y & L.*
      (1993), 8, p. 287.
48   Institute of Medicine, Care Without Coverage, (Washington, D.C.: IOM, 2002), p. 162.

Chapter 7.

Health in Chile: Is the Government Doing Everything it Can to Achieve Social Justice?

Silvia Borzutzky

Introduction

The goal of this paper is to analyze the main characteristics and problems of Chile's health care system focusing specifically on the Plan AUGE implemented by President Lagos in 2004. The paper provides a brief history of Chile's health care policies, as well as a summary of the legacy left by the Pinochet regime (1973-1989) and its market oriented policies. The focus of the paper is on how the democratically elected regimes have dealt with the question of health given the legacy left by the Pinochet regime and its market-oriented policies which drastically reduced the role of the state in the provision of health and other social services. The most serious attempt to solve this problem took place in 2004 through the establishment of the Plan AUGE which contains an innovative approach to health. Since the full implementation of the plan did not begin until mid 2007, the paper can only provide a preliminary analysis of AUGE's effects and prospects.

Although Chile's health statistics are quite good as compared with other countries in the region, this paper argues that given the economic success of the country more could be done to achieve a system that truly accomplishes the goals of social solidarity if a larger amount of resources were dedicated to the health care system. In the long run a healthier population will only increase the country's economic success and prosperity, and create a more just and equitable society.

The Pinochet Regime's Legacy (1973-1989)

Although concerns for public health in Chile can be traced back to the origins of the country, it was in the mid-20th century that the state began to play a very active role in the provision of health. The entire system was based on the separation between blue and white collar workers already existing in the social security system.[1] In 1952, the National Health Service (SNS) was created. Its

---

[1]   R. Merino, "Desarrollo histórico y visión futura de la salud in Chile (Historical Development and Future of Chile's Health System), in R. Caviedes et al, ed., *Síntomas del sistema de salud*

functions were to provide medical attention to blue collar workers and indigents; to supervise the general health conditions of the country; and to be responsible for general preventive medical functions. White collar workers and civil servants received limited medical services through SERMENA (Employees Medical Services), created in 1960. The system expanded dramatically in the next two decades and by 1973, the SNS employed about 120,000 people and provided coverage to about 70 percent of the population. The expansion of medical services and benefits went hand in hand with a general process of expansion of the socioeconomic functions of the state during the mid 20th century. This process ended abruptly with the overthrow of President Salvador Allende on September 11, 1973.

The Pinochet regime's adoption of market-oriented policies reduced the role of the state both in the economy and in the provision of medical services, education, and social security among others. As a result, the Pinochet regime introduced substantial modifications to the Chilean health delivery system. The policies were framed by the idea of the subsidiary state which aimed at withdrawing the state from the provision of social services and regulatory activities, and transferring those responsibilities to the individual and to private health care providers. The policies evolved over time and included not only a drastic reduction of funds, but also a major transformation of the system in the late 1970's.

From an administrative standpoint, in 1979 the government replaced the SNS and SERMENA by the National System of Health Services (Sistema Nacional de Servicios de Salud) which ended the occupational based division and replaced it with units charged with the provision of comprehensive services in a given geographical area. At the same time, primary care facilities were transferred to the Municipalities. Thus while the elimination of the distinction between blue and white collar workers reduced a major source of inequity, transferring some of these functions to the municipalities created a new source of inequality in the nature and extent of the care, given the huge income disparities among the different localities.

The Private System: The ISAPRES

The introduction of market-oriented mechanisms in the area of health began in 1981 with the establishment of ISAPRES (Instituciones de Salud Previsional) which were modelled after the HMO's in the U.S. ISAPRES are "private entities that offer a series of medical insurance and workman's compensation packages in return for a basic 7 percent payroll contribution plus an additional premium of 2-3 percent depending on the size of the package".[2] Until 1998, the government offered a 2 percent subsidy to low income citizens to join an ISAPRE. The subsidy was eliminated due to its negative effects both on

---

  chileno, su diagnóstico y tratamiento (Symptoms of the Chilean Health System: Diagnosis and Treatment) (Santiago: Ciedess, 2002), p. 17-32.

2   Brian Cartin, "The Effectiveness of the Reform" in M. A. Cruz-Saco and C. Mesa-Lago, *Do Options Exist? The Reform of Pensions and Health Care Systems in Latin America* (Pittsburgh: University of Pittsburg Press, 1999) p. 210.

the public health system and on the health of the low income groups, who often were attracted to the ISAPRES by their propaganda and not by the quality or quantity of the services which for many, were worse than the ones offered by the public system, and at a much higher cost. The public system was maintained in order to provide attention to low income groups.

The ISAPRES were created by the Pinochet regime in order to enhance the private health care system and much like all the other market reforms introduced by the regime, aimed at creating a fairly unregulated system where the providers could set the rules of the game and the affiliates had to confront a number of problems, such as persistent discrimination against the elderly and women.[3] Although new regulations have been introduced since the transition to democracy, 2002 data indicated that only 2.5 percent of the affiliates were 69 years or older while only 31.8 percent of them were women. Today there are about 36 ISAPRES, and since 1990 they are regulated by the Superintendencia of ISAPRES. The creation of this regulatory organism reduced most of the abuses and discriminatory practices of the ISAPRES.

In practice, the public system acts as "a catchall" system, since those affiliated in the ISAPRES can at any time transfer to the public system. However, returning to an ISAPRE is much more difficult. Moreover, it has become common practice that individuals who are subscribing to one of the ISAPRES seek medical attention in the public sector, either because the ISAPRE does not cover a particular ailment or because of the poor distribution of services provided by the ISAPRES throughout the country.[4] Thus, by the winter of 1998 about 20 percent of those served by the public system were in fact enrolled in an ISAPRE.[5] 1999 was the worst year for the ISAPRES, since they lost about 12.2 percent of the affiliates and the industry also registered heavy losses.[6] Moreover, public perception of the ISAPRES has deteriorated rapidly due to accusations of fraud and discrimination against the older and the sicker.

In brief, since 1981 the Chilean health system has been formed by a public and a private branch, and employees or workers have the option of depositing the 7 percent health tax either in the public or the private system. The public system is administered by FONASA (Fondo Nacional de Salud, National Health Fund), which in turn provides the insured the option of receiving attention, either through the public hospitals, or through a system of vouchers financed partly by FONASA and partly by the insured; this allows the insured to get attention from participating physicians and hospitals. If the insured chooses the private system, the 7 percent goes to the selected ISAPRE, which in turn offers a variety of plans. Depending on the plan chosen by the insured, his contribution will have to be augmented by at least another 4-7 percent of the wages. Given the cost of the private system, only 26 percent of the insured

---

3   For a discussion of the other reforms introduced by the Pinochet regime, see S. Borzutzky, *Vital Connections: Politics, Social Security and Inequality* (Notre Dame: Notre Dame University Press, 2002).

4   *Ibid.*, p.237.

5   La Tercera Internet, Sept 1, 1998.

6   El Mercurio electrónico, 29 May 2000, and Superintendencia de Institutos de Salud Previsional, Annual Statistics at www.sisp.cl/estd/e-sintes.

receive attention through the private sector; 62 percent through FONASA and 3 percent through the Armed Forces and Police medical services. The public system is also responsible for the provision of preventive medical services, such as vaccination programs, prevention of contagious diseases and the maintenance of water and sewage services.

Transition to Democracy

The Pinochet regime ended in 1989 and the newly elected democratic regimes have maintained the market economic model while dedicating larger funds and new policies to reducing poverty and improving the living standards of Chileans, particularly those in the lower income groups. In the area of health the Pinochet regime's legacy included the reduction in government funding, which by 1985 was 36 percent less than in 1970, and a profoundly unequal system which favoured the upper income groups and the urban areas and gave little to those in the lower income groups and the rural areas.[7]

The Concertación governments (Concertación is the name of the centre-left coalition that has controlled Chile's government since 1990) have over the years significantly increased the fiscal commitment to the health area. By 1997 total health spending amounted to about US $3,600, 000 (about 2/3 of this amount represented public expenditures and 1/3 was spent privately). Total health care spending in 1997 amounted to 5.02 percent of GDP, the private sector spending equalled 2.13 percent of GDP. Between 1997 and 2002 health spending as proportion of GDP grew by about 15 percent, and by 2002, 48 percent of the public health budget was financed through a fiscal subsidy; 33 percent came from taxes paid by the insured and 17 percent came from other sources.[8] Per capita health spending was $303 p/person (official exchange rate) and total health care spending was 7 percent of the Gross Domestic Product. The cost per person was estimated at $133 (official exchange rate). Private health care spending amounted to 54 percent of total health spending, which makes it a very expensive given the small amount of people covered by the system. Within the private health sector, private insurance accounted for 40.3 percent of the cost while 59.6 was directly paid by the users.[9]

By the end of the 1990's, Chile's health system faced a number of major problems which were all rooted in the lack of sufficient funding. Specific problems included deficiencies in the provision of primary care, a very old and decrepit hospital infrastructure, and the need to provide coverage for catastrophic illnesses because Chileans are living longer (life expectancy has increased from 54 years in 1952 to 74 years for males and 81 for females in 2004[10]) and the chances of suffering a catastrophic illness have increased.[11] This problem

---

7   Balance económico y social del régimen militar, Apuntes Cieplan, No 76, 1988.
8   Sistema Regional de Datos Básicos de Salud-Peril de Salud de PAFS 2001-Chile available on www.paho.or/spanish/sha/prflchi,htm, pp. 11 &12.
9   Organización Mundial de la Salud, Core Health Statistics, Available internet.
10   Ibid.
11   M. E. Salazar, "Las enfermedades catastróficas y su cobertura" (Catastrophic Diseases and Coverage) en Caviedes ed., p. 109.

was partially solved in 2000 as the ISAPRES have agreed to include a clause in all their contracts providing basic protection in the case of catastrophic illnesses.[12] The new arrangement defines a catastrophic illness in terms of the cost, and includes all diseases costing more than the deductible. New solutions were also provided by the Plan AUGE analyzed below.

Despite increases in the budget, the most critical problems in the health care system are still insufficient funding and unequal benefits. The 7 percent wage tax is insufficient and does not cover the basic needs of either the public or the private system. In the case of the public system, the wage tax covers only about 50 percent of the budget and the other 50 percent is financed through fiscal subsidies. But this is not enough, and as a result patients have to wait for basic attention; basic resources, such as medicines and equipment, are scarce; and the personnel are poorly paid. In practice, the state system has been left with the task of caring for the poorest economic groups, including about 3 million indigents, as well as the elderly and the very sick (about 95 percent of those suffering from AIDs and people needing dialysis are receiving treatment free of costs from the public system). Both groups have high health expenditures and generate small contributions. Regarding the question of unequal benefits, the system has traditionally discriminated against lower income groups and provided poor services in the rural areas. Thus, while there is ample coverage in upper income neighbourhoods in the large urban centres, in the lower income neighbourhoods and rural areas there have always been long waiting lists for specialized attention and surgery.[13]

Both the Lagos (2001-2005) and the current Bachelet administration have made health care spending a government priority and have significantly increased the health care budget focusing on two key areas: improvement of the hospital facilities and increased access to primary care. The Lagos administration increased health spending by about 15 percent between 2001 and 2003, including a 4 percent increase in the budget for hospitals and a 14 percent increase in the budget for ambulatory care.[14]

President Bachelet, a physician by training, has made a major commitment to improving health care and has substantially increased the health care budget. For instance, the budget for hospitals and equipment increased in 106 percent between 2006 and 2007 in order to achieve the goal of having one hospital per 34, 000 people in the near future. The 2007 budget also contains a 16 percent increase in the budget for primary medical care, and these new resources will allow the public system to provide primary care to another 5 percent of the population (between 2000 and 2007 the budget for primary care has increased in 200 percent). It is also important to note that the government has improved the administration and performance of the public hospitals through the introduction of better administrative practices and notions of competitiveness and autonomy. In brief, between 2006 and 2007 the health

---

12   *Ibid.,* p 119-130 & Superintendencia de ISAPRES circular 59.
13   A. E. Latorre, "La reforma de la salud: Una obligación social", *Foro,* Septiembre 2004.
14   El Mercurio.com 10 Feb, 2003, available on internet.

budget increased by 13 percent to about US $ 4.5 billion.[15] It is important to note here that Chile's current GDP is US$ 202 billion and GDP per capita is about US $12, 000.[16] According to the World Health Organization, spending amounted to 6.2 percent of GDP in 2004, but given the rapid rise of GDP in the last three years the total health spending as proportion of GDP has actually declined.

The Lagos Administration and the Plan AUGE

The health policy of the Lagos administration was characterized by major policy innovations, including the development of an innovative and controversial program called plan AUGE, or Plan de Acceso Universal con Garantías Explícitas (It is important to note that the acronym Auge in Spanish means power, dignity or glory) and the introduction of ideas of competitiveness and self-management to the administration of hospitals, as well as privatizing the construction of new hospitals. While the attempt to privatize the construction and management of new hospitals could not be pursued because of massive opposition of both the government coalition and the opposition, the introduction of the notion of self administration, or auto-gestion, has progressed rapidly, but has not solved the problem of the lack of adequate hospital facilities. We will first analyze the Plan AUGE and then return to hospital-related policies.

In April 2002, the Ministry of Health announced that it would send to Congress a new plan geared to cover 56 basic diseases which include about 1,600 different diagnoses, and that would integrate the public and a private components of the system. Among the main benefits that the plan provides are integral maternity care, including a pre and post-natal subsidy; care for patients with diabetes, hypertension, epilepsy; HIV/Aids; cancer; and neurological diseases, among others. What needs to be emphasized is that together these 56 diseases account for about 80 percent of the health care spending. However AUGE does not involve the provision of new benefits, but simply a new form of financing benefits that the public sector is already committed to providing, but which in practice it cannot afford. It also entails the development of strict protocols to be used by physicians geared to reduce medical costs.

In fact, the plan entails is a set of four guarantees: guaranty of access, according to which the insured will receive attention; guaranty of opportunity, which ensures prompt attention and would eliminate the wait lists (the insured is expected to be given a timetable for the treatment during the first visit); guaranty of quality of care; and a financial guaranty that the money is there to pay for the required services and that the insured will not pay more than 20 percent of the costs of the treatment. Financial responsibility for the co-payment is determined according to income brackets and the system limits

---

15   C. Selman Calavaro, "El presupuesto para inversiones de la cartera es mas del doble del año pasado: El ambicioso portafolio en salud", ElMercurio.com, April 1, 2007, available on internet.

16   CIA, World Factbook, 2007.

the co-payment to no more than the equivalent to two monthly wages for any treatment. Indigents receive free attention.[17] According to its proponents, once AUGE is in full operation (mid 2007), it would both reduce medical costs by limiting the number and type of exams doctors can order for each pathology, and improve basic health statistics since the 56 pathologies covered by the plan account for 80 percent of all deaths in Chile.[18]

The government proposed to finance the plan with new taxes on alcohol, tobacco, gasoline and the IVA, or Value Added Tax.[19] One of the most controversial features of the project involved the idea of forming a Solidarity Fund by taking 0.6 percent of the 7 percent health tax paid to the ISAPRES and using it to finance a new maternity fund; this fund would pay the pre and post-natal subsidy. The fund was the focus of a serious controversy between the government and the ISAPRES and their supporters in the right- wing opposition coalition, the Alianza por Chile. While the government argued that it was justified to create this fund because 80 percent of the money spent in the maternal subsidy went to women enrolled in ISAPRES, the ISAPRES argued that the government was establishing a new tax on the middle class and that it was attempting to destabilize the ISAPRES and their financial system.

While the administration sees the AUGE program as a critical step in the improvement of public health in Chile, for others the plan is nothing but a step toward the entire privatization of the system, since it forces the hospitals to compete in the provision of benefits and services and to make the most efficient use of their resources. According to a study done by a private consultant, CB Capitales, the cost per beneficiary will amount to US $50,000 or US $90 per year and the state contribution to the system will amount to US $785,780 by 2010, which is less than what the state is contributing today. According to the same study, the final goal of the administration is to reduce the fiscal involvement in the provision of health by creating a system in which each institution will be competing for services and prices and the state will only play a subsidiary role".[20]

One of the most vocal opponents of Plan AUGE was the Colegio Médico de Chile, the Chilean equivalent to the American Medical Association. For the Colegio Médico, the plan was destined to fail because it was built on the bases of an already bankrupt health care system which lacks adequate hospitals and technology, and because the association perceives the plan as a way of reducing the government's commitment to the provision of health. The physicians also opposed the establishment of bureaucratic controls on medical decisions and practices in order to contain costs. In fact, the plan contains a detailed system of the protocols that will be used by physicians, including the types and number of exams that can be ordered and the medicines that can be prescribed for each of the covered illnesses.

---

[17] Latorre, *op. cit.*
[18] Ministerio de Salud, "Plan Auge", available on internet www.minsal.cl.
[19] Ministerio de Salud, "Financiamiento del Sistema AUGE", available on internet: www.minsal.cl.
[20] Published in Diario Estrategia (8/05/2002), available on internet.

Physicians also questioned the logic used by the administration in the selection of pathologies included in the plan. For instance, the Chilean Society of Paediatrics and Infant and Adolescent Neurology argued that while the plan covers rare diseases, such as Cystic Fibrosis (there are only 10-15 cases per year), it does not provide any coverage for Attention Deficit Disorder and Depression, which affect about 15 percent of Chilean children and have serious consequences for the educational system and the society as a whole. Dr. Tomás Mesa, the Association's president, argued that "we do not know what criteria were used to select the diseases. We believe that there was a criterion based on cost and incidence, but the scientific societies should have been consulted".[21] The administration's criteria are certainly difficult to understand. For instance, initially the plan only covered depression for women between the ages of 20-44, but it did not provide protection for women over 44 years old, who are much more likely to suffer from depression; it covered drug and alcohol dependency only for those between 15-24 years of age and psychosis only for those between the ages of 15-29.[22]

In July 2004, after months of negotiations, the Health Committee of the Chilean Senate approved a compromise bill. In order to obtain the support of the right wing coalition, the government had to withdraw from the plan the creation of the Solidarity Fund, which imposed a transfer of funds from the ISAPRES to the public sector. According to Pedro García, Minister of Health, the government decided to compromise in order to get support for a bill which otherwise would have died in the committee.[23] In its final form, the bill provided guaranteed attention for 25 diseases in 2005, 40 in 2006 and 56 in 2007. The compromise bill also included a 20 percent maximum co-payment if the actual cost of the treatment is higher than the estimated government cost. Anything over that 20 percent will be paid either by FONASA or the IS-APRE, depending on where the patient is enrolled.[24] The bill also created a system of pre-judicial mediation in cases of malpractice suits in order to contain growing concerns with the high cost of demands for medical negligence, and also to satisfy at least one of the many demands made by the physicians.[25] The physicians continued opposing the plan, arguing that it limits their independence and brings even larger inequities to the health care system forcing them to discriminate among their patients which they considered unethical. The new plan certainly changes the way in which medicine is practiced in Chile and it threatens to reduce the freedom of the physicians. However, physician's opposition did not deter the government and today the plan is in full operation and the physicians have been left with no options but to accept the plan.

---

21 V. H. Durán "Médicos critican baja cobertura mental del Auge" *El Mercurio*, Febrero, 4, 2003, available on internet.

22 V. H. Durán "Nuevo boycot médico contra el plan AUGE" *El Mercurio*, Febrero 1, 2003, available on internet.

23 *El Mostrador.CL*, May 12, 2004, "AUGE, Minsal justifica exclusión de fondo de compensación". Available Internet http://www.elmostrador.cl/.

24 *El Mostrador.CL*, May 19, 2004 and July 12, 2004,"Senado aprobó en general el plan AUGE" and "Alianza retira disputada indicación del plan AUGE", available on internet.

25 *El Mercurio*, July 16, 2004, Comisión de Salud despacha el AUGE, available on internet.

The most important area of controversy was the program's financing. Even members of the administration recognized that there was no political support within the government coalition for an increase of the Value Added Tax (VAT) and that new sources of revenue need to be re-evaluated.

The Plan AUGE in Operation and the Lack of Hospital Beds

Since its inception the plan has expanded coverage first to 40 pathologies and then to all 56 pathologies since mid 2007. By the end of 2006 the Minister of Health, María Soledad Barría was proud to report that over 2.5 million persons had used the benefits provided by AUGE. The Minister also noted that 180, 000 persons had sought care for depression since the benefit was first offered at the beginning of 2006, most of these patients were women.[26] The plan has also added new features and services, including the provision rehabilitation treatment for adolescent drug users whose numbers have increased rapidly (official estimates are that at least 12,000 young Chileans between 10-19 years of age are addicted to the use of drugs). The government has also committed resources to prevention.[27] Included in the new services is natal care.

As the founders of the system look into its future, there are several areas of concern, including the cost and availability of medicines, the lack of hospitals and hospital beds required to satisfy the demands produced by the full implementation of the program, and the long term financing of the program. Much like in other countries medicines in Chile are very expensive and the cost of these medicines amount to almost 2/3 of the total family health care budget and 9.2 percent of the family's expenses. Minister Barría has proposed to augment the access to generic drugs, but there is no government plan geared to do this yet.[28] A poll conducted by the Ministry of Health in 2006 indicated widespread patient dissatisfaction with the access to medicines.[29]

While the government glowingly celebrated the full implementation of the program in July 2007, doctors and experts are accusing the government of not providing sufficient funds to sustain the increased demand for hospital beds. In fact, extremely cold weather at the end of June and the first week of July produced a generalized epidemic of respiratory diseases which showed how unprepared the hospitals were to deal with the increased demand. In the words of Dr. Castro, "during this weekend [the last weekend in June] there were no critical beds in Santiago which could be used for the care of gravely ill patients". As Dr. Castro visited major hospitals in Santiago he could see how patients were treated in the hospital hallways because there were no rooms available. Dr. Castro demanded increased funds for the sector "in order to im-

---

26   D. Varas, "Balance del sistema público de salud: Atenciones a depresivos llegan a mas de 180,000 en 2006", ElMercurio.com, Diciembre 28, 2006, available on internet.

27   P. Elgueda, "Ingreso al plan AUGE: Adolescentes adictos podrían optar a terapias garantizadas", ElMercurio.com, Junio 28, 2006.

28   D. Varas, "Estudio nacional sobre satisfacción y gasto sanitario: Fármacos pesan en el sector salud", El Mercurio.com, Abril 20, 2007.

29   Ministerio de Salud, "Estudio nacional sobre satisfacción y gasto en salud, 2006, available on internet.

plement AUGE under truthful conditions".30 Studies done by health economists and other experts also point to the same problem.

While the government is well aware of the problem and as indicated above has rapidly increased the budget for hospital construction, the full implementation of AUGE is only adding fuel to the fire since more beds will be required to care for AUGE patients which will in turn reduces the availability of beds for critical care. The problem is particularly acute outside Santiago. In the words of Minister Barría, what is needed is "the adequate mixture of infrastructure, equipment and specialists". Thus, while the Ministry is financing new projects geared to improve existing hospitals and build new ones, "the patients simply would have to be patient until these projects are completed".31 The deficit of critical care beds is estimated in about 40 percent.

The question of how to finance the AUGE Plan has been an unresolved issue from the outset. To the extent that the government failed to obtain from Congress the required financing, the Plan has moved along without adequate financing. A study done by Ricardo Bitran and Associates argues that while the government is moving toward the full implementation of the program, the quality of the services provided will certainly suffer given the lack of adequate financing. Bernardo Luque, Alturas Management also point to the same phenomenon.32

Today's problem will only get worse in the future. According to government estimates, the expected costs of the program will increase fourfold by the year 2020 given the fact that the population over 60 will increase to about 3.2 million people (today is about 1.8 million). It is also important to note that the over 60 population today amount to 11.4 percent of the population and that 7.5 percent of them are poor or indigents and cannot pay for their health care.33

In summary, since July 2007, the Plan is covering all the 56 pathologies included in the law and reluctantly doctors have learned how to deal with the system's controls and regulations. While the current administration has dramatically increased the budget still a lot more needs to be done to effectively provide the benefits included in AUGE and to improve the capacity of the hospitals to serve both the AUGE and the non-AUGE patients. If the goal of the program was to advance the quality and availability of medical care in Chile for all and not just a few, these goals will not be accomplished unless more funds are dedicated to the program.

Conclusions

Chile is today a very successful developing country. The country enjoys financial stability, a small foreign debt, low inflation, and a sizeable balance of pay-

---

30   S. Rivas, "Salud y Colegio Médico chocan por el AUGE", *El Mercurio*.com, July 2, 2007.

31   "Crisis hospitalaria en el país: Ministra de Salud pide paciencia" *El Mercurio*, Julio 31, 2006, available on internet.

32   D. Varas, "Duros cuestionamientos de expertos que participan en el desarrollo del plan: Financiamiento pone en jaque al AUGE" Agosto 4, 2006 *El Mercurio*, available on internet.

33   D. Varas, "Estudio de la Superintendencia de Salud; El adulto mayor cuadruplicaría gasto en salud hacia 2020" El Mercurio.com, available on internet.

ments surplus which in 2006 amounted to about 6 percent of GDP, and that the administration has decided to invest abroad in order to avoid the so called "Dutch Disease". While it makes sense for the economic policy makers to pursue conservative financial policies that focus on the need to invest the copper earnings in the successful stock markets in Asia, Latin America and Europe, it would also make sense to increase the fiscal commitment to health.

The Plan AUGE has the possibility of providing care for the treatment of about 80 percent of the country's most serious diseases, but if policy makers do not provide the adequate financing, what AUGE is likely to produce is a number of problems that would only highlight the weaknesses of the system, including the lack of hospital beds, an old and decrepit infrastructure, and a very poor distribution of resources that makes the provision of adequate health in the rural areas a real challenge. The problems experienced during the 2007 winter shows clearly that faced with cold weather and an epidemic of respiratory diseases the hospitals in Santiago, where one finds the largest number of bed per capita, could not service the increased demand for medical care.

The Bachelet administration appears to be committed to reducing poverty, improving health and other social programs geared to create a socially just society. The administration also needs to be commended for having increased the health care budget rapidly, but a lot more needs to be done. AUGE guarantees of prompt attention, adequate care and coverage for about 80 percent of the medical expenses will become a reality only if new monies are dedicated to health care. There is no doubt that the plan is based on the idea of providing equal access to people suffering from the same illnesses. However, the huge differences in quality and availability of care between the urban and the rural areas and the AUGE and non-AUGE illnesses will be solved only if there is a true commitment to funding the program and investing in the infrastructure needed to make the goals of solidarity and social justice a reality.

Part Four

Africa and the right to AIDS treatment

Chapter 8.

Justice and Justiciability: Advancing Solidarity and Justice through South Africans Right to Health Jurisprudence

Lisa Forman

Introduction

The South African Constitutional Court's jurisprudence provides a path-breaking illustration of the social justice potential of an enforceable right to health. It challenges traditional objections to social rights by showing that their enforcement need not be democratically unsound or make zero-sum claims on limited resources. Indeed the South African experience suggests that enforcing health rights may in fact contribute to greater degrees of collective solidarity and justice. While the Court's approach does not guarantee all rights claims, it nonetheless seeks to ensure that the basic needs of the poor are not unreasonably restricted by competing public and private interests. Achieving this balance has meant shifting from traditional liberal rights approaches that atomize individuals from their social context and focus on individual rights to the exclusion of correlative duties. Instead, the Court has adopted an approach to rights more cognizant of the realities of societal interdependence and the socio-economic preconditions of individual autonomy and agency. This novel rights paradigm locates individual civil and social rights within a communitarian framework drawing from the traditional African notion of 'ubuntu,' which denotes collective solidarity, humaneness and mutual responsibilities to recognize the respect, dignity and value of all members of society. This rights approach is providing powerful weapons to the poor for challenging the reasonableness of public and private restrictions on basic health care needs. Yet this jurisprudence also illustrates the limits of litigation as a tool of social transformation, and of social rights that remain embedded in ideological baggage even where they have been constitutionally entrenched and enforced. While the Court's approach mainly bolsters the enforceability of social rights, its cautious enforcement of social rights may nonetheless substantiate persistent objections to these rights.

This paper explores these aspects of the Constitutional Court's unfolding jurisprudence on the right to health, by first providing background to the constitutional entrenchment of a justiciable right to health; second, exploring early Constitutional Court jurisprudence on this right; third, turning to the forceful application of this right in relation to government policy on AIDS treatment; and finally, concluding with thoughts about the strengths and limits of this jurisprudence in light of subsequent case-law.

The South African Entrenchment of a Justiciable Right to Health

South Africa's entrenchment of a justiciable health right is not explicable without being historically located within the country's transition from apartheid to constitutional democracy. Apartheid provided an antithetical model of law devoid of morality or fairness, motivating the construction of a new constitutional order with a strong commitment to an integrated set of human rights, both civil and social. Certainly the African National Congress (ANC) had long supported the protection of social rights, recognizing that civil rights alone would do little to redress the material inequality created and exacerbated by apartheid. This insight was eloquently articulated by Nelson Mandela one year before becoming the first black president of South Africa:

> The right to vote, without food, shelter and health care will create the appearance of equality and justice, while actual inequality is entrenched. We do not want freedom without bread, nor do we want bread without freedom ... A denial of such claims would be to accept the dehumanising effects of deprivation and mass poverty as the lot of the majority of our people.[1]

The final *Constitution* entrenches a range of justiciable social and economic rights, to food, health care, water, social security, housing, education, and children's rights to basic social amenities.[2] These rights are located within an explicitly transformative constitution, with a pervasive foundational commitment to creating a responsive, accountable and open democratic state based on equality, dignity and freedom.[3] In addition to entrenching social rights, the Bill of Rights includes other distinctively progressive provisions, such as a prohibition of discrimination on the grounds of sexual orientation and gender,[4] and a horizontal application to "natural and juristic persons" including corporations.[5]

---

[1] Address of Nelson Mandela at his Investiture as Doctor of Laws, Soochow University, Taiwan, 1 August 1993.

[2] *Constitution of the Republic of South Africa* Act 108 of 1996 (*Constitution*), sections 27 (food, health care, water and social security), 26 (housing), 29 (education), and 28 (children's rights to basic social amenities). While the 1993 *Interim Constitution* did not entrench universal justiciable socio-economic rights, it included a number of rights relevant to health, as well as health rights for specific populations such as children and detainees. See *Constitution of the Republic of South Africa Act 200 of 1993*, assented to 25 January 1994, date of commencement, 27 April 1994, sections 9, 10, 8, 29, 30(1)(c) and 25(1)(b).

[3] See for instance, *Constitution*, preamble, and sections 1(a) and (d); 7(1); 36(1); 39(1)(a); 41(c); 195(1)(f) and (g).

[4] *Constitution*, section 9(3).

[5] *Constitution*, sections 9(3) (equality), 8(2) and 239 (horizontality). On horizontality, see Stephen Ellmann, "A Constitutional Confluence: American 'State Action' Law and the Application of South Africa's Socio-Economic Rights Guarantees to Private Actors" in Penelope Andrews and Stephen Ellmann, eds., *The Post-Apartheid Constitutions: Perspectives on South Africa's Basic Law* (Johannesburg: Witwatersrand University Press, 2001) at 444.

The *Constitution* entrenches a number of health-related rights, including children's rights to basic health care services in section 28(1)(c) and prisoner's rights to adequate medical treatment in section 35(2)(e).[6] The universal health right is contained in section 27, which states:

(1) Everyone has the right to have access to health care services, including reproductive health care ...

(2) The state must take reasonable legislative and other measures, within its available resources, to achieve the progressive realisation of each of these rights.

(3) No one may be refused emergency medical treatment.

The formulation of section 27 provides little indication of the nature or scope of the entitlement which the right to access health care services confers, nor of the extent to which resource limitations and progressive realization could permissibly limit the state's duty to ensure access. Some guidance on the state's obligations is provided by the constitutional mandate that the state must respect, protect, promote and fulfil the *Constitution's* rights,[7] a typology drawn from international law which imposes a range of positive and negative duties under each right.[8] Nonetheless its scope and content remained to be sculpted from these relatively amorphous constitutional provisions through an evolving Constitutional Court jurisprudence.

The Court's enforcement of section 27 was made considerably more difficult given the relative dearth of global socio-economic rights jurisprudence to provide guidance. While health rights are increasingly recognized in national constitutions,[9] these are seldom enforced by courts given widespread perceptions that doing so would irrationally distort budgets and arrogate the executive policy making function, and thereby breach the appropriate democratic

---

6   There is also a right to an environment that is not harmful to health or well-being in section 24(a) of the *Constitution, supra* note.

7   *Constitution,* section 7(2).

8   The duty to respect imposes a negative obligation to desist from interfering with people's enjoyment of rights; the duty to protect requires the state to prevent third party interference with people's rights; and the duty to promote and fulfil describes the state's positive obligation to realize access. The notion of a typology of rights is widely acknowledged to have been developed by Henry Shue and introduced into the international human rights machinery by Asbjorn Eide during his tenure as UN Special Rapporteur on the Right to Food in the early 1980s. *See* H. Shue, *Basic Rights, Subsistence, Affluence and US Foreign Policy* (Princeton, NJ: Princeton University Press, 1980), and A. Eide, C. Krause and A. Rosas, *Economic, Social and Cultural Rights: A Textbook* (Dordrecht: Martinus Nijhoff, 1995). This typology has now been formally adopted within the United Nations machinery overseeing economic and social rights, see for example, CESCR, "General Comment 3: The Nature of States Parties' Obligations" U.N. Doc. E/1991/23 (CESCR, General Comment 3). It is applied in the context of health in CESCR, "General Comment No. 14 (2000): The Right to the Highest Attainable Standard of Health (article 12 of the International Covenant on Economic, Social and Cultural Rights)" U.N. Doc. E/C.12/2000/4, 11 August 2000 (CESCR, General Comment 14).

9   A recent study indicates that over two-thirds of all domestic constitutions have provisions regarding health and health care. See E.D. Kinney and B.A. Clark, "Provisions for Health and Health-Care in the Constitutions of the Countries of the World," *Cornell International Law Journal* 37 (2004), p. 285, 287.

---

separation of powers.[10] The characterization of social and civil rights as positive and negative rights respectively is central to these objections, where positive rights are seen to require extensive state action and resources to be realized in contrast to negative rights that are fulfilled through inaction and limited resources. As a result, judges are often deferent to social and economic policy,[11] and reluctant to recognize and enforce positive obligations pertaining to social welfare.[12] However, social rights commentators have illustrated that there are no sharp distinctions between positive and negative rights since civil rights require extensive resources and government action to be realized.[13] Sharp distinctions between social and civil rights have been further eroded by the growing recognition that all rights impose a range of positive and negative duties.[14] Despite these insights, dichotomous distinctions between these rights persistent, perhaps reflecting a more ideological underpinning: for example, the positive/negative dichotomy fits neatly into the liberal conception of a non-interventionist state that primarily promotes individual autonomy by protecting individual freedoms and private property.[15] The notion of limited government is similarly advanced by prevalent neo-liberal oriented global economic laws which prescribe limited social spending, deregulation and privatization in order to achieve free markets as the primary means of ensuring equitable material distributions.[16] The paradox is that if civil freedoms and property protec-

---

10   These objections are elegantly outlined and addressed in "Economic and Social Rights and the Right to Health: An Interdisciplinary Discussion Held at Harvard Law School in September, 1993" Organized by the Human Rights Program, Harvard Law School, and the Francois-Xavier Bagnoud Center for Health and Human Rights, Harvard School of Public Health (Cambridge, MA,: Human Rights Program, Harvard Law School, 1995).

11   See *Dandridge v. Williams* 397 U.S. 471 (1970), where the U.S. Supreme Court refused to review the way that social grants were formulated or administered, reasoning that "[t]he intractable economic, social and even philosophical problems presented by public welfare assistance programs are not the business of this Court."

12   See *Gosselin v. Québec (Attorney General)*, 2002 4 S.C.R. 429, where the Canadian Supreme Court refused to recognize that the right to security of the body places positive obligations on the government to provide social welfare; *Deshaney v. Winnbago County Dep't of Social Services* 489 U.S. 189, 194 (1989), where the US court held that the State of Wisconsin had no positive constitutional duty to protect a child from a gravely abusive father; and *Andrews v. Law Society of British Columbia* 1989 1 S.C.R 123, at paragraph 194, where Justice La Forest states: "much economic and social policy making is simply beyond the institutional competence of the courts: their role is to protect against incursions on fundamental values, not to second guess policy decisions."

13   See for example, S. Holmes, and C. R. Sunstein, The Cost of Rights (New York: W.H. Norton, 2000) and P. Hunt, *Reclaiming Social Rights: International and Comparative Perspectives* (Aldershot: Dartmouth Publishing Company, Ltd. 1996).

14   See for example, footnote 8 supra.

15   Liberal democracy is defined as "a political system marked not only by free and fair elections, but also by the rule of law, a separation of powers, and the protection of basic liberties of speech, assembly, religion and property." F. Zakaria, "The Rise of Illiberal Democracy" Foreign Affairs (1997), p. 37.

16   These are the tenets of neoliberalism encapsulated in the Washington Consensus, a set of market-oriented economic reforms designed to create economic growth. See John Williamson, "Did the Washington Consensus Fail?" (Speech to the Center for Strategic & International Studies, 6 November 2002), available online at http://www.iie.com/publications /papers/williamson1102.htm.

tion actually require extensive resources and state action to be realized than even a minimal night-watchman state may be interventionist and redistributive, albeit that it may favour the interests of private property and not the poor. Similarly, meeting subsistence needs cannot be inconsistent with philosophies focusing on individual autonomy, given how extensively autonomy depends on adequate food, shelter and health care.[17] The ascendance of liberal-oriented constitutional democracy and neoliberal-oriented global economic laws pose conceptual and strategic challenges to advancing the right to health given their tendency to protect against interference with individual freedoms and free markets. The challenge therefore for ensuring legal entrenchment and judicial enforcement of these rights is to counter both practical and ideological objections to doing so, and to recognize that for policy-makers and judges, the distinction between pragmatism and ideology when it comes to these rights may have become considerably blurred.

Early Constitutional Court Jurisprudence Relevant to Health Care[18]

While the old paradigm of social rights was considerably weakened in South Africa by the constitutional entrenchment of justiciable health rights, judicial choices regarding enforcement remained equally determinative of the extent of their power. At the certification of the *Constitution*, the Constitutional Court rejected arguments that socio-economic rights conferred a task on the courts so different from other rights that it breached the separation of powers.[19] The Court insisted that socio-economic rights were "at least to some extent, justiciable," and at the very minimum, could "be negatively protected from improper invasion."[20] While certainly opening the door to enforcement, this statement also suggests the Court's uncertainty about the extent of the justiciability of

---

[17]   This is animated by Abraham Maslow's hierarchy of human needs which proposed that humans can only satisfy higher needs such as friendship, love and creativity once their basic physiological and safety needs are met. A.. H. Maslow, "A Theory of Human Motivation" Psychological Review (1943) 50, p. 370-396. This insight is similarly advanced in Amarty Sen's capabilities approach, which proposes that human capability is dependent on basic levels of health and education. See for example, A. Sen, *Development as Freedom* (New York: Anchor Books, 2000).

[18]   This article does not explore the decisions of lower courts on and related to section 27. In this regard see the High Court decisions in *Van Biljon and others v. Minister of Correctional Services and Others* 1997 (4) S. Afr. L. Rep. 441 (Cape Provincial Division); *B v. Minister of Correctional Services* 1997 (4) S. Afr. L. Rep. 411 (Cape Provincial Division); *Residents of Bon Vista Mansions v. Southern Metropolitan Local Council* 2001 (Witwatersrand Local Division), Case No: 01/12312 and most recently *Treatment Action Campaign and Others v. Minister of Health Provincial Government of the Western Cape and Others* (Cape Provincial Division) Case No. 7991/2007.

[19]   This was in response to objections to the constitutional inclusion of social and economic rights raised by various civil society groups (primarily business-oriented) at the Constitution's hearing on certification. *Ex Parte Chairperson of the Constitutional Assembly: in re Certification of the Constitution of the Republic of South Africa* 1996 (4) S. Afr. L. R 744 (S. Afr. Const. Crt.), at para. 77 (*Certification decision*).

[20]   *Certification decision*, at para. 78.

these rights, and by implication, about the enforceability of positive duties.[21] The Court therefore concretized a sharp distinction between negative and positive duties as part of its approach to social rights.

The Court's first decision on section 27 hardly appeared to validate this right's justiciability. *Thiagraj Soobramoney v. Minister of Health (Kwa-Zulu Natal)*[22] seemed to illustrate a judicial unwillingness to enforce positive duties and an undue deference to state assertions of budgetary constraints.[23] Mr. Soobramoney approached the Constitutional Court after being refused renal dialysis by a state hospital that rationed treatment for patients with chronic renal failure unless they were also eligible for a kidney transplant. The Court dismissed Soobramoney's claim, finding that the provincial hospital's failure to provide renal dialysis facilities for all people with chronic renal failure did not breach the state's obligations under section 27. While Justice Chaskalson acknowledged the deplorable conditions and great poverty in which millions of South Africans lived, he argued that limited resources and the extent of demand meant that "an unqualified obligation to meet these needs would not presently be capable of being fulfilled," and that both the state's obligations and the corresponding rights themselves were "limited by reason of the lack of resources."[24]

In rejecting Soobramoney's claim, the Court showed considerable deference to the state's averment that there were no resources available to expand access to dialysis. In these circumstances, the Court found the guidelines to be a rational response to scarce resources which maximized the amount of people who could access dialysis.[25] The Court considered that permitting claims for these and similarly expensive treatments could prejudice all other health needs,[26] and indeed the government's ability to meet broader social and economic needs.[27] Balancing competing interests meant that at times government would have to "adopt a holistic approach to the larger needs of society rather than to focus on the specific needs of particular individuals within society."[28]

While this decision appeared to reject an enforceable individual right to access health care services, the Court was careful to suggest that this right was in fact justiciable, albeit within a novel rights tradition premised not on autonomy but

---

21   See former Chief Justice Chaskalson's ex-curiae assertion that these rights sit at "the border of the separation of powers between the judiciary and the executive." A. Chaskalson, "From Wickedness to Equality: The Moral Transformation of South African Law", p. 4 *International. Jnl. of Const. L.* (2003), p. 590-609 at 601.

22   *Soobramoney v. Minister of Health (Kwa-Zulu Natal)* (1998) 1 S.Afr.L.R. 765 (S. Afr. Const. Ct.) *(Soobramoney decision)*.

23   See for example, D. Moellendorf, "Reasoning about Resources: Soobramoney and the Future of Socio-Economic Rights Claims" S. *Afr. Jnl. on Hum.Rts.* (1998), p. 327-333, at 327; and C. Ngwenya, "The Recognition of Access to Health Care as a Human Right in South Africa: Is it Enough?" *Health and Human Rights*, (2000), p. 27-44 at 33.

24   *Soobramoney decision*, at para. 11.

25   *Ibid.*, at paras 24-25.

26   *Ibidem*, at para. 28.

27   *Ibidem*, at para. 31.

28   *Ibidem*, at para. 32.

on human interdependence.29 This new approach would require adapting traditional rights analyses to "provide a broad framework of constitutional principles governing the right of access to scarce resources and to adjudicate between competing rights bearers."30 The implication that the Court would enforce this right is similarly echoed in the Court's indication that "a court would be slow to interfere with rational decisions taken in good faith by the political organs and medical authorities whose responsibility it is to deal with such matters."31

The Court's willingness to interfere with government decisions was borne out in the seminal case on housing rights that followed. In *Government of the Republic of South Africa & Others v. Irene Grootboom & Others*,32 squatters who were forcibly evicted by the state from land earmarked for low-cost housing sued the government on the basis of everyone's right of access to adequate housing in section 26 and children's right to shelter in section 28(1)(c). In its judgment, the Constitutional Court established the constitutional test of reasonableness as the standard for assessing state compliance with its socioeconomic rights obligations. Since the housing right shares the same limitations clause as the right to access health care services, the Court's extensive interpretation of the state's obligations in light of progressive realization within available resources applies equally to section 27.

In a decision delivered by Justice Yacoob, the Court indicated that while reasonableness was determined on a case-by-case basis, given great poverty and the constitutional commitment to equality, dignity and freedom, the state's primary obligation was to act reasonably to provide the basic necessities of life to those who lack them.33 Taking 'reasonable legislative and other measures' required the state to devise a comprehensive and workable plan to meet its obligations, providing for all needs, including short, medium and long-term needs as well as for crises.34 Thus, legislation, policies and programmes that exclude "a significant segment of society" would be considered unreasonable.35 In seeking to ensure that the basic necessities of life were provided to all, the state had to focus in particular on the needs of the most vulnerable, especially the poor, and particularly those experiencing urgent and desperate needs.36 Reasonableness required programs to be balanced and flexible, with national government bearing the responsibility of ensuring sufficient laws and polices to fulfil their obligations.37 While progressive realization recognizes that full

---

29   See for instance, Justice Sachs: "[h]ealth care rights by their very nature have to be considered not only in a traditional legal context structured around the ideas of human autonomy but in a new analytical framework based on the notion of human interdependence." *Soobramoney decision*, at para. 54.
30   *Ibidem*, at para. 54.
31   *Ibidem*, at para. 29.
32   *Government of the Republic of South Africa & Others v. Irene Grootboom & Others* (2000) 11 B.Const. L.R. 1169 (S. Afr. Const. Ct.) (*Grootboom decision*).
33   *Grootboom decision*, at paras. 24 and 44.
34   *Ibidem*, at paras. 38, 40, 42 and 43.
35   *Ibidem*, at para. 44.
36   *Ibidem*, at paras. 35 and 43.
37   *Ibidem*, at paras. 40 and 43.

realization of everyone's right to access health care services is not always immediately possible, the Court emphasized that the state must take steps to effectively meet the basic needs of all in society, and to examine and where possible lower legal, administrative, operational and financial hurdles over time.[38] These steps should be taken as expeditiously and effectively as possible and any deliberately retrogressive measures would need full justification in light of all the rights in the *Constitution* and available resources.[39] The reasonableness of any policy cannot however, be separated from the level of resources available and the state is not required to do more than its available resources permit.[40] This means balancing the goal (of meeting all basic needs) with the means.[41] Equally importantly, trying to meet all needs requires "adequate budgetary support by national government," and requires the state to "plan, budget and monitor" their fulfilment.[42]

It is notable however that the Court rejected arguments by amicus curiae to recognize the international human rights notion of a minimum core within the right to housing.[43] The minimum core concept recognizes non-derogable essential levels of social rights that cannot be limited due to resources and which are not subject to progressive realization.[44] The Court reasoned that recognizing a minimum core required that the Court itself determine its content, a complex task requiring information that the Court lacked in general and in the case before it. While the Court declined to import the core concept, it nonetheless indicated that the minimum core could be relevant to a determination of reasonableness.[45]

The Court found that national housing policy fell short of government's constitutional duties, and declared that section 26 required a comprehensive program to realize the right of access to adequate housing that included reasonable measures to provide relief to those with no access to land, no roof over their heads, and living in intolerable conditions or crisis situations. State housing fell short of compliance for its failure to do so.

The reasonableness standard illustrates the Constitutional Court's innovative effort to balance the institutional and democratic implications of enforcing socio-economic rights with its duty to protect society's most vulnerable members. The decision sent a clear message to both government and civil society that the Court was prepared to subject social policy to judicial review and to order constitutionally compliant policy where it fell short of constitutional

---

38   *Ibidem*, at para. 45.
39   This aspect of the Court's decision directly incorporated the interpretation of the UN Committee on Economic, Social and Cultural Rights of the phrase "progressive realization" in international human rights law. See CESCR, "General Comment 3: The Nature of State Party Obligations" U.N. Doc. HRI\GEN\1\Rev.1 at 45 (1994), at para. 9, cited with approval in *Grootboom decision*, at para. 45.
40   *Ibid.*, at para. 32.
41   *Ibidem*, at para. 46.
42   *Ibidem*, at para. 68.
43   *Ibidem*, at paras. 27-33.
44   The minimum core is defined in relation to social rights in CESCR, General Comment 3, at para.10. It is interpreted in relation to the right to health in CESCR, General Comment No. 14, at paras. 42- 47.
45   *Grootboom decision*, at para.33.

standards. Nonetheless the reasonableness standard read in concert with the rejection of the minimum core raised questions as to whether the entitlement was in fact an individual right that guaranteed particular services rather than an "administrative law model of socio-economic rights" that required "sensible priority setting."[46] To this extent, questions remained about the social justice potential of these rights.

Placing the Right to Health into the Crucible of National AIDS Policy

The force of the right to access health care was definitively put to the test by the government's refusal to provide any forms of AIDS treatment in the public sector. This decision drew strongly from President Mbeki's support of AIDS denialism, which not only disputes that HIV causes AIDS, but views antiretroviral drugs as fatally toxic.[47] To put the human consequences of this decision in context, South Africa has one of the world's largest AIDS pandemics, with an estimated 5.54 million people infected in 2005, approximately 11.7 percent of the total population.[48] AIDS has become the single largest cause of death in the country, with over 300 000 people dying per year,[49] and an estimated 1.2 million deaths from HIV/AIDS to date.[50] One and a half million children are estimated to have been orphaned as a result,[51] and around 80-90 000 infants were being maternally infected every year.

Social contestation over government's resolute refusal to provide treatment coalesced around its delays and active obstruction of public sector use of Nevirapine, an antiretroviral drug with growing efficacy in preventing mother to child transmission (MTCT) of AIDS,[52] and which had been offered to the gov-

---

46   C. R. Sunstein, "Social and Economic Rights? Lessons from South Africa" *Constitutional Forum* (2000) II:4, p. 123, 131.

47   See for example, M. Harvey, "How Can a Virus Cause a Syndrome? Asks Mbeki" *iClinic* (21 September 2000) online: Aegis http://www.aegis.com/news/woza/2000/IC000906.html, M. Cohen, "Mbeki Questions HIV Testing" *The Associated Press* (24 April 2001), and E. Cameron, "AIDS Denial and Holocaust Denial—AIDS, Justice and the Courts in South Africa," *S. Afr. L. J.* (2003) 120:3, p. 525.

48   South African Department of Health, "National HIV and Syphilis Antenatal Sero-Prevalence Survey in South Africa 2005," at <http://www.doh.gov.za/aids/index.html>. Note however that this figure jumps considerably in the demographic of adults aged 15-49 years, where approximately 18.78 percent of people are infected. See Report, p.17.

49   R. E. Dorrington et al, *The Impact of HIV/AIDS on Adult Mortality in South Africa*, Technical Report Burden of Disease Research Unit, Medical Research Council, 2001.

50   R. E. Dorrington, D. Bradshaw, L. Johnson and D. Budlender, *The Demographic Impact of HIV/AIDS in South Africa: National Indicators for 2004* (Cape Town: Centre for Actuarial Research, South African Medical Research Council and Actuarial Society of South Africa, 2004).

51   R. E. Dorrington et al, "The Demographic Impact of HIV/AIDS in South Africa: National and Provincial Indicators for 2006," Centre for Actuarial Research, South African Medical Research Council and Actuarial Society of South Africa, at i.

52   L. A. Guay *et al.*, "Intrapartum and Neonatal Single-Dose Nevirapine Compared with Zidovudine for Prevention of Mother-to-Child Transmission of HIV-1 in Kampala, Uganda: HIVNET 012 Randomised Trial" *The Lancet* (1999) 354, p. 795-802; Daya Moodley, "The SAINT Trial: Nevirapine (NVP) versus Zidovudine (ZDV) + Lamivudine (3TC) in Prevention

ernment at no cost for five years by Boehringer Ingelheim, the manufacturer and patent holder of the drug. Despite government refusals, the expansion of a national MTCT program was well supported amongst the media, public and medical communities,[53] motivated in part by national legal and political advocacy, and the growing protests of health care workers themselves that government policy interfered with their ethical duties towards patients.[54] Responding to these increasing social pressures, in August 2000 the Minister of Health and nine provincial health representatives decided that once Nevirapine had been registered for use domestically, it would be tested for two years at two pilot sites in all nine provinces to assess the operational challenges of introducing a national program and to build the capacity and infrastructure that accompanying interventions such as counselling and HIV testing, revised obstetric practices and infant feeding practices required.[55] No indication was given of when thereafter government would take a decision on a comprehensive national program.

By June 2001 many MTCT research sites were still not operating, and in August 2001 the Treatment Action Campaign (TAC), a national treatment advocacy group, together with doctors working in the public sector and a children's rights NGO instituted legal action against the Minister of Health and Provincial Health departments arguing that the state's delays and refusal to make Nevirapine available in the public sector breached section 27 as well as children's right to basic health services. The government argued that limiting the drug to research sites was reasonable given their concerns about the price of the drug and associated interventions, and about the safety and efficacy of Nevirapine. After the High Court ruled against the government, it appealed to the Constitutional Court, arguing that limiting the program to pilot sites would help it understand the operational demands of a successful program, allowing it to gradually extend the program as resources allowed.[56] However government also now pointedly aimed its appeal at the very act of judicial review of health policy—arguing that the High Court's order made government policy, and therefore violated the doctrine of separation of powers, and that from this perspective the Constitutional Court was only able to make a declaratory rather than mandatory order.

---

of Peripartum Transmission" (2001) XIII International AIDS conference, Durban, South Africa, 9-14 July 2000, abstract no. LbOr2.

53   See for example, "Government Should Provide Anti-retrovirals" *The Mercury* (6 December 2002). (Reporting that a survey had shown that almost all South Africans are in favour of implementing anti-retroviral therapy to HIV-positive pregnant mothers and people living with HIV/AIDS); and S. A. Karim *et al.*, "Vertical HIV Transmission in South Africa: Translating Research into Policy and Practice" *The Lancet* (2002) 359, p. 992-993.

54   See for instance P. Govender, "Doctors defy drug ban" *Sunday Times* (20 January 2002).

55   South African Department of Health, "Protocol for Providing a Comprehensive Package of Care for the Prevention of Mother to Child Transmission (PMTCT) in South Africa", 23 May 2001, at p. 4.

56   South African Constitutional Court, "Media Summary," http://www.constitutionalcourt.org .za/Archimages/2478.PDF.

In July 2002 the Constitutional Court delivered a unanimous judgment in support of the TAC.[57] The Court rejected the government's arguments vis-à-vis constrained resources in toto, given the government's own acknowledgement that confining the drug to training sites was unrelated to drug prices,[58] and evidence lead at the hearing that government had made substantial new allocations for HIV treatment including MTCT.[59] The Court also dismissed government's arguments regarding efficacy and safety given the weight of contradictory scientific evidence and the limited threat posed by resistance.[60] The Court held that the real dilemma was whether it was reasonable to exclude the drug in other public health facilities where testing and counselling were available and the drug was medically required.[61] In this regard, the Court focused on the grave suffering and limited survival prospects of children, and stressed that the case was concerned with newborn babies whose lives might be saved by the administration of a simple and cheap intervention, the safety and efficacy of which had been established, and which the government itself was providing in pilot sites in every province.[62] While the Court recognized the need to assess operational challenges and monitor issues relevant to the safety, efficacy and resistance of Nevirapine, it stressed the "pressing need to ensure that where possible loss of life is prevented in the meantime."[63]

The Court applied several aspects of the *Grootboom decision* to section 27 and the provision of MTCT, holding that programs must not ignore urgent needs nor exclude significant segments of society,[64] and that state policy in this case affected poor people who could not afford to pay for medical services.[65] The Court held that children's:

> needs are "most urgent" and their inability to have access to Nevirapine profoundly affects their ability to enjoy all rights to which they are entitled. Their rights are "most in peril" as a result of the policy that has been adopted and are most affected by a rigid and inflexible policy that excludes them from having access to Nevirapine.[66]

The state's obligation was therefore to ensure that children were able to access basic health care services contemplated in section 28, particularly since this case concerned:

> children born in public hospitals and clinics to mothers who are for the most part indigent and unable to gain access to private medical treatment which is

---

57 *Minister of Health and another v. Treatment Action Campaign and others* (2002) 5 S.Afr.L.R. 721 (S.Afr.Const.Ct) (*TAC decision*).

58 *TAC decision*, at para. 48.

59 *Ibid*, at para. 120.

60 *Ibidem*, at paras. 57-66.

61 *Ibidem*, at para. 50.

62 *Ibidem*, at paras. 71 and 72.

63 *Ibidem, supra* note.

64 *Ibidem*, at para. 68, quoting *Grootboom decision*, at paras. 43 and 44.

65 *Ibidem*, at para. 70, referencing *Grootboom decision*, at paras. 35-7.

66 *Ibidem*, at para.78.

beyond their means. They and their children are in the main part dependent upon the state to make health care services available to them.[67]

The Court found that government policy failed to meet constitutional standards because it excluded those who could reasonably be included where such treatment was medically indicated.[68] It is notable that the Court was careful both not to be seen to overstep its constitutional mandate and to safeguard its capacity to enforce section 27. Thus, on the one hand, the Court firmly rejected amicus arguments to import the minimum core into section 27, arguing that both institutional competence and the appropriate separation of powers militated against doing so. The Court argued that it was "impossible to give everyone access even to a "core" service immediately,"[69] and "[a]ll that is possible, and all that can expected of the state, is that it act reasonably to provide access to the [Constitution's socio-economic rights] on a progressive basis."[70] Yet at the same time, the Court rejected government's arguments that the separation of powers limited it from reviewing health policy and from making anything more than declaratory orders.[71] The Court strongly affirmed that although the state's obligations under the Constitution's socio-economic rights were qualified, the rights were nonetheless justiciable and authorized the Court to review health policy.[72] The Court stood similarly firm on its constitutional authority to grant "appropriate relief"[73] and make "just and equitable orders,"[74] arguing that the constitutionality of mandatory relief and supervisory jurisdiction had been repeatedly confirmed in domestic and foreign jurisprudence.[75]

While the Court declined to exercise supervisory jurisdiction in TAC, its order both declared the government's responsibility to devise and implement a comprehensive MTCT program, and mandated government to immediately remove restrictions on the drug and make it available in the public sector, to provide for the training of counsellors and take reasonable measures to extend testing and counselling facilities throughout the public health sector.

Assessing the Jurisprudential Contribution to Solidarity and Justice

These cases read in concert with later decisions illustrate both the strengths and limits of judicial enforcement of the right to access health care services. While *Soobramoney* seemed to suggest an embryonic approach to balancing rights that favoured collective interests over even compelling individual rights claims, the Court's later decisions indicate that collective interests are not necessarily restricted by individual rights claims, and that a society premised on advancing individual dignity, equality and freedom cannot ignore the needs of

---

67   *TAC decision*, at para.79.
68   *Ibidem*, at para.125.
69   *Ibidem*, at para. 35.
70   *Ibidem*, at para. 35.
71   *Ibidem*, at para. 96.
72   *Grootboom decision*, at paras. 93-4, quoted in *TAC decision*, at para. 24.
73   *Constitution of the Republic of South Africa* Act 108 of 1996, at section 38.
74   *Constitution*, section 172(1)(a).
75   *TAC decision*, at paras. 100-112.

the poor in collective welfare. Thus, in both the *Grootboom* and *TAC decisions*, the needs of poor and vulnerable populations were prioritized over competing government assertions of resource constraints and incapacity.

To some extent, this priority derives from the constitutional entrenchment of justiciable social rights, which considerably bolsters the importance of individual welfare needs in the judicial decision-making process, even against governmental resource constraints. This priority is reflected in the 2003 case of *Khosa and Others v. Minister of Social Development and Others*, where the Court found that excluding permanent residents from receiving social grants violated the state's obligations to provide access to social security for everyone in section 27(1)(c).[76] The Court found that despite the government's averment of constrained resources, financial considerations were far outweighed by "the importance of providing access to social assistance to all who live permanently in South Africa and the impact upon life and dignity that a denial of such access has."[77]

The prioritizing impact of a justiciable health right on public health needs is well illustrated in the 2005 *New Clicks decision*, where several pharmacy chains challenged governmental regulations to reduce medicines prices including through a fixed dispensing fee for pharmacists.[78] The chains argued that the dispensing fee would cause their dispensing services to operate at a loss, thereby reducing access to medicines and harming the pharmacy profession. However the Constitutional Court unanimously held that the legislation permitted regulations to provide for price controls including through setting a single exit price.[79] While the Court was split 6:5 against the appropriateness of the dispensing fee, it upheld the constitutionality of the regulations given the important constitutional purpose of making medicines more accessible and affordable. Indeed, the Court repeatedly validates that the purpose of making medicines more affordable was to enable government to fulfil its constitutional obligations under section 27.[80] The constitutional importance of this purpose meant that when it came to balancing the private and public interests at stake, the Court could find no equivalence between the pharmacists' interests and the public's health needs.[81]

The *New Clicks decision* also adds significant new substantive content to the right beyond the constitutional framework of reasonableness elaborated in the *Grootboom* and *TAC decisions*. In several places the judgment confirms that the

---

76 *Khosa and Others v. Minister of Social Development and Others; Mahlaule and Another v. Minister of Social Development and Others*, Constitutional Court of South Africa, Cases CCT 12/03; CCT13/03, at para. 38 (*Khosa decision*).

77 *Khosa decision*, para. 82.

78 *Minister of Health & Professor D. Mcintyre No v. New Clicks South Africa (Pty) Ltd & Others*, Constitutional Court of South Africa, Case CCT 59/04, at para. 661 (*New Clicks decision*). The legislation in question was the *Medicines and Related Substances Control Amendment Act* No. 90 of 1997.

79 *New Clicks decision*, at paras. 13 and 14.

80 *Ibidem*, at paras. 16, 84, 314, 514 and 519.

81 See for example, Justice Ngcobo's assertion that while "the interests of the pharmacists is a factor to be taken into consideration ... they must yield to the interests of the general public." *New Clicks decision*, at para. 519.

right to health care services includes the right to access affordable medicines,[82] which places a range of obligations on the state in relation to affordability.[83] The Court indicates that the impact of inaccessible medicines on the poor in particular suggests state duties to take "special measures to assist those who are the most vulnerable to disease and, simultaneously the most lacking in resources."[84] Thus the Court recognizes state duties to regulate market activities to protect public health needs, and moreover that the status quo itself may be unreasonable and require active remedial action.[85] These dicta animate the Court's recognition that rights exist within an interdependent social environment and place correlative duties on other social actors. This provides a powerful flip side to the *Soobramoney decision,* where an individual rights claim to expensive treatment was seen to pose unreasonable threats to the collective good. In the *New Clicks decision* (as in the *TAC* and *Grootboom decisions*), the Court conversely ensures that competing public and private interests could not unreasonably restrict individual rights. This approach sees the Court ensuring that individual entitlements are located within a broader notion of collective responsibility towards the poor. Thus, while the Court will seek to ensure a maximum utility for resources, its approach to rights is not utilitarian, and focuses particularly on the impact of public and private actions on the poorest and most powerless members of society. This approach is illustrated in the 2003 *Port Elizabeth Municipality case* dealing with housing rights, where the Court refused to authorize the eviction of the occupiers of privately owned land because the municipality had not taken reasonable steps to find alternative lodging.[86] In its judgment, the Court emphasized that:

> [i]n a society founded on human dignity, equality and freedom it cannot be presupposed that the greatest good for the many can be achieved at the cost of intolerable hardship for the few, particularly if by a reasonable application of judicial and administrative statecraft such human distress could be avoided.[87]

The Court indicated that this approach to rights was based on the traditional African notion of 'ubuntu,' which translates to "humaneness," personhood and 'morality,' and which "envelops the key values of group solidarity, compassion, respect, human dignity, conformity to basic norms and collective

---

82   For example, *New Clicks decision,* at para. 514 and 704.
83   See for example, Justice Sachs holding that "preventing excessive profit-taking from the manufacturing distribution and sale of medicines is more than an option for government. It is a constitutional obligation flowing from its duties under section 27(2)." *Ibid.,* at para. 659.
84   *Ibidem,* at para. 651. See also para. 706, which states that "[p]rohibitive pricing of medicine ... would in effect equate to a denial of the right of access to health care."
85   See for example, Justice Sachs' dicta in the *New Clicks decision,* which indicates that: "the concept of reasonableness should not be used as an apparently neutral instrument which, regarding the status quo as the settled norm, serves to block transformation and freeze challengeable aspects of our public life ... In a society where distributions are manifestly unequal and unjust, it is a defence of the status quo and the failure to make corrective intervention, rather than a re-distributive initiative, that could be open to a charge of unreasonableness." *New Clicks decision,* at para. 660, incorporating text from footnote 84.
86   *Port Elizabeth Municipality v. Various Occupiers,* Constitutional Court of South Africa, Case CCT 53/03, at para. 29 (*Port Elizabeth Municipality decision*).
87   *Port Elizabeth Municipality decision,* at para. 29.

unity."[88] This is a notion which the Court argues "suffuses the whole constitutional order .... [and] combines individual rights with a communitarian philosophy."[89] This approach to rights seeks to ensure not simply that individual rights are realized, but to make doing so an integral part of a collective ethos of mutual respect and humaneness. Thus, although the Court avers a restrained constitutional role, its enforcement of the constitutional social rights provides a powerful mechanism for remediating injustice. While arguably, the Court's enforcement may not be able to remediate the structural inequalities that may considerably restrict the realization of social rights, the Court seeks nonetheless to "at least soften and minimize the degree of injustice and inequity" which actions such as evicting the poor "in conditions of inequality of necessity entails."[90] The Court's decisions have certainly contributed to remediating inequities. For example, the *TAC decision* not only achieved a national MTCT program in over eighty percent of government clinics,[91] but laid the groundwork for a national AIDS treatment program, which was announced in 2003.[92] By October 2006, approximately 165-175 000 people were accessing antiretrovirals through this program.[93]

Yet while the South African jurisprudence illustrates the minimizing impact of litigation on injustice and inequality, it also shows its limits in effecting expeditious and effective policy change, as disparities in the implementation of the *Grootboom* and *TAC decisions* suggest. For example, there was little tangible change in housing policy to cater for people in desperate and crisis situations even one year after the *Grootboom decision*.[94] The picture was considerably different after the *TAC decision*, perhaps because of the power of domestic treatment advocates who effectively used the media to highlight implementation delays, and who also instituted contempt of court proceedings against a provincial premier for not implementing the decision. These differences suggest that if political mobilization by civil society is necessary to ensure timeous im-

---

88   *S v. Makwanyane and Another* 1995 (3) S. Afr. L. Rep. 391 (Const. Crt.), at para 308, referenced in *Port Elizabeth Municipality decision*, at para. 37, footnote 36. For more on ubuntu in the constitutional order, see also *David Dikoko v. Thupi Zacharia Mokhatla*, Constitutional Court of South Africa, Case CCT 62/05; and *Nonkululeko Letta Bhe & Others v. Magistrate, Khayelitsha & Others; Charlotte Shibi v. Mantabeni Freddy Sithole & Others; South African Human Rights Commission and Women's Legal Centre Trust v. President of the Republic of South Africa and Minister for Justice and Constitutional Development Constitutional Court of South Africa*, Constitutional Court of South Africa, Case CCT 49/03, 69/03 and 50/03.

89   *Port Elizabeth Municipality decision*, at para. 37.

90   *Ibid.*, at para. 38.

91   580 880 pregnant women accessed MTCT services in 2006; 74 052 got NVP; 19 758 babies born to HIV positive mothers tested: 16 228 babies tested negative, 3470 tested positive. Ministry of Health, "100% Coverage for Prevention of Mother to Child Transmission of HIV," 12 March 2007.

92   Department of Health, *Operational Plan for Comprehensive HIV and AIDS Care, Management and Treatment for South Africa 19 November 2003*, (Care Plan) online: Government of Republic of South Africa.

93   Another 100-110,000 people receive ARV in the private and not-for-profit sectors. See International Treatment Preparedness Coalition (ITPC), "Missing the Target #3: Stagnation in AIDS treatment Scale Up Puts Millions of Lives at Risk," 28 November 2006, at 45.

94   K. Pillay, "Implementing Grootboom: Supervision Needed" *Economic and Social Rights Review* (2002) 3, p. 12.

plementation, that a stronger judicial approach to implementation is required, including through the use of mandatory orders and supervisory jurisdiction. This is an option which the Court left open in the *TAC decision,* and which the Court may well utilize if state compliance is persistently dilatory or inadequate.

The Court's rejection of the minimum core has been a particularly contentious aspect of its jurisprudence, and has been criticised for leaving large gaps and ambiguities for how government should operationalize the reasonableness standard generally or in health care specifically. For example, the reasonableness standard provides only broad constitutional guidelines to the state, without defining temporal priorities to guide progressive realization, or defining urgency, desperation, and the key populations of the poor and vulnerable.95 Nonetheless, the decisions in *Grootboom, TAC, Khosa* and *New Clicks* illustrate that the abstract nature of the reasonableness standard does not detract from its broader power in protecting the indigent and ill from public negligence or private incursions. Moreover, the *New Clicks decision* illustrates that the Court will incrementally develop the substantive content of these rights in addition to the broad constitutional principles of the reasonableness standard. In this light, the Court's rejection of the core should not be seen to fracture the spirit and intent behind justiciable social rights, but rather to be substantially in harmony with them.

Certainly the Court's enforcement sends a clear message to other legal cultures regarding the justiciability of social rights and positive duties. It illustrates the potential for a judicial role in enforcing rights that answers pragmatic concerns about their zero sum claims and the institutional competence and democratic legitimacy of judicial review of social policy. Yet the Court's cautious and qualified approach to enforcing social rights has not fully addressed ideological objections to social rights, by reifying the notion that positive duties are questionably enforceable and negative duties unquestionably so.96 The Court's response therefore remains rooted in a sharp distinction between positive and negative duties (and ostensibly positive and negative rights) despite the fact that there may not be sharp distinctions between the kind of

---

95   See for instance, T. Roux, "Understanding Grootboom – A Response to Cass R. Sunstein" *Forum Constitutionnel* (2002) p. 41-51, at 46, and S. Liebenberg, "South Africa's Evolving Jurisprudence on Socio-economic Rights" *Law, Democracy and Development* (2002), p. 159. See also, D. Bilchitz, "Towards a Reasonable Approach to the Minimum Core: Laying the Foundations for Future Socio-economic Rights Jurisprudence" *S. Afr. Jnl. on Hum. Rts,* (2002) 19, p. 1-126 and M. Pieterse, "Possibilities and Pitfalls in the Domestic Enforcement of Social Rights: Contemplating the South African Experience" *Human Rights Quarterly* (2004) 26, p. 882-905.

96   This is evident in the Court's elaboration of alternative regimes for enforcing the negative and positive duties that each constitutional right (whether social or civil) is interpreted to hold. Thus, the Court has held that civil rights impose positive duties that should be assessed according to the constitutional standard of reasonableness. On the other hand the Court has held that social rights impose negative duties not subject to progressive realization and which should instead be assessed under the *Constitution's* general limitations clause. See respectively, *Rail Commuters Action Group and others v. Transnet Ltd* Constitutional Court of South Africa, CCT 56/03, at paras. 70 and 88; and *Jaftha v. Schoeman and others; van Rooyen v. Stoltz and Others S. Afr. L. R.* (2005) 2, p. 140 (Const. Crt.).

actions and resources needed to realize these duties.[97] This distinction suggests that the Court has not fully discarded the ideological baggage associated with positive rights and this persistent legal cultural bias may obscure the analytical work needed to attend to rights violations and the structural inequalities that perpetuate and exacerbate them.

Conclusion

The South African jurisprudence reflects the emergence of an innovative African rights tradition more cognizant of the social determinants of individual autonomy and agency than liberal rights approaches that exclude social welfare claims. Instead, the South African judicial approach promises to advance equal access to health care and to mitigate those deprivations of poverty that can reasonably be averted within limited resources. This approach has empowered the right to health against public and private interests that unreasonably encroach on the basic needs of the poor. Yet the judiciary's willingness to give teeth to this right is a highly contingent choice, deeply influenced by legal-cultural conceptions of the legitimacy of social rights, and deeper ideological conceptions of the appropriate role of the state versus the market in material redistribution and remediation of inequality. These deeper influences suggest that if the right to health is to assume judicial force, it must infiltrate these deeper conceptions not simply of law but of governance. This requires not simply targeting the legal education that trains judges in outdated approaches to social rights, but also working towards the broader internalization of this right as collective expectations of appropriate governance and commerce with regard to health and social needs. This approach sees rights becoming potentially transformative tools, providing a moral framework for the achievement of a more humane society in which the basic needs of the poor are not rejected or minimized as a matter of course. While litigation alone will not achieve this outcome, if it can be combined with rights discourse, advocacy and social mobilization, the right to health may become collectively empowered as a remedial tool capable of placing reasonable limits on politics and economics in service of the health interests of the poor.

---

97   See for instance, Henry Shue, *Basic Rights, Subsistence, Affluence and US Foreign Policy* (Princeton, NJ: Princeton University Press, 1980).

Chapter 9.

The Impact of ART Scale-up on Health Systems (De-)Strengthening in Sub-Saharan Africa: Justice and Justification

Stephanie Nixon and Nina Veenstra

"The global recognition of rights to [HIV] treatment reflects a significant shift in mindset. Another shift is now needed to deliver on those aspirations."[1]

Introduction

The scale-up of anti-retroviral treatment (ART) in sub-Saharan Africa (sSA) is unquestionably a positive development. These life-prolonging medicines are finally becoming an essential component of the response to HIV/AIDS in the most highly-affected region in the world, a full decade after they were introduced in rich countries. To be successful, however, scale-up must be understood as more than the technical exercise of delivering pills. A central dimension of the challenge involves the health systems through which services are delivered.

The addition of ART to HIV care in rich countries in the 1990's was a significant development but did not threaten the stability of those health systems. In contrast, the greatly increased scale of the HIV epidemic in sSA married with the region's less resilient health systems is likely to result in a very different scenario. The sub-Saharan African region is experiencing a generalized epidemic with national adult HIV-prevalence rates of above 30% in some instances, which stands in stark contrast to the prevalence rates of less than 1% in most wealthy countries.[2]

Furthermore, health systems in sSA are struggling to evolve while simultaneously attempting to meet demands that far outweigh their capacities. With respect to HIV in particular, the transition in the region from a prevention-only approach to one that embraces combined prevention, treatment and care has shifted demands on and expectations for these struggling health systems. One must therefore be cautious in looking to the West for lessons about how the introduction of ART might affect health systems. Rather, this novel situa-

---

[1]   R. Loewenson and D. McCoy, "Access to antiretroviral treatment in Africa", *British Medical Journal* (2004) 328, p. 241-242.

[2]   UNAIDS, *Report of the global AIDS epidemic 2006*, UNAIDS, Geneva (2006).

tion calls for analysis of ART provision to be located in the context of the strengthening efforts that have been underway in poor countries' health systems for decades. Indeed, recognition of the significance of Africa's fragile health systems to the success of ART rollout is the "shift in mindset" called for by Loewenson and McCoy in the opening quote.

To this end, Part 1 of this paper addresses the question of how the scale-up of ART could impact on health systems in sSA. We conclude that the current expansion of access to ART potentially involves an approach to health delivery that runs counter to many of the aims of health system strengthening in the region.

In Part 2 of this paper, we address the question of whether or not this is justified. That is, knowing that the current scale-up of ART is likely to compromise efforts to strengthen health systems in the region, is it still justified to move forward? We conclude that the potential erosion of health systems strengthening in the region *is* justified, provided simultaneous efforts are undertaken to optimize the possibility for the "AIDS transition" scenario to be realized. We discuss these simultaneous efforts, drawing on recent research to paint a picture of the emerging scenario in sSA.

In Part 3 of the paper, we reflect back on Parts 1 and 2 in order to derive lessons that may inform scale-up of ARV in sSA in ways that, at least, minimize detrimental effects and, ideally, serve to strengthen health systems in the region. We discuss the value of solidarity as a guiding principle for ART scale-up planning, followed by a series of concrete lessons for moving forward.

The Potential Impact of ART Scale-up on Health Systems in sub-Saharan Africa

For countries in sub-Saharan Africa, health systems are a work-in-progress, continuously being reshaped in an effort to become stronger. Ideas about how best to strengthen health systems have shifted over time. Current efforts draw heavily upon the landmark Alma Ata Declaration on Health and the related commitment to 'Health for All by the Year 2000'. At the centre of this vision was the concept of Primary Health Care (PHC), which encompasses a comprehensive approach to health that addresses underlying social, economic and political determinants of wellness and illness.[3] Within this concept, the mandate of health systems is broader than simply the provision of primary health care services. The focus of health systems shifts from disease-specific technology and the culture of curative hospital care toward a more integrated, holistic and proactive approach to wellness. Equity is viewed as a central goal coupled with a human rights perspective as the means by which it can be achieved. The PHC approach to health has received criticism for being idealistic,[4] but the philosophy holds lessons that have stood the test of time.

---

3   *Declaration of Alma-Ata,* International Conference on Primary Health Care, Alma-Ata, USSR (1978).

4   M. Cueto, "The origins of primary health care and selective primary health care", *American Journal of Public Health* (2004) 11, p. 1864-1874.

The health care reforms that followed PHC in the mid-1980's emphasized a different set of principles, notably the economic value of services. The foundation of these reforms was economic neo-liberalism. The approach, therefore, aimed at increasing the role of market mechanisms in health care provision by expanding the role of the private sector, increasing "cost-sharing" and focusing on efficiency.[5] The role of governments was minimised through fiscal limits on public health care spending and through decreased public regulation over health services. Cost-recovery mechanisms, such as user fees, were particularly damaging because of their inequitable impact on health care utilization.[6] The result was an approach to health that went against many of the principles espoused by PCH and lost sight of the goal of health for all.

The neo-liberal economic policy approach remains visible today in both rich and poor countries. In sSA, the approach was adopted by countries largely as a condition of World Bank/IMF loans or as a result of international pressure. However, as the damaging effects of these policies on fragile health systems are better documented, there is renewed passion for many of the values articulated in Alma Ata almost three decades ago.[7][8]

It is within this context that we come to the question of how the greatly expanded roll-out of ART could impact on health systems. For instance, the spotlight on HIV treatment emphasises a medical model focus. It also seems to be leading to centralisation of health care. In South Africa, the response to HIV/AIDS has been shown to prioritise short term delivery objectives established by higher levels of government, which is at odds with the longer term development objective of strengthening local government systems.[9] In Table 1, the first column presents shifts in focus sought through health system strengthening, whereas the second column outlines the likely influences of ART scale-up, which largely operate in less desired directions.

---

5   World Bank, World Development Report 1993: Investing in health, World Bank, Washington (1993).

6   See, for example J. Nabyonga, M. Desmet, H. Karamagi, P. Kadama, F. Omaswa and O. Walker, "Abolition of cost-sharing is pro-poor: evidence from Uganda", *Health Policy and Planning* (2005) 2, p. 100-108.

7   Global Health Watch, Global Health Watch 2005-2006: An alternative world health report, People's Health Movement, Medact and Global Equity Gauge Alliance (2005).

8   People's Health Movement, People's Charter for Health, First People's Health Assembly, Dhaka, Bangladesh (2000).

9   D. Blaauw, L. Gilson, P. Modiba, E. Erasmus, G. Khumalo and H. Scheider, Governmental relationships and HIV/AIDS service delivery, Centre for Health Policy (CHP), University of Wit-watersrand, Johannesburg (2004).

Table 1. How ART Scale-up Might Influence Health System Strengthening Efforts

Desired shifts in focus	Potential influence of ART scale-up
From curative to preventive care	Back to curative care
From medical model to broader determinants of health approach	Back to medical model
From specialized tertiary care to primary care	Back to tertiary care
From centralized, urban care delivery to decentralized care that covers rural regions	Back to centralized, urban care delivery
From focus on short-term concerns to long-term development objectives	Back to focus on short-term concerns
From vertical programming for disease-specific responses to integrated care	Back to vertical programming
From top-down, centralized planning and management to community led, decentralized planning and management	Back to top-down, centralized planning

Of particular note for health system strengthening is the way in which ART scale-up has promoted vertical programming as opposed to a horizontal model. Vertical programming, meaning separate health structures dedicated to the planning, management and implementation of selected disease-specific interventions, is a public health strategy that has been used for decades.[10] The common rationale for verticalisation is to provide greater capacity for a focused effort to reduce morbidity and mortality related to a specific disease.[11] As such, the call for vertical programs is typically stronger where epidemics, poverty and weakened health systems coincide, which is the case for HIV/AIDS in many countries and especially in sSA.

While this argument is compelling, there are hard-learned shortcomings of this approach that are instructive for thinking about the scale-up of ART. Some of these shortcomings are related to the shifts in focus outlined above. In particular, vertical programming often reflects a medical model response, which detracts from a more comprehensive approach that addresses upstream determinants of health.[12] It has also historically assumed a top-down management approach as opposed to one that engages community participation.

---

[10] A. Mills, "Mass campaigns versus general health services: what have we learnt in 40 years about vertical versus horizontal approaches?", *Bulletin of the World Health Organization* (2005) 4, p. 315-316.

[11] V. Oliveira-Cruz, C. Kurowski and A. Mills, "Delivery of priority health services: searching for synergies within the vertical versus horizontal debate", *Journal of International Development* (2003) 15, p. 67-86.

[12] A. Mills, "Vertical vs horizontal health programmes in Africa: idealism, pragmatism, resources and efficiency", *Social Science and Medicine* (1983), p. 1971-1981.

Other concerns stem from the way in which these programmes can promote multiple parallel disease-specific programmes operating in silos and the way in which they are often supported by external funding. The concept of vertical programmes operating in silos and the high levels of donor funding afforded to these programmes often work in tandem to create a set of undesirable circumstances in the health system. In essence, while vertical programmes may be effective in and of themselves, they have the potential to disrupt the efforts of local health systems to deliver comprehensive and integrated essential services.[13] A common harm involves the usurping of often limited supplies of health workers from existing systems to higher salary roles within vertical programmes being sponsored by international health non-governmental organisations and donors.[14] This process may been seen as de-skilling primary care workers as their expertise focuses to achieve narrow goals at the expense of their broader expertise on the health demands of communities.[15] While external funding for ART programming is essential, it also comes with the issue of who is setting health priorities. Responses to HIV/AIDS are designed and delivered at the country level. As such, the strategy created for scaling up delivery of ART within and by countries should drive the allocation of external resources and not *vice versa*.

The resulting picture is one whereby ART scale-up, while crucial in and of itself, holds the potential to frustrate efforts to strengthen health systems in the countries of sSA by shifting foci in less desired directions. It is with this springboard that we turn to the question of whether or not these negative effects on health systems potentially caused by ART scale-up are justified.

Justifying the Impact of ART Scale-up on Health Systems

This exceptional approach to ART scale-up is rooted in the rationale of addressing morbidity and mortality as a matter of urgency and then reducing HIV incidence in the medium term. The reduction in incidence will result in a more manageable disease burden, at which time ART delivery can be assimilated into general health services. If all goes as planned, vertical programmes will give way to horizontal approaches and ART will be integrated into broader health service efforts. This approach and its rationale are not unlike responses to other communicable disease outbreaks. If there were a measles outbreak, for example, special services would be established as a matter of urgency to firstly treat the existing cases and secondly to prevent further spread of the disease. As the spread of the disease is brought under control, measles would again become one of many conditions managed through integrated care.

The justification for exceptional approaches, such as that afforded to ART, is therefore based on a key assumption: that the burden of disease will become

---

13   WHO, The African Regional Health Report: The health of the people, World Health Organisation, Geneva (2006).
14   K. Kober and W. Van Damme, "Scaling up access to antiretroviral treatment in southern Africa: who will do the job?", *The Lancet* (2004) 364, p. 103-7.
15   Global Health Watch, Global Health Watch 2005-2006: An alternative world health report, People's Health Movement, Medact and Global Equity Gauge Alliance (2005).

more manageable for the health system in the foreseeable future. In relation to HIV/AIDS, this means that the number of people living with HIV/AIDS would, in the medium term, be brought down to levels that the general health services could manage. However, the justification is uncertain in the case of HIV/AIDS because of both the long-wave nature of the epidemic and our limited experience with ART programmes in sSA. Uncertainties about factors affecting future demand for care compromise our ability to predict the likelihood of a reduced burden of disease. However, we can reasonably anticipate a range of possible scenarios linked to the introduction of ART.

The most optimistic scenario takes lessons from the demographic transition and has therefore been labelled the "AIDS transition" by economist Mead Over.[16] In this case, mortality due to AIDS declines as people access and adhere to ART. Importantly, new HIV infection rates also decline as ART has a positive impact on prevention through mechanisms that may include reduced transmissibility and decreased HIV stigma. The resulting impact on health systems is an initial increase in the number of people requiring care followed by stabilization as the disease burden becomes much more manageable. The vertical approach to ART delivery will have served its purpose, helping to bring a dire situation under control.

Alternative scenarios, however, lead to more dismal outcomes. For instance, ART programmes may be unsuccessful in achieving and maintaining a reduction in mortality due to programme delivery problems concerned with access, support and adherence. The failure to reduce mortality will in turn negate related benefits for HIV prevention, causing incidence rates to remain high. Assuming there is some initial success in reducing mortality, the result will be an initial increase in the number of people requiring care followed by some stabilization as mortality rates resume. However, the overall burden of care will be higher than in the AIDS transition scenario and, most importantly, the pandemic will continue to flourish.

Even where ART programmes do manage to achieve a sustained reduction in mortality, the AIDS transition may still not transpire. This is because the assumption that ART scale-up has positive effects on prevention may be faulty, with actual outcomes seeing ART having either no effect or a negative effect on prevention. In such cases the incidence of new infections will remain high, the epidemic will continue to grow, and the burden on health systems will be at its highest yet. With each of these alternative scenarios, the introduction of vertical ART programmes becomes more difficult to justify from the perspective of their impacts on health systems. The argument in favour of the exceptional response to ART scale-up is, therefore, tied to the success of the AIDS transition scenario.

How likely is it that the AIDS transition scenario will be realized in sSA? There are assumptions that can be unpacked in order to begin to answer this question. For instance, along with the increased or decreased burden placed on health systems by ART, there are also likely to be shifts *within* health sys-

---

[16]   M. Over, "Impact of the HIV/AIDS epidemic on the health sectors of developing countries", in M. Haacker (ed.), *The Macroeconomics of HIV/AIDS*, (Washington: International Monetary Fund, 2004).

tems that are relevant to managers and policy-makers responsible for prioriti-
zation and resource allocation. One potential shift in the burden of HIV/AIDS
care due to ART would be from inpatient to outpatient services.[17] [18] [19] In sSA,
such shifts have not yet been reported because ART programmes are still quite
nascent, although this is a hopeful goal. The balance of this section reviews
evidence emerging regarding other nuances in the sSA experience that can inform assumptions underpinning the AIDS transition scenario.

Rich countries have witnessed sustained declines in mortality since the advent of ART. The debate over *whether* ART programmes can feasibly be introduced in resource-limited settings[20] [21] has been superseded by questions of
how ART can best be delivered in order to achieve similar clinical
successes.[22] [23] [24] [25] Two key challenges to achieving reductions in mortality in
sSA involve getting people on treatment early and maintaining adherence,
both of which currently carry an uncertain prognosis. Early evaluations of ART
programmes in Africa have demonstrated that their effectiveness has been
compromised by patients presenting late for treatment.[26] [27] [28] However,
decisions about if and when to seek therapy depend not only on affordable
medicines but on a range of social, political and economic factors as well.

17   E. Beck, S. Mandalia, I. Williams, A. Power, R. Newson et al., for the NPMS Steering Group,
      Decreased morbidity and use of hospital services in English HIV infected individuals with
      increased uptake of anti-retroviral therapy 1996-1997, *AIDS* (1999) 13, p. 2157-2164.
18   M. Stoll, C. Class, E. Scuttle, J. Von der Scullenburg and R. Schmidt, "Direct costs for the
      treatment of HIV-infection in a German cohort after introduction of HAART", *European
      Journal of Medical Research* (2002), 7, p. 463-471.
19   I. Dourado, M. Amélia, D. Barriera and A. Maria, "AIDS epidemic trends after the introduc-
      tion of antiretroviral therapy in Brazil", *Rev Saúde Pública* (2006) Suppl, p. 9-17.
20   A. Creese, K. Floyd, A. Alban and L. Guiness, "Cost-effectiveness of HIV/AIDS interven-
      tions in Africa: a systematic review of the evidence", *The Lancet* (2002) 359, p. 1635-1642.
21   E. Marseille, P. Hofmann and J. Kahn, HIV prevention before HAART in sub-Saharan Af-
      rica", *The Lancet* (2002) 359, p. 1851-1856.
22   D. Coetzee, K. Hildebrand, A. Boulle, G. Maartens, F. Louis, V. Labatala, H. Reuter, N.
      Ntwana and E. Goemaere, "Outcomes after two years of providing antiretroviral treatment in
      Khayelitsha", *AIDS* (2004) 6, p. 887-895.
23   P. Farmer, F. Leandre, J. Mukherjee, M. Claude, P. Nevil, M. Smith-Fawzi, S. Koenig, A.
      Castro, M. Becerra, J. Sachs, A. Attaran and J. Kim, "Community-based approaches to HIV
      treatment in resource-poor settings", *The Lancet* (2001) 358, p. 404-409.
24   C. Akileswaran, M. Jurie, T. Flanigan and K. Mayer, "Lessons learned from use of highly ac-
      tive antiretroviral therapy in Africa", *Clinical Infectious Diseases* (2005) 41, p. 376-385.
25   L. Ferradini, A. Jeannin, L. Pinoges, J. Izopet, D. Odhiambo, L. Mankhambo, G. Karungi, E.
      Szumilin, S. Balandine and G. Fedida, "Scaling up of highly active antiretroviral therapy in a
      rural district of Malawi: an effectiveness assessment", *The Lancet* (2006) 367, p. 13335-13338.
26   See for example S. Lawn, L. Myer, C. Orrell, L. Bekker and R. Wood, "Early mortality among
      adults accessing a community-based antiretroviral service in South Africa: implications for
      programme design", *AIDS* (2005) 19, p. 2141-2148.
27   P. Weidle, S. Malamba, R. Mwebaze, C. Sozi, G. Rukundo, R. Downing, D. Hanson, D.
      Ochola, P. Mugyenyi, J. Mermin, B. Samb and E. Lackritz, "Assessment of a pilot antiretrovi-
      ral drug therapy programme in Uganda: patients' response, survival, and drug resistance",
      The Lancet (2002) 360, p. 34-40.
28   M. Bachmann, "Effectiveness and cost effectiveness of early and late prevention of
      HIV/AIDS progression with antiretrovirals or antibiotics in Southern African adults", *AIDS
      Care* (2006) 2, p. 109-120.

The ongoing debates about adherence to ART in Africa have recently been clipped by a meta-analysis that demonstrated higher levels of adherence to anti-retroviral regimes in sSA than in North America.[29] This welcome finding arrived in the context of mixed success with drug regimen adherence for other common diseases in sSA such as malaria and tuberculosis, and health infrastructure constraints that some feared might contribute to 'anti-retroviral anarchy'.[30] [31] However, many of the early ART programmes (which have been the subject of these adherence studies in sSA) have captured a population and a set of circumstances that will not necessarily be the norm as treatment scales up. In particular, they have often been implemented in urban contexts and with extra measures to ensure adherence, such as comprehensive adherence counselling.

Barriers to accessing ART, and the potential for these to be broken down, are at the heart of concerns about late initiation of treatment and poor adherence. In sSA, the most frequently cited barriers across a range of contexts have been stigma and costs.[32] [33] [34] Perceptions of health facilities and the quality of their care have also come into play. There has been an assumption that ART will assist to break down these barriers, however the evidence emerging on low and slow ART uptake in workplace programmes in sSA encourages further reflection on the factors influencing success.[35]

Furthermore, where daily survival is an issue, ART becomes pitched against many other profound challenges. This is perhaps most starkly illustrated in South Africa where people living with HIV/AIDS have been seen to frequently discontinue their antiretroviral treatments in order to maintain a sufficiently low CD 4 count to qualify for a disability grant.[36][37] Challenges as-

29 E. Mills, J. Nachega, I. Buchan, J. Orbinski, A. Attaran, S. Singh, B. Rachlis, P. Wu, C. Cooper, L. Thabane, K. Wilson, G. Guyatt and D. Bangsberg, "Adherence to antiretroviral therapy in sub-Saharan Africa and North America", *Journal of the American Medical Association* (2006) 6, p. 679-690.

30 A. Harries, D. Nyangulu, N. Hargreaves, O. Kaluwa and F. Salaniponi, "Preventing antiretro-viral anarchy in sub-Saharan Africa", *The Lancet* (2001) 358, p. 410-414.

31 W. Stevens, S. Kaye and T. Gorrah, "Antiretroviral therapy in Africa", *British Medical Journal* (2004) 328, p. 280-282.

32 G. Mshana, J. Wamoyi, J. Busza, B. Zaba, J. Changalucha, S. Kaluvya and M. Urassa, "Barriers to accessing antiretroviral therapy in Kisesa, Tanzania: a qualitative study of early rural referrals to the national program", *AIDS Patient Care and STDs* (2006) 9, p. 649-657.

33 A. Padarath, C. Searle, Z. Sibiya, E. Williams and M. Ntsike, *Understanding barriers and challenges to community participation in HIV and ARV services*, 3rd Public Health Conference 2006 'Making health systems work', Midrand, South Africa (2006).

34 S. Weiser, W. Wolfe, D. Bangsberg, I. Thior, P. Gilbert, J. Makhema, P. Kebaabetswe, D. Dickenson, K. Mompati, M. Essex and R. Marlink, "Barriers to antiretroviral adherence for patients living with HIV infection and AIDS in Botswana", *Journal of Acquired Immune Deficiency Syndromes* (2003) 3, p. 281-288.

35 G. George, "Workplace ART programmes: why do companies invest in them and are they working?", *African Journal of AIDS Research* (2006) 2, p. 179-188.

36 S. Leclerc-Madlala, *Juggling AIDS, grants and treatment in South Africa: predicaments of second phase HIV/AIDS*, Anthropology Southern Africa Conference: 'Continuity, Change and Transformation: Anthropology in the 21st Century', University of KwaZulu-Natal, Durban (2005).

sociated with the integration of HIV/AIDS treatment into fragile health systems, as well as the less stable social, political and economic context in sSA, reinforce the need for vigilant monitoring and evaluation as a means through which these challenges can be analysed and addressed.[38]

Central to the AIDS transition scenario described above is a reduction in HIV incidence. The most direct way that ART can lead to a reduction in new infections and hence the number of people requiring treatment in the future, is by decreasing transmission rates through a reduction in viral load. This effect has been demonstrated for both sexual transmission and vertical transmission,[39] [40] however, the impact of such an effect at a population level remains unclear because of factors such as the stage at which people commence treatment and the extent of discordant partnerships. Such factors were investigated in a study of a South African township where the population impact of ART on reducing sexual transmission was found to be small under WHO guidelines.[41]

The introduction of ART could also impact negatively on efforts to reduce HIV incidence by deflecting attention and resources away from prevention efforts. Conversely, the availability of treatment may reduce stigma and give hope, so encouraging uptake of voluntary counselling and testing leading to an improved awareness of status. Early evidence on the latter is encouraging with a large study in Botswana demonstrating significant reductions in stigma. Although several factors were correlated, perceived access to ART was associated with decreased odds of holding at least one stigmatising attitude.[42]

Until now, we have only reflected on how the ART programme might influence the demand for care, yet it will also affect supply side factors by having an impact on the health workforce. This observation is particularly salient considering the current human resource crisis in sSA. Therefore, we need to also deliberate on questions such as: to what extent will health workers be prioritised or encouraged to begin treatment, hence reducing HIV-related absenteeism and attrition? And to what extent will ART improve the motivation and working conditions of health care workers, so discouraging migration from the public health system?

---

37   N. Nattrass, Trading-off income and health: AIDS and the disability grant in South Africa, Centre for Social Science Research (CSSR), Cape Town (2004).

38   M. Egger, A. Boulle, M. Schechter and P. Miotti, "Antiretroviral therapy in resource-poor settings: scaling up inequalities?", International Journal of Epidemiology (2005) 3, p. 509-512.

39   See for example J. Castilla, J. Del Romero, V. Hernando, B. Marincovich, S. Garcia and C. Rodriguez, "Effectiveness of highly active antiretroviral therapy in reducing heterosexual transmission of HIV", Journal of Acquired Immune Deficiency Syndromes (2005) 1, p. 96-101.

40   E. Cooper, M. Charurat, L. Mofenson, I. Hanson, J. Pitt, C. Diaz, K. Hayani, I. Handelsman, V. Smeriglio, R. Hoff and W. Blattner, "Combination antiretroviral strategies for the treatment of pregnant HIV-1 infected women and prevention of perinatal HIV-1 transmission", Journal of Acquired Immune Deficiency Syndromes (2002) 5, p. 484-494.

41   B. Auvert, S. Males, A. Puren, D. Taljaard, M. Caraël and B. Williams, "Can highly active antiretroviral therapy reduce the spread of HIV?: A study in a township of South Africa", Journal of Acquired Immune Deficiency Syndromes (2004) 1, p. 613-621.

42   W. Wolfe, S. Weiser, K. Leiter, W. Steward, F. Percy-de Korte, N. Phaladze, N. Lacopino and M. Heisler, Impact of universal access to antiretroviral therapy on HIV stigma in Botswana, XVI International AIDS Conference, Toronto (2006).

The first question is difficult to answer since, although health worker attrition due to HIV/AIDS is a serious concern in the most heavily affected countries, stigma may prevent the uptake of ART amongst health workers. Evidence has shown that AIDS-related deaths have significantly contributed to health worker attrition in countries such as Zambia, Malawi and Uganda.[43][44] In Zambia, it was estimated that deaths outnumbered resignations and that death rates alone could account for the nurse vacancy rate of 37%.[45] It is also increasingly acknowledged that health care workers are subject to the same stigma and discrimination as the communities they serve, presenting an obstacle to their own efforts to seek required care despite their knowledge of the benefits.[46][47]

The impact of the ART programme on the motivation and working conditions of health care workers has also not been clearly established. According to a newspaper article published just prior to the implementation of South Africa's ART programme: ".....health workers' morale will be boosted as they will no longer be helpless when faced with destitute AIDS patients".[48] Since nurses in particular have been on the front-lines of providing palliative care for those infected with HIV, high rates of depression and burn-out have been identified as contributing to the migration of these health care workers into less stressful and/or more financially rewarding jobs in the private sector and abroad. ART programs were anticipated to change this trend. However, current indications suggest that this shift in attitude has not been realised. Rather, ART programmes have been seen as yet another addition to the health care workers' already heavy workload.[49] The issue of how ART programmes are impacting on health care worker morale requires continued attention.

43   Y. Dambisya, "The fate and career destinations of doctors who qualified at Uganda's Makerere Medical School in 1984: retrospective cohort study", *British Medical Journal* (2004) 7466, p. 600-601.

44   M. Mukati, A. Gonani, A. Macheso, B. Simwaker, S. Kinoti, and B. Ndyanabangi, Challenges facing the Malawian health workforce in the ara of HIV/AIDS. Commonwealth Regional Health Community Health Secretariat for East, Central and Southern Africa (CRHCS/United States Agency for International Development CUSAID/Support for Analysis and Research in Africa (SARA) (2004).

45   F. Feeley, "Fight AIDS as well as the brain drain", *The Lancet* (2006) 368, p. 435-436.

46   K. Kiragu, T. Ngulube, M. Nyumbu, P. Njobvu, P. Eerens and C. Mwaba, "Sexual risk-taking and HIV testing among health workers in Zambia", *AIDS and Behaviour* (2006) 1, p. 131-136.

47   J. Zelnick and M. O'Donnell, "The impact of the HIV/AIDS epidemic on hospital nurses in KwaZulu-Natal, South Africa: nurses' perspectives and implications for health policy", *Journal of Public Health Policy* (2005) 2, p. 163-185.

48   K. Cullinan, "Antiretroviral roll-out could be just the tonic - or a bitter pill", *Sunday Times*, 28 September 2003.

49   M. Chopra, C. Kendall, Z. Hill, N. Schaay, L. Nkonki and T. Doherty, 'Nothing new': responses to the introduction of antiretroviral drugs in South Africa, *AIDS* 20, 1975-1977 (2006).

Lessons Learned for Scaling Up ART in Support of Health System Strengthening

This analysis is concerned with anticipating potential impacts of ART scale-up on health systems in sSA to highlight strategies for minimizing negative effects. The preceding sections have examined how the mass expansion of ART delivery, particularly through vertical programming, might threaten already fragile health systems. We have also explored recent evidence emerging from the region regarding experiences to date. From this platform, we are in a position to highlight a range of lessons for ART scale-up efforts that take into account opportunities for minimizing damage to health systems in the process. Framed in a more productive light, the momentum and resources behind ART scale-up can be viewed as a vehicle for strengthening health systems should this goal be recognized as a priority. This section begins with discussion of the potential role for solidarity as a guiding principle in this effort, followed by concrete lessons for ART scale-up.

At a philosophical level, one way to promote health system strengthening during the era of rapid ART scale-up is to embrace solidarity as a guiding principle. Although the notion of solidarity has a diverse history, Harmon has identified three interrelated propositions that reflect the spirit of this value across its varied definition, and which hold relevance for our consideration of ART scale-up.[50]

First, Harmon notes that solidarity recognizes that individuals are naturally embedded in social contexts in a state of interconnectedness with other individuals, groups and society. Second, solidarity is understood as grounded in compassion with the ultimate goal being to construct a just and fair society through personal and collective actions. Third, Harmon explains that solidarity demands common action to uphold the complex of social relationships that is needed to realize standards of decency and justice. To this end, solidarity emphasizes the role of duties flowing both to and from individuals, communities and broader collectives.

This framing supports an approach to ART rollout that understands such efforts as nested within the context of a broader response to HIV/AIDS that is shared across programmatic, disciplinary and geographic borders. Such a response takes full account of the urgency with which ART scale-up is required, but does not lose sight of the necessarily comprehensive nature of the HIV/AIDS response, which includes not only care and support for people who are living with HIV, but also the equally urgent need to focus on prevention. Such a response recognizes not only the immediate demands of the pandemic, but also the need to prioritize the elements of our long-term response including new prevention technologies such as vaccines and microbicides. Such a response understands the biomedical response of treatment as necessary but not sufficient for adequately contending with a health crisis with such far-reaching social, political and economic drivers. And such a response calls for reflection on the duties that we hold to ourselves and each other that are informed by our

---

50   S. Harmon, "Solidarity: a (new) ethic for global health policy", *Health Care Analysis* (2006) 14, p. 215-236.

diverse disciplinary, ideological and geographic orientations. In terms of ART scale-up, this framing points to a range of practical lessons (see Box 1).

Box 1. Lessons for Preserving and Strengthening Health Systems in the Context of ART Scale-Up in sub-Saharan Africa

---

(1) Build indicator mechanisms into ART plans to monitor impacts to health systems
(2) Seek a balance between and, ideally, integration of treatment and prevention efforts
(3) Ensure commitment to GIPA so that planning is inclusive and practical
(4) Focus on community input and a rights-based approach to the rationing of scarce resources
(5) Embrace creative ways of addressing the human resource shortage, including caring for caregivers
(6) Establish ongoing, comprehensive comparative research to measure and evaluate roll-out.

First, ART programme plans ought to take account of health system targets. This can be achieved through the intentional inclusion of activities in vertical programme plans that are designed to counteract potential harms to broader health systems. Another proactive approach would see all national HIV/AIDS programmes and global initiatives held accountable for not only minimising harms to health systems, but also to health system strengthening through the inclusion of system indicators in their monitoring and evaluation frameworks.[51][52] Similarly, new initiatives could be expected to conduct systems impact assessments at the outset to identify potential damages before they begin. For instance, vertical programmes could fortify elements of the general health service infrastructure that are required for the vertical delivery to be successful, such as laboratory facilities and drug supply chains.[53]

Second, the medical model approach inherent in ART provision must not eclipse attention to the social, political and economic forces that influence how well people will be able to access, tolerate and adhere to treatment. Moreover, a successful AIDS transition requires simultaneous investment in HIV prevention programming at individual, community and structural levels in order to mount a comprehensive response to HIV. This point cannot be overemphasised, since modelling has demonstrated unsustainably high levels of treatment required in the event that an overly narrow focus on treatment under-

---

[51] R. Atun, F. Lennox-chhugani, F. Drobniewski, Y. Samyshkin and R. Coker, "A framework and toolkit for capturing the communicable disease programmes within health systems: tuberculosis control as an illustrative example", *European Journal of Public Health* (2004) 14, 267-273.
[52] Global Health Watch, supra note 15.
[53] P. Travis, S. Bennet, A. Haines, T. Pang, Z. Bhutta, A. Hyder, N. Pielemeier, A. Mills and T. Evans, "Overcoming health-systems constraints to achieve the Millennium Development Goals", *The Lancet* (2004) 364, p. 900-906.

mines prevention programmes.[54] Synergies between treatment and prevention are many. For example, when treatment is linked to the prevention of mother-to-child transmission as delivered through maternal health services, the likelihood increases that the mother will have enhanced access to treatment, that social stigma will be reduced amongst women, and that the general maternal health services will be strengthened.[55]

Third, the top-down management orientation that is typical of vertical programming has lessons to learn from alternative approaches to HIV/AIDS efforts. The principle of GIPA, or the Greater Involvement of People with HIV/AIDS, is a fundamental component of effective and human rights-based responses and must remain at the centre of treatment programming. Engagement of people infected and affected by HIV in all stages of planning can result in outcomes that are not only more effective but also delivered more equitably.

Fourth, additional efforts are required to counteract or manage rationing trends that impact negatively on equity objectives. In many cases, rationing is inadvertent and stems from the quest to roll out treatment rapidly. People who are easier to access, such as those with higher incomes and/or in urban areas, are preferentially targeted. The result is a widening of existing health care inequities.[56] [57] In other instances, treatment might need to be rationed intentionally because of limited resources. There are few easy answers regarding rationing except to engage communities in helping to determine how scarce resources will be distributed in line with the principles of a human rights-based approach.[58]

Fifth, ART programmes can be used to maintain and strengthen health system capacities through efforts that support health workers to obtain HIV/AIDS care and treatment for themselves as required. A reduction in health worker attrition due to HIV/AIDS can moderate the excessively high post vacancy rates that are a symptom of the human resource crisis in sSA. Unfortunately, ART programmes have also been contributing to this crisis by relying on cadres of health workers that are in short supply. Therefore, efforts are required to explore creative ways of using different health personnel to effectively deliver ART care.[59] The composition of the clinical team responsible for the delivery of ART is one of the most important elements characterising

54 J. Salomon, D. Hogan, J. Stover, K. Stanecki, W. Walker, P. Ghys and B. Schwartländer, "Integrating HIV prevention and treatment: from slogans to impact", *PLoS Medicine* (2005), e16.
55 R. Loewenson and D. McCoy, "Access to antiretroviral treatment in Africa", *British Medical Journal* (2004) 328, p. 241-242.
56 M. Egger et al., supra note 38.
57 R. Stewart, A. Padarath and C. Milford, "Emerging threats to equitable implementation of ART in South Africa", *Acta Academica Supplementum* (2006) 1, p. 286-308.
58 M. Roseman and S. Gruskin, *HIV/AIDS & human rights in a nutshell,* Harvard School of Public Health and International Council of AIDS Service Organisations (ICASO), Toronto (2004).
59 S. Gimbel-Sherr, M. Micek, K. Gimbel-Sherr, T. Koepsell, J. Hughes, K. Thomas, J. Pfeiffer and S. Gloyd, "Using nurses to identify HAART eligible patients in the Republic of Mozambique: results of a time series analysis", *Human Resources for Health* (2007) 5, p. 7.

different models of care currently undergoing evaluation.[60] Ultimately, an appropriate model of care, along with sustainable financing to support the chosen model, will determine the long term success of ART programmes and the impact they have on the health system.

Finally, multi-site and multi-level research using common indicators across ART programmes is required to provide ongoing analysis of the effectiveness, efficiency and equity in ART roll-out efforts.[61]

Completing the quote from Loewenson and McCoy that opened this article: "Health systems cannot be built from a patchwork of non-governmental, vertical and *ad hoc* services around a crumbling public sector core." If efforts to enhance the capacity of Africa's health systems are seen as a priority in ART scale-up, there is potential to harness the influx of resources, knowledge and energy accompanying treatment efforts to strengthen these public sector cores and build the base for addressing HIV/AIDS and other health concerns in the years to come.

---

[60] See, for example, D. Pienaar, L. Myer, S. Cleary, D. Coetzee, D. Michaels, K. Cloete, H. Schneider and A. Boulle, *Models of Care for Antiretroviral Service Delivery*, School of Public Health and Family Medicine, University of Cape Town, Cape Town (2006).
[61] M. Egger, et al., supra note 38.

Part Five

Australia and Asia

Chapter 10.

The Continuing Contest of Values in the Australian Health Care System

Stephan Duckett

Introduction

For the last quarter century, the equitable underpinning of health care in Australia has become so well accepted that overt political challenge to the institutional framework has proven to be not viable as an electoral strategy.[1] Since 1984, when Medicare, Australia's universal health insurance scheme, was introduced, its high level of public support has meant that there has been no overt challenge to its place as the principal mechanism for assuring access to hospital and medical care. But Medicare has not been without covert challenges, threats and subtle undermining as health care politics in Australia continues to be bedevilled by a contest of values about support for universal versus targeted or segmented policy approaches. (Elliot contrasts universalism with "selective (targeted) and residual (safety net)" policies in the Australian health system).[2]

The principal objective of Medicare is to remove (or reduce) financial barriers to access to health care for all Australian residents and, from a patient perspective, it provides security of access to care. Medicare is also an important part of the health policy landscape in Australia because it provides the mechanism for financing two key provider groups: hospitals and doctors.

In this chapter I will first briefly describe key elements of the institutional framework for health care in Australia, then outline the critical value choices that have dominated political debate in Australia and describe the value choices made in each of the recent Australian political eras.

Health care in Australia

Australia has a federal system of government with the six states and two territories, (collectively in this chapter called 'states') and the (central) Common-

---

[1] M. R. L. Wooldridge, *Health policy in the Fraser years - 1975-83*, MBA thesis, Monash University, Melbourne (1991).

[2] A. Elliot, Is Medicare Universal? Research Note No. 37 2002-03, Canberra, Department of the Parliamentary Library (2003).

wealth government having overlapping roles in health care governance and financing. Another layer of complexity is added because Australia has a thriving private hospital sector, underpinned by (voluntary) private health insurance. Private health insurance also provides insurance for access to dental care, allied health professional and other 'ancillary' services. Further information on the Australian health care system may be found elsewhere.[3]

Development of health care and health policy in Australia has been strongly influenced (both negatively and positively) by experience in the rest of the English-speaking world. Because of Australia's colonial antecedents, the medical profession developed strong links with their counterparts in the United Kingdom, often proceeding there for advanced training. Indeed, the Australian organisation of doctors was a branch of the British Medical Association until the early 1960s, with members receiving copies of British medical publications and absorbing the antipathy to 'nationalised medicine' that pervaded many of those sources. Doctors today often look to the United States for training and experience, although few would wish to emulate any of the organisational aspects of the American health system. Two Australian health economists (John Deeble and Dick Scotton) studied Canada's universal health insurance arrangements and became the vector to transform that knowledge into the design of Australia's health insurance arrangements.[4] Australia's arrangements are unique; indeed Richardson has described private health insurance as rivalling the platypus and the echidna as Australia's contribution to the library of the strange but true.[5]

In terms of performance, Australia ranks relatively well against other OECD countries: ranking in the top quartile on measures of life expectancy and self rated health. Performance on cause-specific mortality is somewhat more mixed but ranking above the median for practically all causes. Australia spends just under 10% of GDP on health, almost exactly as predicted given its GDP per capita.

Historically, hospitals developed as a state responsibility and the Commonwealth's hospital Medicare policies are thus implemented via the states. The Commonwealth government has entered into agreements with each state that provide for Commonwealth funding to the states for hospital services. In return for these grants, the states agree to abide by a number of conditions including:

- to provide a network of public hospital services (about two thirds of all patients are treated in public hospitals); and
- to allow all eligible people (essentially Australian citizens and permanent residents) to be able to access inpatient services in these hospitals as 'public patients' free of any cost to the patient. (Doctors treating public patients are paid by the hospital and so the patient does not face any fee for those ser-

---

3   S.J. Duckett, *The Australian Health Care System.* (3rd ed.) (Melbourne: Oxford University Press, 2007).

4   R. B. Scotton, and C. R. Macdonald, *The making of Medibank,* Sydney: School of Health Services Management, University of NSW (1993).

5   J. R. J. Richardson, 'Social values, efficiency and Medicare' presentation to seminar at Australian Health Policy Institute, 22 May (2003).

vices. About 90% of patients in public hospitals elect to be treated as public patients).

The states are also required to provide a network of specialist outpatient services at no charge to patients.

The agreements provide that states are responsible for the full marginal cost of any increase in hospital budgets during the term of the agreement. Conversely, states accrue the full benefit of any reduction in hospital budgets over this period. Commonwealth Medicare funding is formula-driven during the course of an agreement with the formula being unrelated to actual hospital budgets, adjusting only for exogenous factors such as population growth and ageing.

The Commonwealth plays a more direct role for medical services, with medical funding being directly administered by a Commonwealth agency, Medicare Australia. Medical care outside hospitals is principally provided by independent practitioners, reimbursed on a fee-for-service basis and Medicare is thus structured to provide financial support for that mode of service organisation. Medicare provides rebates for the cost of medical care against a published fee schedule at differing rates: 75% for private patients in hospitals, 85% for specialist care out of hospitals, 100% for general practitioners. But medical practitioners are not constrained to charge these published fees so patients may face out-of-pocket costs. There is a safety net where Medicare can pay up to 100% of any gaps where total family expenditure exceeds certain limits. The Commonwealth updates the fee schedule and gap limits on a regular basis. Doctors can send their bill to Medicare Australia through a process known as 'bulk' or 'direct' billing, in which case the medical practitioner must accept the rebate in full settlement of the account with no patient co-payment. Alternatively, doctors can bill patients who then obtain a rebate from Medicare Australia for the relevant percentage of the government schedule fee (and any gap payment).

Medicare is funded from general taxation. However, Australia's income tax laws provide for a 'Medicare levy', currently 1.5% of taxable income. Differential low-income thresholds (below which no levy is payable) are set for individuals, single parents, and couples. The Medicare levy is not intended to cover the full cost of Commonwealth health expenditure (or indeed total expenditure on health) but rather was introduced as a financing measure to raise additional revenue to pay for the introduction of Medicare in 1984. The levy is not a 'hypothecated' tax; that is, Medicare levy collections are not specifically allocated to the health portfolio, although the need to increase health spending has been used as a political justification for increasing the levy. Nor does the levy represent a form of social insurance or contribution; the levy is thus simply another tax that flows into the pool of funds from which Commonwealth expenditure derives.

Up till the early part of this decade, direct billing has been the principal mechanism for assuring no financial barriers to access to medical care. Direct billing for general practitioner attendances increased each year from the introduction of Medicare up to 1996 where it peaked at an average rate of around 80 per cent for all general practitioner services across Australia (see figure 1).

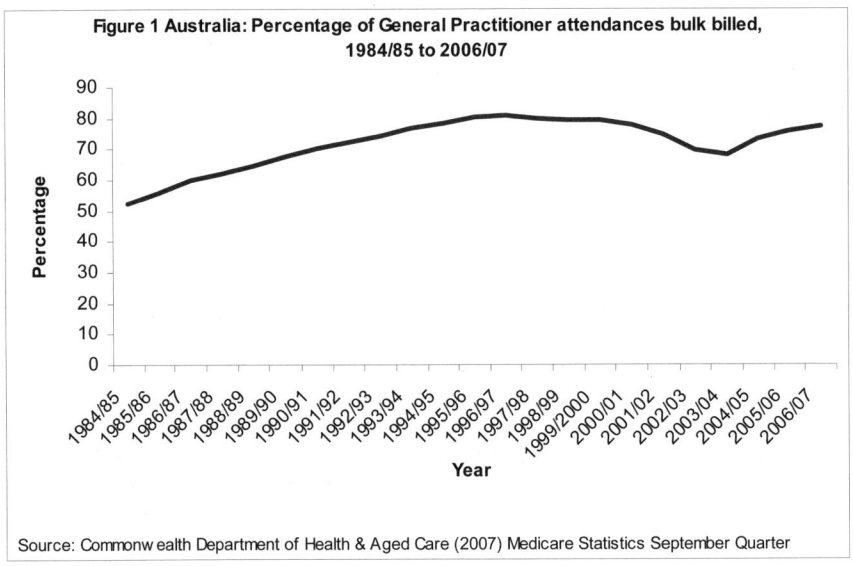

Figure 1 Australia: Percentage of General Practitioner attendances bulk billed, 1984/85 to 2006/07

Source: Commonwealth Department of Health & Aged Care (2007) Medicare Statistics September Quarter

The subsequent decline in direct billing (and the consequential increase in out of pocket costs for consultations) was politically contentious, evincing a government policy response that reversed the decline. The nature of the government response represented a challenge to Medicare's universalist ethos, and is discussed later in this chapter.

Private health insurance

Prior to the introduction of Medicare in 1984, private health insurance was an important way of protecting most consumers against the cost of hospital care. It played an important role in health financing and accounted for about 20 per cent of all health expenditure. Immediately following the introduction of Medicare (1984/85), the health insurance share of expenditure declined precipitously to 8.8 per cent of health expenditure, with a further decline since then, partly associated with increased government subsidies and partly with declining participation in the major insurance products.

Australia's policies about private health insurance change with changes in government. Labor governments emphasise universal coverage and public sector access, Coalition (conservative) governments place greater emphasis on supporting the private sector, particularly through private health insurance. The outcome of these policies is reflected in health insurance coverage statistics (see Figure 2. The break in the series is caused by a discontinuity in the published data).

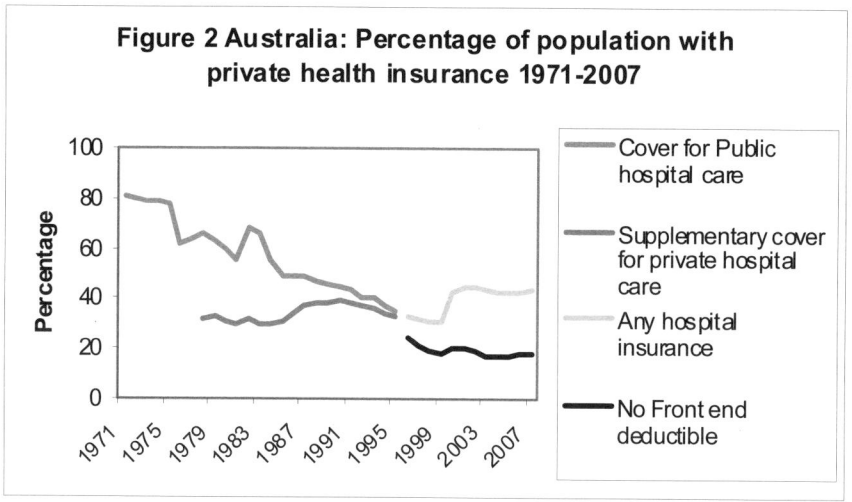

Figure 2 Australia: Percentage of population with private health insurance 1971-2007

Analyses of health insurance trends typically focus on the headline number: the total proportion of the population with health insurance, the top line throughout the period.[6][7][8][9] We see the slow decline over the whole period, with two aberrations: the upswing during the latter part of the Fraser government (1981-83), associated with means testing of public hospitals and the Howard upswing of 2000 coinciding with the introduction of life time cover.[10]

But health insurance policy is more complicated than that. Up to the mid 1990s private health insurance organisations offered two products: 'basic table' insurance which covered the costs of shared rooms in public hospitals and 'supplementary' insurance, which offered cover against the costs of the small number of single rooms in public hospitals and of treatment in a private hospital. Supplementary insurance, as its name implies, was taken as a second, additional supplement to the basic table product. The trends for the two products are quite different. The introduction of Medicare reversed the early 1980s aberration of increased insurance uptake with a resumption of the secular trend of a decline in basic insurance, which is the public hospital cover product. As Medicare now provided access to public hospital care, what basic table insurance offered was only 'choice of doctor' in public hospitals, apparently a product with perceived declining value in the market. Supplementary insurance offered something different: the opportunity to by-pass hospital waiting

6   J. Hall, R. De Abreu Lourenco, et al. "Carrots and sticks - the fall and fall of private health insurance in Australia." *Health Economics* (1999) 8, p. 653-60.
7   S. Willcox, "Promoting private health insurance in Australia." *Health Affairs* (2001) 3, p. 152-161.
8   J. R. G. Butler, "Policy change and private health insurance: Did the cheapest policy do the trick?" *Australian Health Review* (2002) 6, p. 33-41.
9   R. E. Moorin, and C. D. J. Holman, "Development of a health care policy characterisation model based on use of private health insurance." *Australia and New Zealand Health Policy* (2005) 2.
10   Supra note 8.

lists and to access the higher amenity in private hospitals. This product was valued and the mid 1980s saw an upswing in supplementary table coverage, probably in part stimulated by the absolute decline in premiums for basic table insurance associated with the introduction of Medicare. Data published in Annual Reports of the Department of Health, for example, show that NSW basic table premiums (without the ambulance levy) declined 20% from 1983 to 1986, in the face of non-health inflation for the period of 23%. Consumers took the opportunity of cheaper cover to upsize without having to increase their total spending on health insurance.

As Figure 2 shows, the proportion of the population with any form of health insurance declined up to the late 1990s but there was a differential rate of decline in the prevalence of insurance across different population groups, leading to a change in the composition of the insured population. Middle-income families were more likely to drop insurance relative to high income and lower income families, and younger families were more likely to drop insurance relative to older families.[11]

A number of studies have shown that health insurance is unevenly distributed in the population: the insured are wealthier, better educated, and older than the uninsured.[12][13][14][15][16][17][18][19] Because of the greater take-up of health insurance among the wealthy, rebates/subsidies to health insurance are inherently inequitable.[20]

Values at Play

There is no Australian consensus about the relative roles of the public and private sectors in health care nor is there consensus on the role of government. Certainly there has been strong and continuing support over the last quarter century for Medicare. However the role of private hospitals is still somewhat

| 11 | D. Schofield, The distribution and determinants of private health insurance in Australia, 1990, Discussion Paper No. 17, Canberra: National Centre for Social and Economic Modelling, University of Canberra (1997). |

12 A. C. Cameron, P. K. Trivedi, F. Milne and J. Piggott, "Microeconometric model of the demand for health care and health insurance in Australia", *Review of Economic Studies* (1988) 55, p. 85–106.

13 A. C. Cameron and P. K. Trivedi, "The role of income and health risk in the choice of health insurance: Evidence from Australia", *Journal of Public Economics* (1991) 45, p. 1–28.

14 S. Willcox, "A healthy risk? Use of private insurance. Background Paper No. 4", Melbourne National Health Strategy (1991).

15 C. Burrows, K. Brown and A. Gruskin (1993), "Who buys health insurance? A survey of two large organisations", *Australian Journal of Social Issues*, (1993) 28, p. 106–23.

16 Australian Bureau of Statistics 1994, Apparent determinants of private health insurance, Canberra: ABS

17 A. C. Cameron and J. McCallum, "Private health insurance choice in health: The role of long-term utilisation of health services", in *Economics and Health*: 1995, (Sydney: School of Health Services Management, UNSW, (1996), p. 143–57.

18 S. Hopkins and M. P. Kidd, 'The determinants of the demand for private health insurance under Medicare', *Applied Economics* (1996) 28, p. 1623–32.

19 Supra note 11.

20 J. Smith, 'Tax expenditures and public health financing in Australia', *The Economic and Labour Relations Review* (2001) 2, p. 239–62.

contested: are private hospitals direct substitutes for public hospitals providing complementary services or are they supplementary services providing additional amenity over and above that provided in the public sector? There has been no values debate within Australia that might inform or generate such a consensus. One reason for the absence of debate is that it is not necessarily in the interest of key groups to articulate clearly their value agenda and hence their interests may be better served by confusion in the debate or by creating a 'veil of vagueness' to use Gibson and Goodin's term.[21] There is a strong egalitarian ethos in Australia and policies that are overtly elitist and exclusionary rarely attract policy support.

The critical dimensions of the values debate are the extent to which financing and delivery of services should reflect these egalitarian values and social solidarity, versus the extent to which finance and delivery should reflect individual or market values. Moreover, these polar choices play out in different ways in different sub-sectors of Australian health care (hospitals, medical service and so on).

Financing

Social solidarity in health care financing is demonstrated by mutualisation of financing arrangements where all, or part, of the population share the risks of the costs of health care. One way in which the values debate is played out in Australia is in terms of the mutualisation pool: should government subsidies be focussed on pooling risks for the whole population, and does the subset of the population with private health insurance (and thus with differential access to health care) also warrant government support?

The extent of mutualisation of financing (or risk sharing across individuals) is a critical distinguishing factor in health policy across the political spectrum, between sub-sectors of health care and over time. The argument for mutualisation of health care financing is strong and can be advanced on a number of bases.[22] Illness, sickness and disease are unevenly distributed for individuals over time and between groups with different incomes, employment status and other social characteristics. For individuals, health care expenditures can be large and lumpy and so there is a benefit for the individual in smoothing expenditure over time through insurance. Because of increasing health expenditure in older age groups, lifetime health costs are unevenly distributed and on average, occur more heavily in the post-retirement years. There is also an argument that society as a whole benefits from ensuring that all groups within the community have access to an agreed suite of health services, although the definition of the suite varies over time and in different countries. Most medical and hospital services are always within any definition of services for which public mutualisation of funding is seen as legitimate. Cosmetic surgery is of-

---

21   D.M. Gibson and Goodin, R. E., The Veil of Vagueness: A Model of Institutional Design, in M. Egeberg and P. Lægreid (eds.) *Organizing Political Institutions*: Essays in Honour of Johan P. Olsen, (Oslo: Scandinavian University Press, 1999), p. 357-85.
22   K. J. Arrow, "Uncertainty and the welfare economics of medical care", *American Economic Review* (1963) 53, p. 941-73.

ten excluded from what is regarded as appropriately mutualised or supported
with public funding and pharmaceutical, dental and other aspects of health
care are not subject to the same level of consensus about the extent of mutualisation of financing.

In Australia there has been a strong tradition of portraying private health
insurance as a mechanism for mutualisation of financing and private health
insurance has been subsidised by government to a greater or lesser degree
over the past 60 years. The alternate method of mutualisation, through government funding, has been effected in Australia since 1984 via Medicare (and
through a brief period in the 1970s, through Medicare's predecessor, Medibank). Health policy debates in Australia have been dominated by the policy
and value choice: to what extent should mutualisation be across the whole
population (typically effected through government funding), and to what extent should mutualisation be a matter of individual choice through private
health insurance arrangements where individuals choose (or are encouraged
to participate) in the mutualisation pool.

Different parts of the Australian health care system have ended up with different types of mutualisation and the scope of mutualisation for key services
has shifted over time. Private health insurance in Australia emphasises individual choice of both treating doctor and place of treatment, and is strongly
aligned with support for private sector delivery methods. In contrast, mutualisation through government funding has been used to directly support private
sector delivery, as well as public sector delivery.

About 43% of the Australian population has private health insurance but
private health insurance is unevenly distributed by income and location (see
Figure 3).

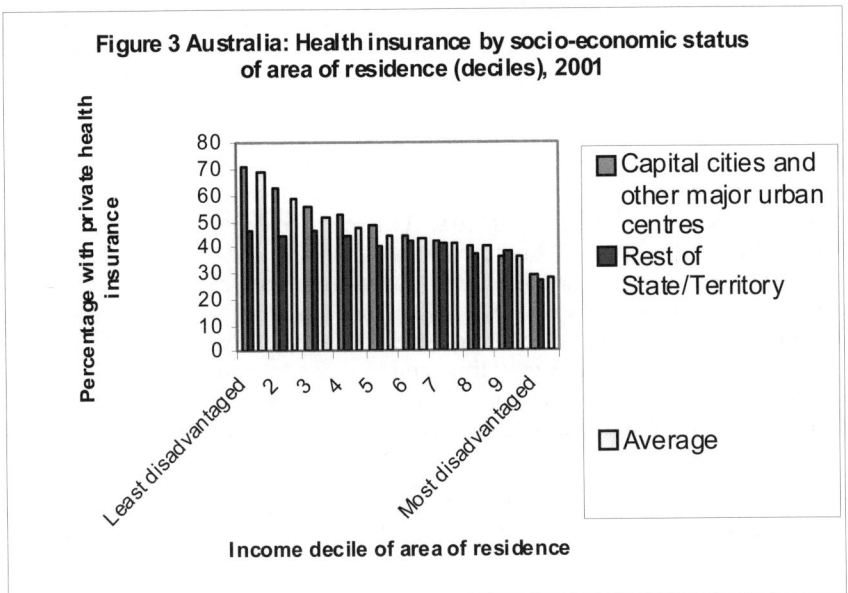

184   Maklu

Prevalence of private health insurance monotonically decreases with decreasing socio-economic status of area of residence, with prevalence in the highest income areas almost two and a half times that of the most disadvantaged areas (69% vs 28%). Residents of urban areas are significantly more likely to hold private health insurance than residents of the rest of the state, with income gradients apparent in both types of geographic areas. Australia is one of the most urbanised countries, and thus the average tends to reflect the urban position.

Private health insurance in Australia, because of its voluntary nature and differential distribution, is thus not an agent of social solidarity in the same way as it might be perceived in Bismarckian countries, where universal insurance arrangements ensure that mutualisation occurs across the whole population rather than within a subset of the population. Private health insurance in Australia is marketed as a product that obviates one's reliance on public sector services and circumvents public sector constraints. Few private hospitals provide emergency care and so, despite the marketing claims, access to the network of public hospitals is still relied on by those with private insurance. Private health insurance marketing emphasises the exclusive nature of the product and even intimates that health insurance is a 'merit good', with those participating in the private health insurance market assisting in reducing demand on public hospitals. These exclusivist claims and differential take up diminish rather than enhance social solidarity.

The role of health insurance is also different in different sub-sectors of the Australian health care system. Figure 4 shows the source of financing for key elements of the health care sector.

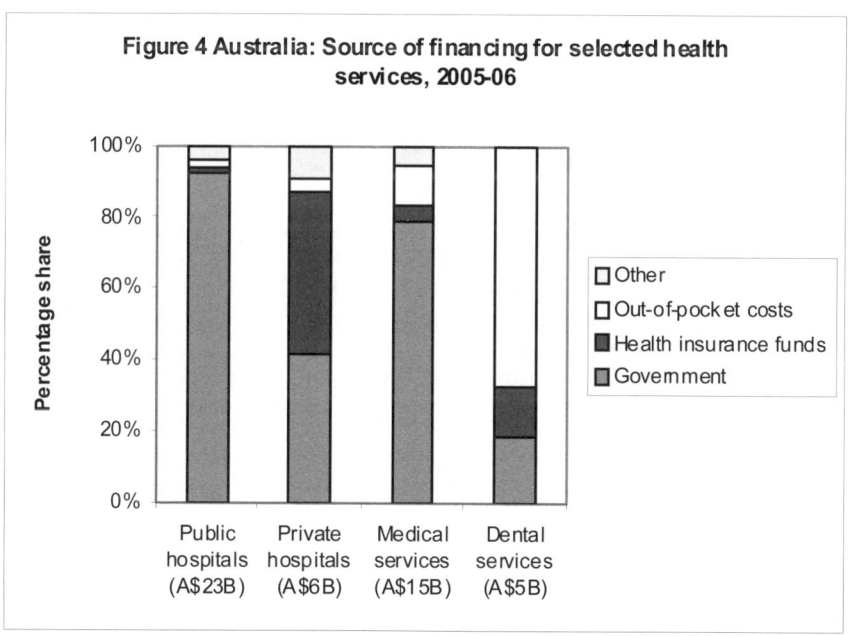

Figure 4 Australia: Source of financing for selected health services, 2005-06

Public hospitals have high levels of government funding (over 90% of funds from this source) with very low levels of financial support from health insurance or out of pocket costs (for public hospital the 'other' sources of funding are principally third party insurance arrangements such as schemes for motor vehicle crashes or work-related injury and illness). In contrast, the revenue for private hospitals relies heavily on private health insurance (46%) and government support (41%, primarily mediated through subsidies to private health insurance). Dental services show a third pattern where there is a moderate level of mutualisation through health insurance (14% of revenues from this source) but there remains significant out of pocket costs for those without health insurance and, because of the extensive use of front end deductibles, even for those with health insurance, over two thirds of the costs of dental services are met by individuals directly. Consistent with Medicare's provision of rebates against the cost of medical care, almost 80% of funding for doctor services is sourced from government.

Delivery

Delivery structures can have a powerful influence on the experience of patients as well as often shaping what is regarded as appropriate and legitimate in terms of mutualisation of finance or financial support. The full spectrum of different ownership or delivery structures can be seen in the Australian health care system including:
- Solo practice of individual professionals who effectively act as small businesses;
- Group practice of professionals;
- Not for profit corporate provision;
- Private corporate provision; and
- Government provision.

The market structure in different parts of the health sector reflects different balances of these different corporate types.

About 60 per cent of all private hospitals are for-profit, and this sector of the industry is expanding in share. Over the period 1996/97 to 2003/04, the number of beds in for-profit hospitals increased by 18 per cent while beds in not-for-profits declined by 3 per cent. Admissions to for-profit hospitals increased faster than not-for-profits (63 per cent versus 21 per cent). The 1990s saw a restructuring of the private hospital industry, with the emergence and increasing importance of for-profit hospital groups in the industry, and a corresponding reduction in the number of free-standing 'independent' for-profit hospitals.[23] [24] The for-profit groups of hospital chains are often companies listed on the Australian stock exchange.

In contrast, specialist medical practice has remained bifurcated with some specialists principally practicing full time in public hospitals (either as em-

23 Productivity Commission, Private hospitals in Australia, Commission Research Paper, Canberra: Ausinfo (1999).
24 M. A. O'Loughlin, "Conflicting interests in private hospital care", *Australian Health Review* (2002) 5, p.106–17.

ployees of a public hospital or as university employees), but a majority of specialists being in private professional practice either solo or in very small groups of colleagues in the same specialty (or with family links).

Private pathology practice is now almost totally dominated by a small number of private corporations. General practice is currently moving through a transition period of consolidations, with solo practice amalgamations to group practice, and an increasing role of corporate ownership and provision.

The delivery structures have significant implications for values and the way in which the health sector operates. Medical interest groups, principally the Australian Medical Association, strongly emphasise individual, autonomous private practice: the small business ethos of the medical profession has a pervasive influence on policies advocated by the medical profession. This small business, solo practitioner delivery model reinforces, and is based on, a value system of individual participation in the market. The market relationship is essentially that of an individual doctor contracted by an individual patient. The individual professional typically feels accountability to individual patients for continuity of care, on call arrangements and so on but, most importantly, the relationship is seen as dyadic with very limited peer or government influence to shape the nature of the relationship. The profession almost always sees "interference" in that relationship as reducing quality of care.

Despite working in a corporate or small business structure, the discourse of the medical profession typically de-emphasises the role of the individual professional as a small business, and the profit orientation of provision, emphasising instead medical practitioners' role as "professionals".

The market based ethos shapes what the medical profession might regard as appropriate types of intervention by government. Any intervention perceived as providing competitive pressure on that relationship (by strengthening the consumer's hand) is seen by the medical profession as inappropriate, with the discourse emphasising weakening of the "doctor-patient relationship". Because of the information asymmetry involved in almost all aspects of medical care, once the relationship has been established there is an inherent power imbalance in a patient's relationship with the medical professional.

This is not to say that the medical profession sees all types of government intervention as inappropriate. Subsidies paid to consumers to meet out-of-pocket costs are now an accepted part of the policy landscape. But payments directly from government to the provider (for services rendered to consumers) are still seen as less appropriate than payments via consumers, even when consumers can claim a rebate from government. A medical indemnity crisis in Australia in the early part of this decade generated another type of government intervention seen by professionals as legitimate: weakening consumers' ability to seek legal redress for negligence and increasing government subsidies to indemnity organisations.

Medical service provision in some specialties is now almost entirely provided by large corporations (pathology being the prime example but also imaging).Despite this, government support for these specialties is still framed in terms of individual private professional practice with an uncapped fee for service model of provision. The alternative frame, contracting or tendering for corporately provided services, is not currently on the policy agenda.

Delivery mechanisms have a profound influence on dominant values in health care in Australia. The emphasis on individual practice is necessarily accompanied by de-emphasis on a "community service" ethos of provision, of a citizen's entitlement to provision rather than market participation as the basis for access to health care. For general practice, people unable to meet high out-of-pocket costs are forced to defer care or seek care in a public hospital emergency department, thus suffering a quality loss by lack of the continuity of care assumed to be a feature of primary medical care. In the case of specialist services, those who are not able to participate in the specialist market must rely on public hospital outpatient services for specialist access. These services have a much lower service orientation than private specialist provision, with patients often facing long waits for access to a specialist, and consumer unfriendly provision arrangements (large waiting rooms, consumer unfriendly scheduling arrangements and so on).

Dual Modes of Practice

The service delivery structure thus militates against equity in service delivery, with differential waiting times and a different service orientation pervading specialist care. Many specialists practise in both the public and private sectors. This creates potential conflicts of interest: to the extent that individual doctors (or the medical profession collectively) are able to influence waiting time in the public sector, they are also able to influence the size of the private market to their advantage. Longer waiting lists in the public sector increase the number of patients willing to participate in the private market, in spite of the out of pocket costs entailed in visiting a specialist privately to avoid long waits. In addition to increasing market size, this results in higher remuneration as time in the private sector tends to be more profitable to the specialist than public sector time.

There is evidence internationally and, in a cross sectional study, for Australia that mixed public and private provision is associated with longer waits in the public sector.[25] The same holds true when one looks at the dynamics of the market for surgical procedures. Figure 5 shows data about the change in the proportion of elective procedures undertaken in the private sector against the change in the median waiting time for those same procedures over the period 2001-02 to 2005-06. (The data are drawn from the Australian Institute of Health and Welfare, the procedures selected are all those for which published data are available for both metrics).

---

25   S. J. Duckett, "Private care and public waiting." *Australian Health Review* (2005) 1, p. 87-93.

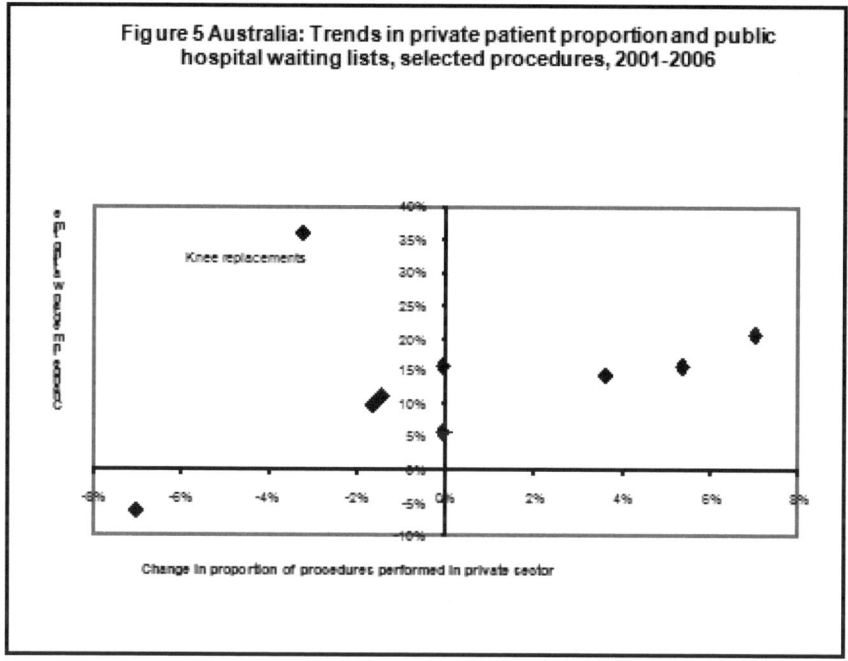

Figure 5 Australia: Trends in private patient proportion and public hospital waiting lists, selected procedures, 2001-2006

With the exception of knee replacements, there is an almost perfect linear relationship between the change in private sector proportion and the change in the median waiting time: as the private sector grows relative to the public sector, so too do public sector waiting times (even including knee replacements in the equation still leaves a statistically significant positive relationship between the two variables). But how does this relationship work and what is the direction of causation? The data give us no leads here. Over the short run (e.g. the period reviewed), the supply of surgeons to undertake any procedure is relatively fixed, or at best grows in line with population change (and thus demand). With fixed relative supply, shifts to private provision have, as a necessary corollary, a reduction in public provision, leading to longer waiting times. Similarly, increasing public sector waiting times will increase the number of patients willing to pay in the private sector to bypass the public sector capacity constraints. What is clear is that intentionally or unintentionally, surgeons benefit from constraining public sector supply by shifting patients to the somewhat better remunerated private sector.

The relative size of the private market is critically important from a solidarity and justice perspective. Part of the attractiveness of private financing and provision to consumers is that these allow them to circumvent public sector constraints in terms of both amenity and waiting times. But, as shown above, an increase in the size of the private sector impacts adversely on the public sector by reducing the availability of scarce resources (particularly surgeon time) to the public sector. This then increases waiting times for public patients and reinforces private sector growth.

The increasing size of the private sector has a more insidious impact: to the extent all patients rely on the public sector, all citizens have a vested interest in the health of the sector. Governments, in turn, have a political stake in the public sector in terms of quality and resourcing. Social solidarity is thus undermined by strengthening the role of the private sector with large segments of the population, especially the most vocal political elites, no longer relying on the public sector for their care, the personal salience of the public health care sector is reduced.

There is a parallel argument about private health insurance. A strong private insurance market is a necessary underpinning of private provision and the future of the financing and delivery sides are intertwined. A decline in private health insurance thus weakens the political importance of that market directly and indirectly that of the private hospital market. Similarly, with 43% of the population participating in private health insurance, it is difficult for government to redistribute funds away from the private sector to improve public sector provision.

The Value Struggle as expressed in electoral politics

Consensus has not been reached on the dominant values in Australian health policy, the place of universal programs versus targeted support or the role of the private sector. As a result there has been contestation about values over the last 50 years leading to gyrations in policy about private health insurance and medical care.

The Australian Labor Party has generally been the guardian and promoter of communitarian and collectivist values and in general has supported this by emphasising public sector financing. The Labor Party has had a much more ambivalent approach to market based arrangements but from the late 1960s has accepted the structure of private medical practice and the role of private hospitals. In contrast, the conservative Liberal and National parties (who form a coalition in government nationally) have de-emphasised mutualisation or collectivisation of finance across the whole population and have emphasised the role of voluntary private health insurance. Similarly they have promoted private provision of health services.

These different political views have led to different policy stances in the different political eras in Australia summarised in table 1.

Table 1: Values choices in health policy in Australia, 1949-2007

Political period	Policy choices	Underpinning values
1949-1972 Liberal-National	• Support for private health insurance for both hospital and medical care	• Individual self reliance • Selective and residual policies
1972-1975 Labor 'Whitlam'	• Introduction of Medibank • "Universal health insurance"	• Mutualisation/risk sharing across whole population • Strong equity and universalist emphasis

THE CONTINUING CONTEST OF VALUES IN THE AUSTRALIAN HEALTH CARE SYSTEM

1975-1983 Liberal-National 'Fraser'	• Dismantling of Medibank • Narrowing of eligibility for access to public subsidies/support	• Mutualisation through private health insurance • Segmented/targeting of subsidies
1983-1996 Labor 'Hawke/Keating'	• Reintroduction of Medibank under new name, Medicare	• Mutualisation/risk sharing across whole population • Strong equity and universalist emphasis
1996-2007 Liberal-National 'Howard'	• Extensive financial and policy support for private health insurance and private delivery • Targeting of financial support for medical services	• Strategic support for private sector delivery • Segmented/targeting of subsidies

1949-1972

The Liberal and National parties (throughout this period the National Party was called the 'Country Party') dominated the political landscape from 1949 to 1972. Health policy in this era has been characterised as "private practice publicly supported".[26] Government support for access to hospital care was means tested, with the emphasis of policy being on political (and to a limited extent, financial) support to private health insurance.[27] Government policy throughout the period emphasised self-reliance with moderate subsidies to private health insurance as a way of assisting individuals and families to manage the costs of health care. The health insurance arrangements became increasingly complex over this period and by the late 1960s, public disenchantment with private insurance arrangements forced political responses in terms of introduction of a national fee schedule (based on the 'most common fee') and a rationalisation of private insurance offerings. A resurgent Labor Party in the late 1960s put further pressure on the Government by abandoning national health service style policies and articulating a new policy for universal health insurance.[28] [29]

1972-1975

Following its election in 1972 the Labor government proceeded quickly to introduce, under the name of Medibank, its policy of universal health insurance for medical services and access to public hospitals without any co-payment. On

---

26 T. Fox, 'The antipodes. Private practice publicly supported' *Lancet* (1963) 1, p. 875-9, 933-9, 988-94.
27 T. H. Kewley, *Social security in Australia 1900–72*, (Sydney: Sydney University Press, 1973).
28 E.G. Whitlam, 'The alternative National health programme'. *Australian Journal of Social Issues*, (1968) 4, p. 33-50.
29 Supra note 4.

the medical side these policies represented mutualisation of finance across the whole population but effectively supported the small business orientation in terms of delivery.

Nevertheless, the policies unleashed bitter political opposition: they were vehemently opposed by the medical profession, the private health insurance industry, and the Liberal and National parties. Well-funded campaigns by doctor groups and the private health insurance industry attacked the policies and Bill Hayden, the politician charged with implementation. The policies were originally blocked in the Senate (the upper house in the Australian bi-cameral legislature) but passed at a historic joint sitting of both houses following Labor's re-election in 1974.[30] Conservative state governments for a time opposed the federal support for free public hospital care.

Medibank enshrined universalist values: the policy aim was to eliminate financial barriers to access to health care for everyone. All Australians were to have equal access to rebates against medical fees and access to public hospitals without means tests. Criticisms at the time challenged these universalist underpinnings arguing that change of this size and style was not necessary because only a small proportion of the population was not covered by existing arrangements and they should be supported through specific subsidy schemes.

Following approval at the joint sitting, Medibank was implemented over the next 14 months as the new medical insurance arrangements and negotiations with states to implement the new public hospital arrangements were finalised. Thus Medibank was still relatively new when a change of government occurred 10 weeks after implementation of the public hospitals arrangements in the last state.

1975-1983

Despite promising at the 1975 election that a Liberal National government would 'maintain Medibank', the Coalition government proceeded to dismantle Medibank's key elements in stages over the next six years.[31] The election of the conservative Coalition parties represented a return to political dominance of those supporting market-based and means tested solutions to coverage and access issues. This was a return to the narrow mutualisation across voluntary private health insurance of the fifties and sixties. The broader mutualisation and communitarian values that had characterised the Labor years were demonised as financially excessive and representing "socialised medicine".

The key changes introduced in these years were:
- October 1976: Introduction of a 2.5% levy on taxable income but those with private health insurance could opt out of the levy.
- May 1978: Reduction in rebate payable from 85% of medical fee schedule with maximum gap between fee and rebate of $5 (85%/$5) to 75%/$10.

30   S. Bennett, "The 1974 joint sitting of Parliament: thirty years on" Research Note (7) 2004–05, Australian Parliamentary Library. Also at http://www.aph.gov.au/Library/; accessed 27 December 2007).

31   S. J. Duckett, "Structural interests and Australian health policy", *Soc Sci Med*, (1984) 11, p. 959-66.

Bulk billing rebates were reduced and restricted to pensioners (85%/$5) and 'socially disadvantaged'with a lower rebate payable (75%/-).
- November 1978: Further reduction in rebate for general population to 40%/$20 (paid through health insurance funds whether member or not)
- May 1979: General population: rebate only for that part of schedule fee in excess of $20 (0%/$20).
- September 1981: Rebates restricted to those with medical insurance, paid at 30% of schedule fee (30%/-). Universal "free" public hospital care abolished and replaced with introduction of fairly restrictive means test for access to free public hospital care.

The attacks on social solidarity were of two kinds. First, the changes dismantled the universalist principles of Medibank by re-introduction of means tests first for medical services (bulk billing changes of May 1978) and subsequently for access to hospital care (September 1981).

Secondly, the changes were designed to reduce population reliance on Medibank and encourage membership of private health insurance and hence reinforce private market provision of health care (levy opt out of October 1976, convenience changes of November 1978, restrictions on payment of medical benefits in May 1979, and September 1981 changes). Although the slow reduction in benefits for medical costs was also expected to increase take up of private health insurance, it was only the September 1981 hospital changes which caused many people to take out private health insurance cover, possibly because medical costs are generally low but even a single episode of hospitalisation could have a very significant impact on family finances.

The government justified the changes on fiscal grounds, but the reversals in policy in this period sometimes *increased* government outlays and can be better explained when viewed through an ideological lens.[32] This is best illustrated by the government justification for the 1981 changes: that they were designed to 'ensure the continuation of private medical practice'.[33]

1983-1996

A new cycle of health policy commenced with the election of the Hawke Labor government in 1983.[34] The return of Labor was again associated with political dominance of communitarian values and emphasis on risk sharing across the whole population. The new government acted swiftly to reintroduce universal health insurance and restore universal access to public hospital care. The new "Medicare" arrangements, as they were termed, were a key part of the new government's broader social policy and were foreshadowed in an 'Accord' negotiated with the union movement prior to the election. The Accord involved the unions agreeing to moderation in money wage demands in exchange for improvements in the social wage, a key component of the latter being the rein-

32   S. J. Duckett, "Chopping and changing Medibank part 2: An interpretation of the policy making process", *Australian Journal of Social Issues*, (1980), p. 15, 79-91.
33   Supra note 31.
34   S. J. Duckett, "Making a difference in health care", in S. Ryan and T. Bramston (eds.) *The Hawke government: A critical perspective*, (North Melbourne: Pluto Press, 2003), p. 215–24.

troduction of universal health insurance and thus savings to workers by obviating the perceived need for people to take out private health insurance.[35] [36]

Private health insurance attracted little policy attention during the Hawke and subsequent Keating governments. Government policy changes were designed to improve industry functioning through improved product design, introduction of front end deductible packages in 1985, and attempting to reduce out-of-pocket costs by allowing insurance funds to negotiate prices with hospitals in 1996.[37] Health insurance funds appear to have been slow to respond to this latter opportunity,[38] perhaps because it was easier to persuade the incoming Liberal government to reintroduce subsidies!

Without the Labor government in the early 1980s, Australia is unlikely to have had universal health insurance. As the subsequent Howard period demonstrates, if the Fraser Liberal government had continued, it would have remained responsive to the interests of the private health insurance organisations and the organised medical profession. Patch up arrangements for health insurance would have continued with an emphasis on subsidising private health insurance rather than having a systematic, universal arrangement that provided cover for all Australians.

The Labor period in office represented a remarkable period of stability of health policy. Possibly because of this stability, public support for Medicare (both in terms of medical and hospital services) grew over this period to the extent that the Liberal and National parties subsequently abandoned their overt opposition to Medicare.

1996-2007

Paralleling the Fraser commitment to 'maintain Medibank', John Howard, the leader of the Liberal-National coalition at the 1996 election promised to maintain 'Medicare in its entirety'. Howard's attack on Medicare was subtler than Fraser's demolition of Medibank. The underlying ideology and philosophy of the Liberal National parties was to support private market solutions in all policy fields and means tested social support rather than universality. Although there was no winding back of government support for universal medical insurance during the Liberal National period, there were a series of policy initiatives designed to strengthen the role of the private sector, reflecting the Coalition government's predilection for targeted rather than universal programs.

The most significant and expensive policy changes in the Howard years involved those designed to increase the uptake of private health insurance. Here the government introduced both extensive subsidies to private health insur-

35   L. Sonder, 'The Accord, the communique and the budget', *The Australian Quarterly*, (Winter) (1984), p. 153-162.

36   S. Carney, *Australia in Accord. Politics and industrial relations under the Hawke Government*, (South Melbourne: Sun Books, 1988).

37   S. Gath, "Enhanced consumer rights in private health care: Have the "Lawrence Amendments" delivered?" *Journal of Law and Medicine* (1999) 6, p. 241-252.

38   S. Willcox, "Buying best value health care: Evolution of purchasing among Australian private health insurers." *Australia and New Zealand Health Policy* (2005) 2, p. 6. Available at: http:/www.anzhealthpolicy.com/content/2/1/6.

ance (known as the health insurance rebate) as well as a restructure of community rating principles to place a strong incentive on consumers to take out health insurance before the age of 30. Higher income people were given tax incentives to take out private health insurance. The major private health insurance policy initiatives were as follows:

- July 1997:
  Surcharge of 1% on Medicare levy tax introduced for those with individual incomes of over $50,000 p.a. or household income over $100,000 p.a. who did not have private health insurance. These income limits were not indexed for inflation so affect an increasing proportion of the population over time. The effect of the levy surcharge was to make it cheaper for high income individuals and families to take out private health insurance than pay the levy. This policy has had the additional effect of pushing high income people (generally lower users of health services) into the health insurance risk pool, thus improving the pool's profile.
  Capped means tested rebate for private health insurance. This policy had very limited impact in terms of increasing take up of private health insurance.39
- January 1999: Capped means tested rebate replaced by uncapped 30% rebate on private health insurance premiums without means test. As with the July 1997 subsidy arrangement, this policy had a very limited effect on private health insurance take-up.
- July 2000: Regulation of private health insurance premiums changed to introduce differential premiums based on age at which the contributor first took out health insurance ('life time community rating'). People/families joining private health insurance after age 30 faced a 2% premium increase (up to age 70) for each year over 30 when they joined.
- April 2005: Health insurance rebate increased to 35% for people 65 to 69 years; 40% for people 70+

The most significant of these policy changes in terms of impact on private health insurance was the July 2000 introduction of 'life time community rating'.40 41 42 This change led to a 50% increase in the number of people who had health insurance, with prevalence of health insurance increasing from around 30% to 45% of the population. The policy discourse and marketing of the new scheme were at odds. The policy discourse emphasised that financial support for private health insurance would in some sense provide relief for public hospitals by reducing demand on the public sector as more people could afford to use private hospitals. The government thus attempted to portray itself as supporting the role of the public hospitals. In contrast, the marketing arrangements for the new policies, both by government and private health insurance organisations, emphasised that private health insurance

---

39   Supra note 10.
40   Supra note 8.
41   L. Segal, "Why is it time to review the role of private health insurance in Australia." *Australian Health Review* (2004) 1, p. 3-15.
42   R. E. Moorin and C. D. J. Holman, "Modelling changes in the determinants of PHI utilisation in Western Australia across five health care policy eras between 1981 and 2001." *Health Policy* (2007) 2-3, p. 183-94.

would allow patients to by pass the queue for elective surgery and/or hospitalisation. This represented a subtle attack on the universalist/communitarian approaches of the previous government, and implied that the population could no longer rely on the Medicare public system for timely access to care.

The government marketing program emphasised the importance of taking out insurance by the deadline set for implementing new age-at-entry based premiums.[43] People and families who had health insurance prior to the cut off date were deemed to have entered at age 30. The marketing slogan was 'Run for cover' and had images of patients on beds rushing past other patients queuing for public hospital care. As Deeble concluded:

the 'run for cover' campaign associated with 'lifetime health insurance' had a dramatic effect. Its basic message was that the government could not provide universal access to an adequate standard of hospital care through Medicare and that the only way to ensure personal coverage was to take private insurance now. That would not only advantage new members, who would otherwise pay more in the future, but also benefit those who could not afford to be insured. It was an aggressive campaign and in terms of membership growth alone, a very successful one.[44]

Subsequent evaluations of the policy have demonstrated quite clearly that the substantial subsidies to private health insurance did little to take any pressure off the public hospital system,[45] [46] [47] [48] [49] [50] [51] [52] although the life time cover changes may have shifted about 100 000 patients per annum from public hospitals to private hospitals, mostly for same day procedures.[53] [54] [55]

43   S. Carter and S. Chapman, "John's $12 tonic: Press coverage of the government's selling of a private health insurance rebate." *Australian and New Zealand Journal of Public Health* (2001) 3, p. 265-71.

44   J. S. Deeble, The private health insurance rebate: Report to State and Territory Health Ministers, National Centre for Epidemiology and Population Health, The Australian National University (2003).

45   S. J. Duckett and T. Jackson, "The new health insurance rebate: An inefficient way of assisting public hospitals", *Medical Journal of Australia* (2000) 9, p. 439–44.

46   Richardson, J. R. J. and L. Segal, "Private health insurance and the Pharmaceutical Benefits Scheme: how effective has recent government policy been?" *Australian Health Review* (2004) 1, p. 34-47.

47   L. Segal, "Why is it time to review the role of private health insurance in Australia." *Australian Health Review* (2004) 1, p. 3-15.

48   D. Hindle and I. McAuley, "The effects of increased private health insurance: a review of the evidence." *Australian Health Review* (2004) 1, p. 119-138.

49   K. Brameld, D. A. Holman, et al., "Possession of health insurance in Australia-how does it affect hospital use and outcomes?" *Journal of Health Services & Research Policy* (2006) 2, p. 94-100.

50   R. E. Moorin and C. D. J Holman, "Does federal health care policy influence switching between the public and private sectors in individuals?" *Health Policy* (2006) 2-3, p. 284-95.

51   R. Moorin, K. J. Brameld, et al., "Health care financing and public responses: use of private insurance in Western Australia during 1980-2001." *Australian Health Review* (2006) 1, p. 73-82.

52   Supra note 42.

53   N. Owers, V. Sundararajan, et al. "The effect of increased private health insurance coverage on Victorian public hospitals." *Australian Health Review* (2003) 2, p. 6-10.

54   S. J. Duckett, "Living in the parallel universe in Australia: public Medicare and private hospitals." *CMAJ* (2005) 7, p. 7.

At the same time as the private sector (health insurance and hospitals) were given extensive subsidies (the subsidy to health insurance is now greater than industry assistance to mining, manufacturing and agriculture combined), Commonwealth support for public hospitals was being whittled away. The 2003-2008 Australian Health Care Agreement was more parsimonious than predecessor agreements. Previous agreements had provided a five-yearly re-balancing of Commonwealth and state contributions to public hospitals: the Commonwealth typically contributing above 50% of costs in the first years of an agreement with the proportion reversed in later years as excess hospital cost inflation took its toll on state spending. The 2003-8 agreement was different, negotiated acrimoniously and yielding a saving to the Commonwealth of about $1 billion on the Budget Forward Estimates, used to fund the changes to bulk billing described below.[56] Approaching the end of the agreement period, the Commonwealth share of public hospital spending has reached a new nadir of 41%, demonstrating the Coalition's priority of support for the private sector.

The second cluster of policies introduced by the Coalition government undermined social solidarity by introducing targeting of financial support for access to medical care, thus weakening a critical attribute of Medicare, its universality. From its introduction Medicare had been a universal health insurance scheme with the whole population being treated equally in terms of government support.

However, the government schedule fee is not linked to fees actually charged and the value of this government support was eroding (for all people) as the schedule fee represented a declining proportion of the fees commonly charged by general practitioners. Responding to political pressures from this decline in bulk billing and consequential increasing out of pocket costs for medical services, the government introduced a number of targeted "safety net" arrangements for particular, politically or socially salient parts of the population. Particular population groups and geographic areas were targeted including residents of rural and outer metropolitan areas (the latter probably included because of the electoral importance of these areas). The specific changes introduced were:

- February 2004: Additional $5 rebate for bulk billed general practitioner services for concession card holders and children under 16
- May 2004:
  Additional $2.50 rebate for bulk billed general practitioner services for concession card holders and children under 16 in regional, rural and remote areas and in Tasmania. (The total additional rebate from 1 February and 1 May changes in these geographic areas was $7.50)
  Safety net threshold of $300 expenditure per annum for families who receive a specific Family Tax Benefit and for concession cardholders, and threshold of $700 per annum for all other individuals or families, after which Medicare will meet 80% of out of pocket costs.

---

55   A.E. Walker, et al., "Public policy and private health insurance: distributional impact on public and private hospital usage." *Australian Health Review*, (2007) 2, 305-314.
56   S. J. Duckett, "The Australian Health Care Agreements 2003-2008."*Australian & New Zealand Health Policy* 1: http://www.anzhealthpolicy.com/cntent/1/1/5, (2004).

- January 2005: 100% rebate (against schedule fee) for most general practitioner services. This change undermined incentives for doctors to bulk bill, with the rebate available whether or not a co-payment was required from patients.

As shown in Figure 1, these changes arrested the decline in bulk billing, but at the cost of reconceptualising bulk billing as a program for targeted segments of the population rather than a universal entitlement.

2007+

The Labor government elected in 2007 has promised to retain many of the policies introduced by the Coalition government including the health insurance rebate, lifetime cover and the Medicare safety net. But in contrast to the Coalition's policy priorities, the new government also emphasised direct support for rebuilding the public hospital system and has moved swiftly to provide additional (albeit once off) funding to states to reduce waiting lists. The 2008-09 budget lifted the threshold for the Medicare levy surcharge to $100,000 annual income for individuals and $150,000 for families, changing the dynamic of the declining value of the threshold and restoring it as a surcharge on the 'wealthy' rather than drifting down to capture a larger segment of the population. The changes threshold arrangements are likely to reverse the very recent rend of increasing take up of private health insurance.

Conclusion

The Australian health care system has been described as a 'strife of interests'57, but these interests have not only pursued their own financial and sectional interests but have also been pursuing quite different value positions about the place of equity and universality. The role the market should play in providing access to hospital care has also been highly contested. The medical profession has had a particularly important role in the contest about values with the principal interest group, the Australian Medical Association, being dominated by a private free market ethos, possibly stemming from the industry structure as small business operators. The professional clinical colleges (such as the Royal Australasian College of Physicians) have not been dominated by this ethos to the same extent, possibility reflecting that in some of the clinical colleges there is a much greater influence of medical staff employed in academic roles or on salary in public hospitals.

The sectional interests have had advocates in the political sphere and the different political parties have placed different emphasis on values of communitarian versus individual self-reliance when in office. As demonstrated in this chapter, despite any promises made as part of election campaigns, Coalition governments have acted consistently to support the private sector over the public sector, and pursued policies which segment or target population groups rather than emphasise social solidarity or universality.

---

57   S. Sax, *A Strife of interests: Politics and Policies in Australian Health Services*, North Sydney, Allen and Unwin, 1984.

What does the future hold? For the foreseeable future Australia will have mixed public and private sector provision with a continuing significant role for government in financing. Private health insurance, which is a critical underpinning of private hospital provision, has maintained its market share above 40% of the population. This is a significant minority group and no government can afford, politically, to alienate this segment of the population. The industry has been successful in persuading contributors to private health insurance that public support for private health insurance is reasonable and deserved. Although there are some signs that the private health insurance market is again unstable and beginning to suffer from adverse selection, it is unlikely that a Labor government will invest significant resources in further subsidising this industry. The future of the medical market is more uncertain and the small business nature of the medical market is under challenge from industry consolidation and larger providers. This will not change the ideological stance of the industry but may weaken its popular appeal.

The election of a Labor government may return the policy focus to universalist and egalitarian values in Australia, but the strengths and successes of the countervailing forces suggest that there will be a continuing contest of values in Australia into the future.

What lessons for other countries? This chapter has demonstrated the importance of electoral politics in influencing the shape of the health care system. The weak values-based consensus about the place of universality in the health care system in Australia allowed the re-emergence of targeted and segmenting policies during the Howard years. Australia's experience also demonstrates the ability of the medical profession to shape policy, with many aspects of policy under Fraser and Howard being driven by professional values and political power of the profession rather than bureaucratic or health economics rationality.

The importance of the medical profession in the Coalition periods should not be overstated: the profession was speaking to governments that were sympathetic to its message. Indeed, it has been argued that health policy in the Fraser period can be better understood by considering wider ideological issues than by looking to explanations within the health sector itself.[58] Certainly, the contestation of values in health policy reflected similar contestation in other areas of public policy over these periods.

Finally, the Australian experience demonstrates some constraint on governments. The strong electoral support for Medicare developed over the Hawke/Keating years constrained the Howard government in its attack on universalism.

---

[58]   Supra note 32.

Chapter 11.

Public Identity, Private Behaviour – Causes, Consequences, and Remedies for Health Sector Reforms in China *

Vivian Lin and Hongwen Zhao

Introduction

With the founding of the People's Republic of China in 1949, the first National Health Conference was convened and the four guiding principles of health development were formulated in 1952. The four principles were to: 1) serve the workers, peasants and soldiers, 2) put prevention first, 3) place equal importance to traditional Chinese medicine and Western medicine, and 4) mobilise all sectors of society for health work. Within three decades, life expectancy increased by 10 years, and health resources tremendously increased (see Table 1). This achievement during the planned economy was the successful accomplishment of what has been termed the 'First Health Revolution'. Compared with other countries of similar per capita income, health status attainment in China was better than expected.[1] China therefore became an international model for primary health care.[2]

---

*   Research assistance by Emily Brink in the preparation of this manuscript is gratefully acknowledged.

1   World Bank, *China: Strategies for reducing poverty in the 1990s.* (Washington DC: World Bank, 1992).
2   WHO, Declaration of Alma-Ata (International Conference on Primary Health Care), 1978.

Table 1 Health Status and Resources in China in 1950, 1980 and 2000

Indicators	1950	1980	2000
Life Expectancy (years)	57.0	67.9	73.0
Infant Mortality (/1000 live births)	80.8	34.7	15.3
Hospitals	4179	12,227	19,246
Hospital Beds	294,700	1,508,600	2,560,40
Health Professionals	1,039,200	3,410,900	4,624,140
Township Health Centres	N/A	47,387	40,791
Total Population	614 million	987 million	1,321 million (2007)
Indicators	1950	1980	2000

Sources: Ministry of Health (MOH), Chinese Health Statistical Digest;
N/A = Reliable information not readily available.

Since 1949, the development of the Chinese health system can be characterised as three rounds of health reforms – with each addressing the causes and consequences of the previous policy action. If this first phase of egalitarian health development, occurring between 1949 and 1979, can be seen as addressing the availability, accessibility and affordability of health care, under the broad ideological framework of equity and political solidarity, then the subsequent developments might be depicted as:

- First round of health reform 1980-1996: Sharing of health care responsibility by individual, collective and government, within the policy context of fiscal decentralisation and corporatisation, and with the consequences of "public identity, private behaviour";
- Second round of health reform 1997-2006: Attempt to mix planning and market approaches, but without adequate government financing for basic public services nor other market-oriented policy levers, leading to the failure of health reform, with solidarity undermined and subsequent social outcry;
- Third of health reform 2007- 2020: Renewed goal statement about health care access, adoption of government financing as part of overall strengthening of public services and reform towards a service-oriented government, with emergence of health rights.

In other words, the initial round of reforms, as part of the opening of the economy and move towards a market-based system destroyed features of the previously successful Chinese health system. In effect, the initial reform was about partial privatisation of financing, with corporatisation in health care management and operations, and decentralisation of ownership (and investment) responsibilities. In its place emerged symptoms of systemic problems which are best characterised as 'public identity, private behaviour' – where ownership remained notionally public, but provider behaviour reflected a strong for-profit orientation. Since the 1990s, various attempts were made to redress the problems of high cost, inequitable access, and poor quality, which came to become the dominant traits in the Chinese health system.

This chapter first reviews the causes, consequences, and remedies to address the disastrous consequences of the first round of health reforms, focusing on the issues of justice and equity and the emerging discussion of health rights. It provides evidence and analysis of the impact of the reform. It then discusses the second round of health reform and its policy measures, and the failures and successes. Then the policy objectives and directions of the third and current health reform are considered, particular in its attempt to address the severe problems of inequities that had arisen. The chapter concludes with discussion about the challenges for achieving current reforms, and what remains to be done. Finally, the chapter suggests that a benchmarking tool is needed to monitor and assess the fairness and performance of the China health system.

Causes and consequences of health system change

The first round of health reform started concurrently with economic reform in the early 1980s. Indeed, economic reforms and public sector reforms were the driving force for health reforms, as fiscal decentralisation, corporatisation of state-owned enterprises (SOEs) and other public sector units meant the shedding of welfare functions of SOEs (such as health care). At the same time, to maintain social stability, price controls and labour allocation systems were maintained, resulting in an incomplete transition from planned economy to market economy.

Consistent with the program of economic reform and fiscal decentralisation, all health institutions were corporatized, having to pay their own way, rather than survive on the basis of the 'iron rice bowl'. MOH policy direction focused on holding hospitals fiscally accountable in order to boost their economic efficiency. To make up for decreasing government financing for hospitals, new policies were implemented over time to provide incentives to modify provider behaviour. These policies allowed for the reintroduction of private medical practices (1980); the pricing of services based on real cost (1985); the implementation of a service contract system, and the allowance of sideline commercial activities to compensate for inadequate budgetary financing (1989).[3] However, no systematic policy reform package emerged from MOH till the mid 1990s. More often, policy practice was an ad hoc response to market-orientation innovations and the reform strategy can be summarised by one word – decentralisation – a central word throughout China in the years of economic reform in the 1980s.[4]

Under such policy directions, cost recovery and expansion of revenue earning services were the main strategies adopted by hospitals. Health providers were inclined to respond to the financial incentives embedded in fee-for-service payments by providing more services, thereby earning more for themselves and their institutions. They pursued their own 'survival' agenda by increasing user charges and favouring expensive prescriptions for new medical technologies and pharmaceuticals. The distorted financing arrangement, at the

---

3   H. Zhao, *Governing the Health Care Market: Regulatory Challenges and Options in the Transitional China.* (PhD thesis, La Trobe University, School of Public Health), (2005), p. 27.
4   *Ibid.* p. 25.

system level, resulted in unhealthy competition at the institutional level. 'Public identity, private behaviour' emerged, with revenue maximization overshadowing traditional ethical standards.[5]

Incentives to over-service in the health system have produced services of questionable quality, particularly where workforce capacity is limited. At the same time, competition in the medical marketplace has increased the concentration (and wastage) of resources in the urban tertiary sector. The shift in government spending can be seen in Table 2:

Table 2: Government spending in urban and rural areas (in millions yuan)[6]

Year	1978	1993
Urban hospital operating expenses	1,794	4,183
Subsidies to rural cooperative medical system (CMS)	89	27

These competitive pressures resulted in medical care cost escalation. With limited regulatory activities and absence of pricing policy, drug prices increased up to 85 percent.[7] The hospital accreditation program, commenced in 1989, largely evolved into a facility building program.[8] Consumer dissatisfaction around issues such as reduced benefits of previously publicly funded insurance schemes, poor attitudes of doctors, and poor quality of hospitals and physician services, has been increasingly reported.[9]

Health care violence became an increasingly serious problem,[10] with complaints of violent disputes between doctors and patients notified to the China Consumers' Association having increased tenfold over a three-year period in the 1990s. Zheng et al reported that one study found 65% of hospital staff in two large urban hospitals had experienced physical or psychological violence because of dissatisfaction with the standard of care provided.[11]

As a result of these changes in financing, by the 1990s, most urban hospitals were receiving less than 10 percent of their total revenue from the government budgetary allocation while generating 60 percent of their revenue by selling pharmaceuticals.[12] With this incentive, an estimated 30-40 percent of

---

5   *Ibid.* page 37.
6   World Bank, *Financing Health Care: Issues and Options for China.* (Washington DC: The International Bank for Reconstruction and Development / The World Bank, 1997).
7   D. Yu, Changes in health care financing and health status: the case of China in the 1980s. Beijing, Paper in circulation (1992).
8   L. Pei, *Hospital management in a time of change: the need for management training and policy reform in three teaching hospitals in Yunnan* (PhD thesis), 1998.
9   Supra note 3, p. 30.
10   P. Zheng, T. Faunce, et al., "Public hospitals in China: privatisation, the demise of universal health care and the rise of patient-doctor violence." *Journal of Law & Medicine* (2006) 4, p. 465-70.
11   *Ibid.*
12   D. Dai, "A review of the health care reform (wei sheng gai ge hui gu)." *Chinese health Economics* (1993) 2: 26-28.

drug consumption was thought to comprise inappropriate or unnecessary utilisation, at a cost (to the public) of more than 30 billion yuan per year.[13]

The consequences of corporatisation were particularly devastating on health care access in rural areas. The demise of people's communes, as part of the economic reforms, meant there was no longer a system for organising rural health services. The rural cooperative medical system (CMS), the community financed and organised delivery system introduced in the 1960s, collapsed, leaving rural residents to pay out-of-pocket for health care. Barefoot doctors drifted away or turned to other work, and those who stayed became private village doctors. The three-tiered network disintegrated, clinical supervision activities disappeared, and the relationship between county health institutions and township health centres was dominated by competition. Increasingly the rural poor are becoming impoverished through costs incurred due to serious illness.[14] Lack of resources, perverse incentives, and dysfunctional managerial mechanisms had become the central issues of rural health development.[15]

By 1993, the increasing inequity between urban and rural areas became noticeable.[16] For example, average per capita health spending (public and private) was 110 Renminbi (RMB) per annum, but the average for rural areas was 60 RMB per capita compared to 235 RMB for urban areas. Furthermore, the proportion of health expenditure from public funds was much less in rural areas than in urban areas. Per capita health expenditure in the officially designated poverty counties (28 percent of all counties in China) was less than half the national average, but 80 percent of this expenditure (twice the national average) was out-of-pocket. Hospital facilities proliferated while primary care services declined. Between 1979 and 1993, the number of villages with health stations reduced from 71 percent to 55 percent. Concurrently, the number of tertiary hospitals in urban areas grew from 9,478 in 1980 to 14,771 in 1995.

The rural-urban divide is further exacerbated by the nature of the health workforce, with inadequate levels of training among rural health care staff, and an overemphasis on specialisation in the urban centres. The number of senior level health professionals, working generally in urban areas, increased by 234 percent in the decade from 1980 and a further 142 percent from 1990 to 1995.[17] With the relaxation of job allocation by the state, and as incomes come to rely on institution-generated revenues, more experienced and better trained staff have sought work in the more financially rewarding county or urban hos-

---

13   Xinhua News Agency, The waste of health resources is serious (wei sheng zi yuan lang fei yan zhong). *People's Daily.* Beijing (1996).

14   E. van Doorslaer, O. O'Donnell, et al., *Paying out-of-pocket for health care in Asia: Catastrophic and poverty impact* - EQUITAP Working Paper #2. Rotterdam, Erasmus University (2005).

15   C. J. Liu, *Closing the Gap Between Policy and Reality: A study of community health services in Chengdu and Panzhihua* (PhD thesis) (2003)

16   Y. Liu, W. C. Hsiao, et al., "Equity in health and health care: the Chinese experience." *Social Science & Medicine* (1999) 10, p. 1349-1356.

17   *Ibid.*

pitals. In affluent areas there has also been growth in private sector health care which offers competitive prices and amenable services.[18]

Although urban residents fared relatively better than rural, the proportion of out-of-pocket payments increased significantly for both populations due to changes in the financing arrangements for the Government Insurance Scheme (GIS) and the Labour Insurance Scheme (LIS). Data from national household health surveys in 1993 and 1998 indicate that health insurance in urban areas declined during that period from 54 percent to 39 percent.[19] According to World Bank estimates in 1981, 29 percent of China's population were uninsured.

The financial barriers and urban-rural inequities in health care access translated into decreased health status. Although economic development contributed to overall improvements in population mortality rates, the gap between urban and rural populations widened.[20] The gendered nature of health care access is exacerbated for rural women, as evidenced in decline in rate of reproductive health examinations.[21] Migrants from rural areas are particularly disadvantaged, given their lack of entitlements to urban health services. Migrant women are thus further disadvantaged. A study in Shanghai revealed high rates of still-births among internal migrants due to limited antenatal care.[22]

In relation to vertical public health programs, various reports suggested that there was a reversal of gains in maternal and child health (MCH) care, reduced immunization coverage, and relapse of TB and schistosomiasis in rural areas. New public health threat such as AIDS and re-emerged old diseases such as STDs became prevalent in the 1990s.[23] The rural poor were the hardest hit during this period of transition to a market-oriented system, due to shrinkage of public health services. Affordability to basic preventative health services exacerbated pre-existing rural-urban differentials in health status and health care access. Evidence has suggested that women were proportionately affected for the sake of inability to pay for services.[24]

The crisis in 2003 around SARS can be traced to the dysfunctionality of a health system subjected to market-based reforms without adequate regulatory or governance oversight. When public health institutions have to earn their own keep, public good functions, such as surveillance systems and community education, are not attended to. When there is no revenue to be earned, hospi-

---

18   G. Bloom, and X. Gu, "Health sector reform: Lessons from China." *Social Science & Medicine* (1997) 3, p. 351-360.

19   J. Gao, and S. Tang, "Health insurance and hospitalisation in urban China: bending to the wind of change." *World Hospitals and Health Services* (2000) 3, p. 23-26,36,38.

20   J. Gao, J. Qian, et al., "Health equity in transition from planned to market economy in China." *Health Policy and Planning* (2002) S1, p. 20.

21   L. Chen, and H. Standing, "Gender equity in transitional China's health care policy reforms." *Feminist Economics* (2007) 3/4, p. 189.

22   S. Zhan, Z. Sun, et al., "Economic transition and maternal health care for internal migrants in Shanghai, China." *Health Policy and Planning* (2002) S1, p. 47.

23   L. M. Lee, V. Lin, et al., *Public Health in China: history and contemporary challenges. Global Public Health: a new era.* R. Beaglehole. (Melbourne: Oxford University Press, 2003).

24   Ministry of Health (MOH), *China national health Survey - the Third NHS Analysis Report.* (Beijing: China Union Medical University publisher, 2004), p. 314.

tals do not report disease occurrences. When the public have to pay out-of-pocket for care, they delay care-seeking and prevention is not seen as important. Furthermore, rural migrants to urban areas were not eligible for household registration and had no entitlement to health services. The successful control of SARS, in the end, was due to the aggressive and cultural- and political-specific approach adopted, using 'inspiration plus punishment' methods akin to public health campaigns conducted prior to the economic reforms. Such success was built upon the existing centralised top down structure and depended less on technical strategies.[25]

Changes in medical ethics represented the more profound transformation brought by misguided health policies. The combination of low salaries for doctors and providing bonuses to doctors (and profits to hospitals) from excessive use of expensive drugs and unnecessary diagnostic procedures has led doctors away from the earlier socialist value of 'serve the people' to the pursuit of profit. The economic reforms unleashed irregularities and improprieties in professional practice and with this emerged new values which contradicted those of the past.[26] [27] [28]

New policy measures – with provider regulation failures

The looming crisis in the health system instigated the second round of health reform, which started in 1996 when the Second National Health Conference was convened by the State Council to discuss the emerging issues in the health sector. The key objectives of the second round health reforms were:[29]
- Promote the viability of institutions, through reforming the health administration system and the service system;
- Recognition that health care should be of a public welfare nature with government implementing certain welfare policies, and health development must be coordinated with the national economy and social development;
- Institutional reform should aim to balance social and economic benefits, in other words, put social benefit first to prevent unilaterally seeking economic benefit; and
- By year 2010, the health system should be consistent with the socialist market system.

Reflecting the new climate of health reform, the policy objectives for the MOH in the Tenth Five-Year Plan (2001-2005) placed emphasis on rural health (both provision of basic services and new CMS development); health sector reform (including regional health planning, hospital management, sale and management of pharmaceuticals, and development of community health

---

25 C. Liu, "The battle against SARS: a Chinese story." *Australian Health Review* (2003) 3, p. 3-13.
26 P.-K. Ip, "Developing Medical Ethics in China's Reform Era." *Developing World Bioethics* (2005) 5(2).
27 L. Chen and H. Standing, "Gender equity in transitional China's health care policy reforms." *Feminist Economics* (2007) 3/4, p. 189.
28 R. Fan, "Corrupt Practices in Chinese Medical Care: The Root in Public Policies and a Call for Confucian-Market Approach." *Kennedy Institute of Ethics Journal* (2007) 2, 111.
29 H. Zhao, supra note 3, p. 33.

services); and on new and re-emerging disease (including HIV/AIDS/STDs, non-communicable disease and tuberculosis).

Regional health planning was intended to redress the imbalance in the health system – between tertiary and primary care, between urban and rural services, between treatment and prevention. Under national policy guidelines, provinces were asked to develop planning standards, while cities were to develop and implement plans. Given decentralised financing and authority, absence of delegated authority to the city health bureau, lack of legislative framework for regulating health care markets, this policy was nothing more than good intent.[30]

The government announced the hospital classification policy in 2000, which was to formally address the issue of profit-earning behaviour of hospitals with "public identity". The policy classified hospitals into for-profit and non-for-profit organizations, with the aim of defining the taxation status of previously government affiliated hospitals, which had already become financially self-governing institutions as part of the fiscal decentralization program instituted in the mid of 1980s. It was hoped that the hospital classification policy would clarify the profit orientation and re-orient the 'private behaviour'. Unfortunately, the policy was not accompanied by effective implementation and thus measures to regulate provider behaviour. Hospitals continued to operate in accordance with past administrative practices while acting like a private agent in an unregulated premature health care market. Without socially accepted professional norms for public services, "public identity, private behaviour" mode of medical practice persisted.[31]

As hospitals were earning much revenue from drug mark-ups to compensate for loss of government financial subsidy, the pharmaceutical management reform policy adopted in 2000 was to introduce separation of prescribing from dispensing and to de-link the incentives of doctors to prescribe more expensive drugs for their own earnings. However, the pharmaceutical industry in China had evolved into market-oriented operations earlier than hospitals, and joint ventures formed with multinational pharmaceutical corporations and had disrupted the traditional government distributional chain for drug supply. Imported drugs, backed by strategic business planning and advertisements, filled hospital pharmacies. Without government compensation through increased budget subsidies and regulatory oversight, hospitals continued to prescribe expensive drugs in order to cover their routine operation costs.[32] [33]

Community health services were hailed as a new approach to re-establish primary care and preventive services in urban communities. In the same way as other initiatives, the policy intent was laudable – to improve equity by increasing access to primary care services – but the fundamental and systemic conditions necessary for policy implementation were not present. The lack of qualified doctors to practice (and to be trusted by the consumers) at the com-

---

30   H. Yang, V. Lin, et al., *Regional Health Planning. Health Policy In Transition: The Challenges for China.* (Beijing: Peking University Press (forthcoming), 2008).
31   *Ibid.*
32   *Ibid.*
33   H. Zhao, H. Yang, et al., *Impact of Hospital regulation policies Health Policy In Transition: the Challenges for China.* (Beijing: Peking University Press (forthcoming), 2008).

munity level and the need for these small-scale institutions to generate revenue, along with the increased presence of a relatively unregulated private sector, constrained the development of urban community health services as intended.[34]

There was rhetorical recognition for the importance of state vision and policy direction. Yet the health administrative system has remained unchanged and fragmented across different ministries in the second round of health reform, and the organisational interests proved to be a barrier for a systemic focus. For example, in relation to the health protection system, the administration of the rural cooperative medical scheme is under the Ministry of Health, the urban basic medicine insurance scheme is under jurisdiction of the Ministry of Labour and Social Security, and medical assistance is under the Ministry of Civil Affairs. In terms of health delivery system, the rigid boundary between the rural health and urban community health care system, reinforced by the financing and decentralised administration arrangements, have proven to be a barrier for access for an increasingly mobile population. The structure of these governing organs and the health delivery system remain largely inherited from the 1998 government institution reform, and it is not likely to be reformed again in a short period of time.

In the 1990s, there was illicit privatisation of hospital ownership, with contracting out of clinical departments, along with this; local government formally privatised rural hospitals in order to be relieved of the financial burden of subsidising health services as a result of decentralisation.[35] These developments further widened inequalities in service accessibility and eroded service quality. Even Chinese doctors were dissatisfied about themselves, the Chinese health care system, and their professional life.[36] Doctors reported concerns about quality and safety, especially in the growing but poorly regulated private sector.

A decade of reform since 1996 has seen more criticisms than success. The 2005 State Council Development Research Centre report on health reform effectively declares the reforms of the 1980s and 1990s a failure. As a result, health financing, emerged as a high government priority in 2006. This is because analysis has shown that the government has continued to steadily reduce its financing role in health in the past two decades (see Table 3). With fiscal decentralization since the early years of the 1980s, government expenditure on health has decreased steadily from 37% in 1981 to 18% in 2006, while the private health expenses on health has increased steadily from 24% in 1981 to 49% in 2006.

34 G. Liu, D. Legge, et al., Community Health Services. Health Policy in Transition: The Challenges for China. (Beijing: Peking University Press (forthcoming) (2008).

35 W. Tam, *Privatising Health in China: Adverse consequences and De-Privatisation.* Conference on Reasserting the public in Public Service Delivery. National University of Singapore (2007).

36 M.-K. Lim, H. Yang, et al., "China's evolving health care market: how doctors feel and what they think." *Health Policy* (2004) 69, p. 329-327.

Table 3: Total Health Expenditures (THE) in China 1981-2006 (in million USD, current price)[37]

Year	THE	THE ($)/capita	Govern-ment*	%of THE	Socie-tal*	%of THE	Indi-vidual*	%of THE
1981	9391	9.38	3500	37	3662	39	2230	24
1985	9501	8.98	3666	39	3132	33	2703	28
1990	15625	13.67	3915	25	6128	39	5582	36
1995	25807	21.31	4638	18	9194	24	11974	58
2000	55405	43.71	8571	16	14157	26	32677	58
2006	123477	93.94	22314	18	40279	33	60884	49

* Government means total government expenditures in health, societal means social and other health insurance contributions, and individual means private health expenses.

Given that the state run and subsidized health systems have developed perverse incentives, driving out-of pocket costs up, the emerging private sector has provided a means of cheaper and thus more accessible health care. The private sector plays an increasing role in ambulatory care for example, although it is not included in any social insurance benefits. As such, it primarily serves self-paying patients; however it appears to serve disproportionately the low-middle income groups rather than higher income groups and is thought to be due to its lower relative costs.[38] Although this is true, public perception of private sector care is that it is of lower clinical quality, even though the service and staff attitude to consumers may be better.[39]

The decline in trust in the health system has become a major challenge for the government in attempting to restore the rural cooperative medical service (CMS) on the basis of modest voluntary contributions from farmers. Furthermore, the rapid economic transition period has led to declining community level social capital, which further influences farmers' willingness-to-join.[40]

Some success in increasing access

Despite these setbacks, there were some successes during the period of the second health reform that point the way to the future. These relate, in the main, to measures to decrease financial access barriers to health care, particularly for the poor and for rural populations.

The new rural cooperative medical scheme (NCMS) was announced in 2003, after several years of piloting. Based on the old cooperative medical scheme developed during the planned economy, the government ultimately

---

37 China National Health Economics Institute, China National Health Accounts Report 2007.

38 Y. Liu, P. Berman, et al., "Health care in China: the role of non-government providers." *Health Policy* (2006) 2, p. 212-20.

39 M. K. Lim, supra note 36.

40 L. Zhang, H. Wang, et al., "Social capital and farmer's willingness-to-join a newly established community-based health insurance in rural China." *Health Policy* (2006) 76, p. 233-242.

accepted that intergovernmental financial transfers were needed. The contribution rate of yuan per household of the new insurance scheme is that the central government contribute 40 yuan, the local government contribute 40 yuan, and that the farmer contributes 10-20 yuan, with the policy aim to have full coverage by 2010. That the government contribution is larger than household contribution is a signal to the community that government recognises its responsibility for primary health care. Unresolved issues remain, however, such as community trust in providers, proper management of the scheme, and the migrated rural population working in urban areas.

The urban basic medical insurance system, designed to cover formal sector employees, was initially piloted in 1994 and expanded in 2000. The urban household medical insurance system, which aims to cover family dependents and non-employed urban residents initially not covered by the system, was introduced in 2007 with government subsidy contributing roughly 60 yuan per household. This followed from pilots which suggested improvement in equity of health care access.[41] [42] [43] Once again, the population of rural migrants working in urban areas are also not covered by the urban insurance scheme.

A health safety net is being established for both rural and urban poor. The medical relief fund was successfully trialled in many urban and rural communities across the country.[44] [45] Currently the Ministry of Civil Affairs is preparing a policy document to formally establish the method of managing a medical relief fund operation.

In addition to health care access, the government also responded to the crisis in public health with additional financing measures including free treatment for HIV and TB, and free access for antenatal care.

The government has also tackled personnel reforms, by appointing contract managers, based on merit selection. Some successes have been seen in rural areas[46] but how successful it can become is still in question at the moment.

Nonetheless, with the government making the decision in 2002 to provide intergovernmental financial transfers for the new rural CMS, the policy stance can be seen as a form of de-privatisation. Local governments at the county level have begun to reassert control over village and township clinics and health

[41]   G. Liu, Z. Zhao, et al., "Equity in health care access to: assessing the urban health insurance reform in China." *Social Science & Medicine* (2002) 55, p. 1779-1794.

[42]   G. G. Liu and Z. Zhao, "Urban employee health insurance reform and the impact on out-of-pocket payment in China." *The International Journal of Health Planning & Management* (2006) 3, p. 211.

[43]   J. S. Akin, W. H. Dow, et al., "Did the distribution of health insurance in China continue to grow less equitable in the nineties? Results from a longitudinal survey." *Social Science & Medicine* (2004) 2, p. 293.

[44]   X.-M. Sun, H. Liang, et al., "Survey for the medical financial assistance schemes of the urban poor in Shanghai." *International Journal of Health Planning and Management* (2002) 17, p. 91-112.

[45]   Z. Zhang, L. Fang, et al. *The Rural Health Protection System in China. Health Policy in Transition: The Challenges for China.* (Beijing: Peking University Press (forthcoming), 2008).

[46]   Y. Liu and G. Bloom, *Rural Health System Reform in Poverty Areas.* (Beijing: Peking University Press (forthcoming)).

centres.47 Some rural health services are now fully funded by government budgets. Regulations have even been introduced to ensure a zero-profit margin on drugs.

Current developments and debates in policy reforms

The third round of health reform was triggered by a combination of the State Council Development Research Centre report in 2007, the general outcry by society calling for reduced burden on individuals seeking medical care, the media prompting public discussion on health issues, and experts providing evidences of health reform both in China and abroad. The third wave of health reform has also been ushered in under a new political context, following government change in 2003, and the new determination to invest in social sectors (in line with the call for the construction of a harmonious society and the concept of scientific development).

The social orientation of the new 'people-centred' market socialism and the notion of 'small state, big society' were enunciated in the 11th Five-Year Plan (2006-2010), which aims to put people first; change the concept of development; and carry out the 'five balances'(i.e. these consist of a balance between: urban and rural settings, different geographical regions, economic and social values, built and natural environment, and domestic development and opening-up beyond China's borders). It appears that in China, 'market institutions', constitutionalism, and the 'Rule of Law' have now become the key national policy goals for the next half-century".48

There is now in-principle agreement for government to increase financing for public health and primary care and the government is likely to adopt both demand side and the supply side financing strategies. In 2008, the plan of the third round of health reform is going to be launched after the March National Peoples' Congress. It is expected that a nation-wide open discussion will be organized through the government before the reform plan is finalised. The objective of the reform is to provide universal basic health services coverage to all Chinese people by 2020. It includes four elements:

- To develop a public health system, maintaining that all public health institutions are fully funded, providing public health services without user charges;
- To strengthen the rural health and urban community service delivery system and to develop appropriate basic health services facilities so that they can provide services at low cost;
- To reform hospital management and operation systems, and to ensure public hospitals provide in the interest of public good, i.e. to ban supply side induced demands for self profit; and

47   W. Tam, *Privatising Health in China: Adverse consequences and De-Privatisation*. Conference on Reasserting the public in Public Service Delivery. National University of Singapore, 2007

48   M. Wang, "The phase change: development trend and policy orientation of the Chinese economy (zhong guo jing ji de jian duan bian hua, fa zhan qu si he zhen che fang xiang)." *China Development Review* (2002) 1, p. 1-18.

- To develop a health protection system, this basically consists of three insurance schemes, a Basic Medical Insurance (BMI) for the urban employees including civil servicemen, an urban residence medical insurance for the urban informal sectors, and a rural new CMS for farmers. In addition, the medical relief system will be developed by the Ministry of Civil Affairs for low income population groups.

This policy agenda is focused on health financing, with the recognition that state intervention is needed to correct market failure. From a financing perspective, however, there are still elements which appear to require further consideration. New CMS and urban BMI (Basic Medical Insurance) are founded on limited redistribution across population groups, and coverage is primarily for inpatient, catastrophic illnesses. From the viewpoint of equity and social solidarity, there is a question about the extent to which cross-subsidisation should occur for all forms of health care for poor and vulnerable population groups.

Despite in-principle policy decisions for government to finance public health and primary care, there has been little discussion about how to ensure efficiency, effectiveness, and equity in the health system through purchasing functions, by either the state or by other purchasers (such as health insurance, or medical assistance funds). Without conscious, planned use of financing levers, it would be difficult for the government to achieve system-level policy objectives related to efficient use of limited resources and equitable distribution of benefits.

The success of these reforms, thus, may be at risk if the focus is limited to health financing. To date, limited consideration has been given to the linkages that are needed across demand side and supply side measures, and about governance issues. The government is still exploring technical approaches to financing through either the demand side or the supply side, but it needs to consider how to ensure quality and equitable access, and improved health outcomes, and how they can be incorporated into government purchasing of services. Furthermore, a purchasing approach should be accompanied by an arms-length relationship between government and providers, with independent corporate governance arrangements for hospitals and other health services.

A comprehensive and robust legislative framework remains largely absent for the health system. China has no overarching health law per se; rather there are quite a number of sub-sector laws such as Maternal and Child Health law, food and pharmaceutical law, and physician law. These need to be knitted together to address all aspects of health system governance and performance. The new primary health care law presently under consideration may be an opportunity to establish a regulatory framework for health however the debate remains focused around the level of financing for health.

The absence of effective regulatory arrangements, by government or through other social institutions, particularly for the behaviour of doctors, is another significant policy gap. Transition from an administrative rule-based system to a rule-based market system is never easy. China lacks regulatory tools and monitoring systems for regulation.

With or without regulatory mechanisms, more attention is needed on ethics and value formation in medical education and in the health workforce more generally. Market-oriented economic reform has fundamentally changed the value of society, including for the health workers. A major challenge for successful reform is to revitalise the medical profession, re-establish trust in the health care system, and instil a new form of medical ethics that will form in the market economy as well as build on traditional social norms. Traditional Confucian ethics of benevolence can be supported with adequate compensation and appropriate prohibitions against profit-seeking.49 Harmony and person-oriented development are new philosophical perspectives underpinning current government policies. For the health workforce, increased government financing and adjustments in the incentives for doctors should be accompanied with a professional code of conduct.

The transition to a market-oriented system also requires reconfiguration of the relationship between state and civil society, including the policy-making process. As yet, the development of civil society voice and representation has been limited. To receive and respond to citizens' views will be necessary for restoration of trust in the health care system and legitimacy of government's health policy. This may mean profound social change that ultimately will produce benefits in health improvement and health equity.

Where to next?

Health development in China, since it's founding in 1949, has proceeded along three waves of health reform, in the early 1980s, in 1996, and in 2008. In summary:

During the planned economy in 1949 -1979, health development in China developed basic health service facilities and human resources, and an employment-based health insurance system. Its emphasis was on equity, availability and accessibility as the primary development objectives in the health sector. The first health revolution was successful in China through primary health care provision and control of infectious diseases.

The first wave of health reform in 1980-1995 aimed to boost health provider efficiency though cost-recovery strategy and other market-oriented measures that reduced government financing. The consequence was high cost, low quality care, as well as increased rural-urban disparity in health resource distribution and health service utilization. Coupled with population ageing and epidemiological transition, China has faced numerous health challenges by the mid of 1990s, particularly in relation to health equity.

The second wave of health reform in 1996-2007 aimed to continue market-oriented but top-down reform. Its failure was related to bureaucratically fragmented health administration systems and inadequate government financing for essential public goods, leading to increasing distrust in the health care system.

The third round of health reform began in 2008 and has emphasized the financing role of government. The current health reform may be a watershed

---

49   R. Fan, "Corrupt Practices in Chinese Medical Care: The Root in Public Policies and a Call for Confucian-Market Approach." *Kennedy Institute of Ethics Journal* (2007) 2, p. 111.

for China health for its serious technical discussion, financial support by the government, and the political commitment by top leadership.

The problems in the Chinese health sector have occurred because the initial reforms were driven from the requirements of the macro economy, rather than through a consideration of health policy. These economic reforms have led not only to problems of health care access, cost, and quality, but also to loss of trust in the health sector. The concern, and need, for revenue generation overrode traditional moral orientation. The limited regulatory frameworks, coupled with underqualified and underpaid regulators, resulted in a true laissez-faire market for health care.

Current reforms aim to remove financial barriers to access, with particular attention to the poor. Intergovernmental financial transfers are a necessary step in order to exert a common policy framework in a market economy. Government financing, however, is an insufficient response. The restoration of trust and legitimacy of the health system requires measures from government that redress equity concerns. The re-establishment of trust at the level of the clinical encounter requires development of informal regulation approaches, affected through social institutions that have yet to be realised.

To focus on the equity dimensions of current health policies, Benchmarks of Fairness[50] could be usefully adapted to the Chinese reforms. The benchmarks in Table 4 would provide a useful framework for ensuring a balanced set of policy measures are adopted, rather than a singular focus on financing. Making monitoring data available to the community will further enhance citizen participation and restoration of trust.

Table 4: Benchmarks of Fairness[51]

OBJECTIVES OF FAIRNESS	BENCHMARK
Equity	Intersectoral public health
	Financial barriers to equitable access
	Non-financial barriers to access
	Comprehensiveness of benefits and tiering
	Equitable financing
Efficiency	Efficacy, efficiency and quality improvement
	Administrative efficiency
Accountability	Democratic accountability and empowerment
	Patient and provider autonomy

As there is no model of successful health reform in the world, health development and reform in China may avail itself for critical review by the world. Moving into the future, in the context of new policy reform measures, the question will have to be raised about whether old policy institutions (and health care system design) remain appropriate in the new economic and social context. In the days of the planned economy, the health system was run as a

---

50   N. Daniels, W. Flores, et al., "An evidence-based approach to benchmarking the fairness of health sector reform in developing countries." *Bull World Health Org.* (2005) 7, p. 7-14.
51   *Ibid.*

command-and-control system. In a socialist market economy, given a public/private mix, what policy tools are needed, especially if health and social equity are to be improved? Who participates in the governance of the health system and how will a variety of voices be heard? If changes do not occur in the policy process and the governance arrangements, what will be the cost to society and economy? The answers to many of these questions cannot yet be written but only when there is a consciousness about equity, participation, and trust in public institutions can these issues start to be addressed.

Chapter 12.

Access to Health Care in Korea

Minah Kang Kim

Introduction

The year 2007 was the 30th year since the inception of the National Health Insurance (NHI) system in Korea. During the past 30 years, Korea has built an impressively comprehensive health security system. Now, nearly everyone in the population is insured under the NHI,[1] or the Medical Aid.[2] Yet, it is noteworthy that in a recent conference that was held to celebrate the 30th anniversary, much attention was focused on the problems of inadequate and inequitable access to health services in the current Korean health care system.

With a universal social insurance system, in which everyone has a mandatory coverage, it is surprising as to why there are still such problems of inadequacies. In most of the health systems, universal access is usually considered as a fundamental feature of the health care systems to ensure necessary access and coverage for their population, and therefore, was considered as an important objective for a health system to pursue. The EU Charter of Fundamental Rights (Article 35) specifies that "everyone has the right of access to preventive health care and the right to benefit from medical treatment under the conditions established by national laws and practices." Likewise, in Korea, where nationals are mandated to be insured under the NHI (or the Medical Aid for the poor), universal access to health care is guaranteed by law.

However, what is seen on the surface may not necessarily represent the reality underneath. The Health ACCESS report[3] astutely interprets this discrep-

---

[1] The National Health Insurance (NHI) program of Korea is one of the major parts of the Korean social insurance system. The NHI, under the supervision of the Korean Ministry of Health and Welfare, is expected to guarantee the access to necessary health care for the Korean patients. Insurance benefits are provided by reimbursing private entities under contract with the National Health Insurance Corporation (NHIC). Enrolment is mandatory for Koreans residing in the Korean territory. As of December 2007, the system covered about 47,820,000 out of 49,672,000 people (96.3%).

[2] The Medical Aid, as a part of the Korean public assistance program, is a public insurance program, which covers health care costs for people who are indigent or belong to the low-income brackets. As of December 2007, the system covered about 1,852,000 (3.7%) of the national population.

[3] The report examines access to health care issues and formal cross-border arrangements for health care among the 10 member states of the European Union (EU). The states examined

ancy by pointing to the differences between coverage and access. When we perceive the term "universal" coverage, we assume that access to health care is protected within the system, considering that "coverage" and "access" are identical. However, when we have a deeper look into the reality, we can find that in many cases "universal coverage" and "guaranteed access" are not always synonymous. We can detect numerous barriers to access services, which may exist in a system of universal coverage.

Korea is a good example. Even with the universal health insurance scheme, a large proportion of patients still report that high medical bills are intense burden for them.[4] Some critical services are not covered in the benefit package,[5] and cost sharing is still at a burdensomely high rate for many people. As a result, on an average, a patient's out-of-pocket expenses amount to about half of the total health care costs. Geographical distribution of services is not well coordinated as some have greater difficulty in accessing health care than the others. Furthermore, lack of coordination in organizing and operating the delivery system results in other hurdles to access, such as long waiting lists to the services in tertiary hospitals. Despite equal entitlement, unequal access to necessary health care services and the resulting consequences in the health status and mortality have been frequently documented in various studies.

Equally significant is the presence of universal coverage that has distracted our attention from the fact that our system still has a coverage gap – population groups in the so-called "dead zone." People with income just above the poverty line, consequently are not eligible for the Medical Aid programs and experience serious barriers to accessing the necessary health care services. In addition, people with uncertain residential status (refugees and failed asylum seekers) as well as illegal immigrants remain without coverage and adequate access to health care.

The goal of this study was to analyze the past developments and the current status of the health care system, with respect to the health care access in South Korea. The study begins with a general discussion regarding the access to health care from a theoretical perspective and provides a framework for subsequent analyses. Consequently, several indicators that measure the access to health care are discussed in this study. After a brief overview of the Korean health system as a policy environment, the current status of access to health care is analyzed. Finally, the conclusion section presents the overall assessment of health care access in the Korean health care system, along with a discussion on the remaining issues and future challenges to the system.

---

in the study are Austria, Belgium, France, Germany, Hungary, Ireland, Italy, the Netherlands, Poland, and the United Kingdom (focusing on England and Northern Ireland).

4   In a survey (Suh et al. 2007) comprising a nationally represented sample of 2000 Koreans, 40% of the respondents said that the medical bills were serious economic burden for them. About 54% reported that both out-patient and in-patient bills were unduly high for them.

5   In the same survey, 60% of the respondents agreed that many medical treatments and services were not covered under the NHI scheme.

"Access to care" as a policy and statutory issue

Since the inception of compulsory medical insurance system in 1977, health policy agenda in Korea was inordinately focused on the universalization of the NHI scheme. In 1977, the Korea NHI system started with a compulsory medical insurance system for large businesses hiring 500 or more workers and achieved the universal coverage in 1989, only after 12 years from its inception. In July 2003, separated health insurance funds between the employees and self-employed insurance programs were fully integrated, completing the structural and substantive integration of the system. Despite the remarkable achievement, the system is still considered as incomplete in guaranteeing adequate and equitable access to health care services and fulfilling the statuary promise of "protecting the citizen's health".

A part of the reason for this gap may be due to the frequent misunderstandings of considering coverage and access as identical concepts. So far, the policy community in Korea has been focused on the expansion of insurance coverage, first in population coverage and then recently, in benefit coverage, based on the assurance that a universal public insurance coverage would guarantee adequate and equitable access to care for everyone. However, Peabody et al. (1995), in their evaluation of the Korean health care system aptly commented that "since health coverage is virtually universal in Korea, the critical issue of how well their system functions is more easily answered by looking at access rather than coverage. Looking at access, several groups appear to be underserved." In accordance with their statement, we can observe that despite the universal insurance scheme, a significant proportion of populations are underserved, namely people below the poverty line, those who live in the rural areas, as well as the elderly group.

The Health ACCESS report indicates that such confusion on this issue is not unique, but commonly observed, stating that:

> "On the basis of the broadly defined term 'universal' coverage, access has often been assumed to exist, on the basis that 'coverage' and 'access' are identical. However, 'coverage' and 'access' are not the same, and barriers – or more specifically 'hurdles' – to access services may exist despite the presence of universal coverage."

The report further indicates that even in the presence of universal coverage, access to health care may not be guaranteed owing to various reasons, such as exclusion of some necessary services in the benefit package, unavailability of services even if listed in the benefit packages, burdensome cost-sharing policies, geographical barriers to the services, and organizational and operational barriers like waiting lists.

Moreover, it appears that the little attention given to the issue of adequate and equitable access to care in the Korean policy communities also arises from the current practice of defining the concept of "access to care" in narrow terms. An expanded definition encompasses multiple dimensions, including comprehensive benefit package, lack of or low economic burden, minimal geographical barriers, etc. By applying the inclusive concept of access, Mossialos' (2007) diagnosis on the Korean health care system illustrates a similar occurrence, which draws our attention. In his evaluation of the Korean health system in three dimensions (width, depth, and height), the system was described as the one with a *wide* coverage of the population, a *shallow* benefit provision, and a *high* cost-sharing element.

In Korea, the citizens' right for their health is entitled by the Constitution, which states that "The health of all citizens is protected by the State."[6] The Basic Law on Health and Medicine Article 10 also declares that all citizens have the rights for their health to be protected by the State and their right to health shall not be discriminated based on gender, age, social status, religion, and economic status. In the same law, Article 4 quotes that both the State and the local government are responsible for fulfilling the basic medical needs equally among the citizens. At the same time, the State and the local governments should plan and implement policy plans to provide adequate medical services to the medically vulnerable population and particularly to the elderly, people with disabilities, workers, students, women, and children.[7] Also, the State and the local governments should plan adequate and equal distribution of medical resources across regions[8] and over a specific time.[9]

At least by law, every Korean citizen has guaranteed access to and benefit from health care services, regardless of their social, economic, and regional position. As described in the following section, this account however is superficially accurate but potentially misleading. An even more fundamental problem here is that despite the entitlement, we lack social consensus on what constitutes the "adequate and equal" access to "necessary" health care services. Still, not much attention is given to how we define "adequate" or "equal" access to medical services, or in understanding what the "necessary" health care services are.

Indicators to measure access

In this section, the current status of access to health care services is evaluated with a set of indicators. The systematical evaluation of the size and changing nature of access problems, their causes, and their effects allow us to move beyond the often quoted and blanket description of insurance coverage, and suggest what we should specifically do to achieve the goal of adequate and equal access. Particularly, indicators that are based on multiple dimensions of access allow us to focus on conditions of the hidden part of the society, predominantly among the vulnerable groups.

In this section, accessibility was evaluated along the three points on the health care provision continuum – structures, utilization, and outcomes. First, the structural aspect of a health care system, such as population coverage for health insurance, benefit coverage, cost-sharing arrangements, and geographi-

---

6   Constitution Article 36: Marriage, Family, Mothers, Health. For complete description, please refer to http://www.servat.unibe.ch/icl/.
7   The Basic Law on Health and Medicine Article 45, No. 1.
8   *Ibid.*
9   *Ibidem* and No 2.

cal barriers were examined.[10] Second, the access to care was indirectly measured by the utilization of health care services – how much and what services were used, and whether used in adequate and equitable patterns or not. Due to data limitation, it was hard to discern the access to appropriate services, determining whether specific services and treatments were adequately provided in both qualitative and quantitative terms, and hence, was excluded from this study. Instead, recent accretion of studies on inequality in the amount of medical utilization was cited. Also, survey responses to "unmet needs" and "delayed care" were used to evaluate "perceived" access to necessary services. Though the assessment of access with survey responses was criticized for its subjectivity, it was frequently used, because people's real experiences as well as apprehension and worries about potential adversities due to illness are well captured with these measures.[11] Finally, to observe the consequences of inadequate and inequitable access to health care in a system, trends of and changes in inequity in health status, both nationally and between groups with different socio-economic status were evaluated. In addition, to assess economic consequences due to inadequate protection, recent studies on catastrophic health expenditure were also cited.

The health care system in Korea

The Korean health care system is characterized by the unique combination of health care service provision and health financing. Based on the historical and cultural heritage of individual responsibility for health and family loyalty, as well as the increasing public demands for better protection from unexpected illnesses, a unique system was developed where health services are provided by commercial sectors and financed by semi-commercial (or public/private mix) mechanism. In Table 1, we can observe a pattern of service provision and financing that follows Esping Andersen's classification of the welfare states (Esping-Andersen 1990). The public financing of private service provision is commonly observed among the so-called Christian democratic countries. A combination of public financing with public service delivery is found among the socio-democratic countries. The public–private mix in both financing and delivery is a common practice among the liberal states like the USA and the Netherlands.

---

[10]   In the Health ACCESS report, access is defined in terms of six barriers: population coverage, benefit coverage, cost-sharing, geographical barriers, organizational barriers, and utilization of services. I took the report's approach, but organizational barriers like waiting list was not included in this analysis, as it is a relatively minor problem in the Korean health care system. Details of each indicator follow in the next section.

[11]   In the USA, a number of systematic surveys including the MEPS (Medical Expenditure Panel Surveys), the CTS (Community Tracking Surveys), and the NHIS (National Health Interview Studies) include questions on "unmet needs" and "delayed care" as subjective measures of access to care.

Table 1 The Categorization of OECD Health Care Systems: By How It Is Financed and Who Provides the Services

		Service provision		
		Public	Mix	Private
Financing	Public	Ireland, Spain, Denmark, Finland, Portugal, Norway, Sweden, Italy, UK	Belgium, France, Germany, Austria, Luxemburg, Japan, New Zealand	
	Mix		US, Canada, Netherlands, Greece	Korea

Source: (Kim 2007).
Note: Financing scheme of a system is classified as "public" if more than 70% of the funding is obtained from public sources. Similarly, service provision is classified as "private" if more than 70% of hospitals in the country are operated by private providers.

Korea is a unique example of universal health insurance system where service delivery entirely relies on the private sector while financing is in the form of public and private mix. In Korea, in terms of service provision, most health care services are rendered by private providers. More than 90% of the hospital beds in Korea are in private health facilities. Ownership of the hospitals and clinics are almost exclusive to the private sector. In most of the cases, physicians own as well as manage these facilities. Public providers play a residual role. Public provision of services is very limited, targeting the most disadvantaged.

With respect to financing, Korea maintains a mandatory public health insurance system, where the entire population is covered under one public insurance scheme. The country has achieved the universal public health insurance in a remarkably short period of time, just over a decade, between 1977 and 1989 (Figure 1). The concept of the NHI system originated from the Medical Insurance Act, which was legislated in 1963. During that period, Korea was a poor under-developed country with limited financial resources, where the per-capita GNP was still under US$100, and consequently, the system was started on a voluntary basis with firms having 300 or more employees. Later, in July 1977, the government launched the universal medical insurance by making large businesses that hire 500 or more workers to join the scheme. With gradual, but rapid, extensions of coverage to smaller firms and other sections of the population – from large to medium and small-sized companies, from employed to self-employed individuals, and from cities to rural areas, the medical security for the whole population was completed in 1989. Before 1998, there were 227 regional medical insurance associations and 139 workplace medical insurance associations, in addition to government and private school medical insurance associations. By 2000, after long and painful periods of debates, the system was merged into a single insurer system, the National Health Insurance Corporation (NHIC), thus structurally ending the era of multiple insurers. Finally, in July 2003, separated health insurance funds between employee and self-employed insurance programs were integrated, completing the structural and substantive integration of the system.

Achieving a major policy system in such a short period, however, almost always involves systemic vulnerabilities. In Korea, this rapid adoption of the universal health insurance system with limited economic and human resources brought long-term consequences, such as heavy dependence on the private sector for service provision and funding. Under the tightly controlled fees (that are considered necessary to prevent rapid increase in the health care expenditure) with fee-for-service payment mechanism, private providers naturally brought the expansion of an exclusively curative health system – increasing the frequency of office visits and hospital admission as well as the intensity of services without evidences of clinical effectiveness or cost-efficiency.

Figure 1 Number of Years to Accomplish Universal Coverage

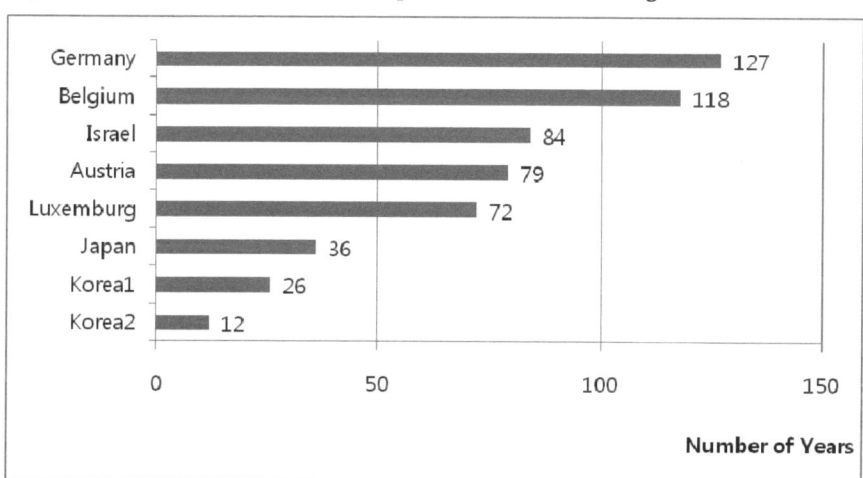

Source: (Carrin and James 2005)
Note: Korea1 defines the years between 1963 and 1989. As described earlier, in 1963, the NHI systems started on a voluntary basis. Korea2 defines the number of years between 1977 and 1989. The year of 1977 is when the mandatory NHI was implemented.

Also, private providers with strong economic incentives tend to focus on high profit-generating services and high-cost curative care. Some of those services are not covered under the NHI package and thus accessible only for those who can afford to pay. In an environment where expensive medical technologies proliferate and curative health services are predominant, coupled with higher user fees and shallow coverage, the health system gradually skewed away from fulfilling the needs of the poor and low-income groups and deterred the expansion of preventive and promotive care. However, once established, this process becomes difficult to reverse, owing to the vested interest embedded in the political and economic structure of health provision. In particular, powerful professional associations play key roles in maintaining the current system.

Table 2 Number of Caesarean Operations among Selected OECD Countries (per 1000 live births)

Country	Rate
Korea	352.3 (2004)
Belgium	177.6 (2004)
Denmark	194.4 (2005)
Finland	163.0 (2002)
Italy	374.5 (2004)
Mexico	393 (2005)
Netherlands	136.4 (2004)
Norway	152.0 (2004)
Sweden	172.0 (2003)
UK	233 (2005)
US	291.0 (2004)
OECD Average	239.3 (2005)

Source: OECD Health Data, 2007

Furthermore, with respect to the compensation of low reimbursement rates to the providers, the health provision in the Korean health care system has been minimally regulated. For example, the government implicitly permitted the practice of charging special consultation fees (extra payments for specialists and senior doctors) and frequent prescriptions of services and treatments outside the NHI benefit package that aid in high-profit generation. The lack of planning and regulation of health care provision brought extreme proliferation of the purchase and diffusion of medical technology in Korea. In 2005, the number of CTs (computerized tomographs) per 1,000,000 persons reached 32.2 (an increase from 12.2 in 1990) and MRIs taken per 1,000,000 persons increased from 1.4 in 1990 to 12.1 in 2005. This made Korea a leading country in terms of medical technology adoption along with Japan. Another example is the extremely high rate of caesarean operations in Korea (Table 2). Among the selected Organization for Economic Cooperation and Development (OECD) countries, Korea ranked the third highest, after Mexico and Italy. The alarming increase in the volume and intensity of both the insured and uninsured services are responsible for the current distorted mix of medical care for treatments, which contributes to the rapid increase in the health care expenditure as well as heavy financial burden on patients. Overall, while the Korean health care system expanded and evolved ostensibly for the last 30 years, the system is still denounced as "partially successful," for not being effective in addressing the intrinsic problems of high patient burden and shallow coverage.

Current status and past trends of access to care in Korea

Population coverage

With a universal and compulsory public health insurance scheme, the Korean NHI system covers the whole population. According to the National Health Insurance Act, which was promulgated in 1999, "Korean nationals who reside in the country," except those who are specified, "shall become the insured or the dependents of the health insurance" (Chapter II. Article 5). As of 2006, the total number of people covered by NHI exceeded 47 million, covering 96.3% of the total population. The remaining 3.7%, about 1.7 million from the low-income households, are covered by the Medical Aid program (Table 3). The insured persons under the NHI program are classified into two categories: the employed insured and the self-employed insured. The law categorizes the workers and employers of all workplaces (except the daily-wage earners with less than 80 hours per month of employment), the public officials, and the school employees and their dependents as employed.

It is fair to state that after the inception of NHI system, there has been a remarkable improvement in the accessibility to medical care and reduction in the burden of medical costs for the population. The number of people who were covered by the public insurance increased from 8.8% of the total population in 1977 to 24.0% in 1980, and reached 93.9% in 1990. In the year 2000, the coverage was 96–97%. A research conducted in 1975 by the Korean Development Institute (KDI) reported that the percentage of people who had disease, but could not use any medical services, reached up to 40% nationally. After the implementation of the universal health insurance, the medical utilization increased at a striking rate. Comparison of statistics from the survey conducted in 1975 and 2006 revealed that over the past 30 years, the percentage of patients who could not get necessary medical care was reduced from 40% to 7% of the respondents.

Table 3 Population Coverage of Korea NHI (Unit: 1000 persons, 2006)

	Insurer	The insured	Number of persons	Proportion
Total population			49,238	
National Health Insurance Program	Sub-total		47,410	96.3%
	National Health Insurance Corporation (NHIC)	Employee insured Self-employed insured	28,445 18,965	57.7% 38.6%
Medical Aid Program	Local Government	Low-income households	1,829	3.7%

Source: MOHW White Paper, 2006

Nevertheless, the actual protection of access to necessary health care of some vulnerable groups is still not complete. Most notably, there are people in the "dead zone" (gaps in coverage) of social protection, because of their inability to pay the insurance premium. It has been reported that a considerable proportion of the non-eligible poor households (just over the poverty line and thus, not eligible for Medical Aid, or those who are reported to have supporting family member, but in reality cannot get any support) or potentially poor households (currently over the poverty line, but due to their medical expenditure move to the poverty status) are not protected with adequate access to care when in need.

For example, according to the National Health Insurance Act Article 48(3), "The Corporation may not provide the insurance benefits to the insured who has been delinquent in paying contributions... until such a time as when the contributions is paid in full." In 2006, about 2 million households were reported delinquent for more than 3 months in paying their insurance premiums. According to a survey with people whose premium payments were more than 3 months delinquent, about 68.4% of them reported economic burdens as the main reason for the delinquency. About 34% of them reported that they could not visit doctors or pharmacies and 25.5% said they had to pay all the expenses out-of-pocket. Recently, based on a survey of households with delinquent premium payment, Lee (2007) argued that the premium subsidy for the poor and low-income group would increase the health care access to a disproportionate degree in the population.

Also, the eligibility criteria for the Medical Aid program as a safety net for health are often criticized for not being inclusive enough for the program functions. Furthermore, the administrative process for becoming the beneficiaries of the Medical Aid program is known to be complicated and poorly coordinated.[12] In the current system, only 3.7% of the total population is covered by the Medical Aid program, while the proportion of people under the 120% of the poverty level is estimated to be between 10% and 15%, thus the program covers only between 1/3 and 1/5 of the population in need.

In recent times, lack of access to health care for illegal immigrants has also become a policy concern. The number of foreigners and immigrants has increased at a fast rate, from 50,000 (0.1% of the population) in 1990 to 910,149 (1.88%) in 2006, excluding the undocumented. Currently, foreigners can be covered with the NHI program after fulfilling certain conditions for enrolment. In 2005, it was reported that 215,198 foreigners were covered, in which about 143,833 were self-insured and 55,238 were employee insured. Despite the recent changes in law in 2006, which directed compulsory insurance coverage for the employers or the employees of workplaces in Korea, the proportion of the insured among foreigners are estimated to stop at about 60% among those who are eligible.

---

[12] As the Medical Aid program is a part of the Minimum Livelihood Protection Program of the Korean welfare system for the poor, the program is operated and managed separately from the NHI. Therefore, determination of the eligibility of the Medical Aid program beneficiaries is carried out by local governments, while management and operation of the system are the responsibilities of the NHIC.

Benefit coverage

Having started with a policy that holds the priority of expanding the population coverage at the expense of comprehensive benefit coverage, the adequacy of the NHI benefit coverage has been one of the reoccurring policy agenda. In social health insurance, the benefit package is not merely a list of services and treatments that are covered under the insurance. But, it is a specification of what constitutes "the entitlements to health care for citizens", and is a key indicator to determine whether the NHI truly fulfils its major roles in guaranteeing the appropriate level of access to necessary health care for the insured.

According to Article 39 of the National Health Insurance Act, the standards of health insurance benefits, regarding methods of health care, procedures, scope and ceiling, etc., are determined by the regulations of the Ministry of Health and Welfare. The benefits are standardized and are the same for everyone. There are no differences between the benefits for the NHI and the Medical Aid program. Basically, services for diseases that do not cause difficulties in the daily activity or at work (such as plastic surgery, warts, acne, impotency, and simple snoring) are excluded from the list (Article 39(3)). However, in reality, a number of treatments and services that are necessary for medical recovery are not yet included in the current benefit coverage, thus posing a serious burden on patients and their families.

According to the law, the out-of-coverage services are divided into two categories: "authorized out-of-coverage" and "discretionary out-of-coverage." "Authorized out-of-coverage" services are those that are found to be medically necessary and cost-efficient but are not included in the NHI benefit package due to fiscal reasons. Examples include the preventive services, extra-charge rooms, some oriental medicines, etc. "Discretionary out-of-coverage" refers to the medical services and treatments that are not yet authorized to be provided to the patients. Examples are the "off-label use" of drugs and new technologies or procedures, for which safety or cost-effectiveness is not validated.

In Korea, decisions about which services and treatments are to be included in the benefit package have been made on the basis of fiscal and political reasons, rather than based on cost-effectiveness evidences, especially in the early years of the NHI.[13] As aptly indicated by Ikegamy in his comparative observation of the Japan and Korean systems, the coverage decisions that are not based on objective evidences are vulnerable, chiefly because providers can persuade patients by stating that better outcomes are likely if they purchase out-of-coverage services. As these uncovered services are often more expensive and more profitable for the providers, this would cause heavy burden on patients who do not have enough understanding and knowledge to make their own judgment and consequently, follow their doctors' prescription and purchase the recommended out-of-coverage services.

---

[13]   It is said that the former authoritarian political regime had introduced NHI for the sake of political legitimization and welfare development (Kwon and Tchoe 2005). Therefore, the government preferred low contribution rates for the sake of rapid extension of population coverage, and to minimize the potential burden of health insurance on the industry and the economy.

Table 4 A Trend of Patient Out-of-Pocket Payments, By Provider Type (2004–2006)

Type	2004			2005			2006		
	Public share	Patient co-sharing	Out-of-service coverage	Public share	Patient co-sharing	Out-of-service coverage	Public share	Patient co-sharing	Out-of-service coverage
Total	61.3	23.1	15.6	61.8	22.5	15.7	64.3	22.4	13.3
Tertiary Hospitals	43.8	20.8	35.4	52.9	17.7	29.4	57.2	16.9	25.9
Large Hospitals	51.7	22.6	25.7	55.3	21.2	23.5	59.5	20.6	19.9
Hospitals	51.6	22.8	25.6	55.4	19.4	25.2	56.6	19.9	23.5
Clinics	67.5	24.3	8.2	64.4	23.6	12.0	69.1	22.8	8.1
Dental Hospital	22.2	16.9	60.9	35.7	24.3	12.0	23.6	15.5	60.8
Dental Clinics	38.3	15.5	46.2	47.5	19.9	32.6	45.4	19.6	35.0
Oriental Medicine Hospitals	20.6	9.4	70.0	28.6	13.9	57.5	31.9	12.0	56.1
Oriental Medicine Clinics	66.4	19.5	14.1	63.2	17.9	19.0	65.4	22.5	12.1
Pharmacy	73.0	25.0	2.0	70.8	26.5	2.7	71.5	27.1	1.4

Source: Choi, et al. 2007.

In a system of fee-for-service payment scheme and a tightly controlled fee schedule for the services, the problem is that providers who have strong incentives continuously develop such out-of-coverage services (whose prices are not controlled, and thus, usually expensive and highly profitable) and recommend their patients to purchase them. This becomes a more serious problem when there are no systematic ways to determine the safety, effectiveness, and efficiencies of the new technologies and services based on scientific evidences, and therefore, patients do not have information resources to make valid judgment.

Table 4 shows data from surveys that were conducted by the NHIC with health services providers on out-of-package benefits and services between 2004 and 2006. As observed in Table 4, the total coverage by the NHI somewhat increased between 2004 and 2006. At the same time, the proportion of payments for the out-of-coverage services was reduced by 2.3 percentage points, largely due to the policy changes that included hospital meal costs in the NHI benefit packages in 2006. With respect to service types, the coverage rate for hospitals was about 57–59% and for clinics services, it was 69.1%. On the other hand, coverage rates for dental services and oriental medicine were disturbingly low. In 2006, the patient out-of-pocket burden in using dental services and oriental medicine treatment remained high and amounted up to 76.4% for dental hospital, 54.6% for dental clinics, 68.1% for oriental medicine hospitals, and 34.6% for oriental medicine clinics.

In terms of determining what constituted the patient burdens for out-of-coverage services, the survey revealed that after the policy change in the NHI benefit package in June 2006, by including the hospital meal costs, the composition was changed dramatically between the year 2005 and 2006 (Table 5). For in-patient services, the proportion of hospital meal costs became an ignorable size, while the relative proportion of special consultation fees were doubled.

Special consultation fees refer to the additional fees over and above those set by the fee schedule for a visit to senior doctors. This practice has been under continuous criticism and concerns for several reasons. First of all, in theory, while these fees should be applied only to a few senior distinguished doctors, they are now applied to a large proportion of doctors. Currently, the proportion of "special" doctors has reached to 80% of the total doctors. Even worse is that patients are often charged for the fee without their knowledge. While in theory, patients are allowed to choose regular doctors and need not pay the special consultation fees, in reality, numerous cases have been reported where patients had to pay such fees, sometimes owing to lack of other choices and at other times without their knowledge. Special consultation fees range from additional 20% to 100% of the treatment item cost. In total, the fees amount up to US$400 million (€400 billion), which is about 7–8% of the nation's total hospital revenues. As shown in Table 5, the proportion increased by almost seven folds for out-patient treatments between 2004 and 2006.

Table 5 A Trend of the Composition of Patient Out-of-Pocket Payment (2004–2006)

Type	In-patient			Out-patient		
	2004	2005	2006	2004	2005	2006
Extra-charge rooms	23.5	22.6	23.3	-	-	-
Special consultation fees	13.1	17.6	25.9	3.2	5.1	21.8
Hospital meal*	20.7	19.8	0.6	-	-	-
Injection	6.7	4.9	10.7	10.3	8.4	6.4
Surgery(IP)/ Medicine (OP)	3.6	3.1	4.6	5.1	11.0	4.1
Lab tests	5.2	4.6	6.6	18.8	23.1	13.4
MRI	5.4	2.4	3.4	5.6	5.1	12.8
Ultrasound	11.0	5.2	6.4	24.4	19.3	20.4
Materials (IP)/ CT and X-ray (OP)	5.1	13.9	11.1	7.0	7.0	1.8
Others	5.8	5.9	7.4	25.6	21.0	19.3
Total	100%	100%	100%	100%	100%	100%

Source: Choi, et al. 2007.
*Hospital meal cost became a part of the NHI benefit package in 2006.

For in-patient services, extra-charge room still takes a large proportion (about a quarter) of the patient's payment. Part of the reason for this is the insufficient number of regular rooms in the Korean hospitals. In a survey, 71.5% of the respondents who used extra-charge rooms reported that they had to stay in such rooms against their will, owing to the shortage of regular rooms.

Co-payment arrangements

As in most of the other systems, under the Korean NHI scheme, the patients are required to pay a certain proportion of their total payment as co-payment for the insured medical services, together with a non-trivial amount for the out-of-coverage services. In general, for out-patient services, patients have to pay 50% of the treatment cost that occurred in tertiary care and general hospital, 40% for hospital services, and 30% for out-patient services at clinics and out-patient drugs (Table 6). For in-patient services, patients have to bear 20% of the total in-patient treatment cost. Considering that the average number of out-patient care visits is significantly high in Korea, which was 14.13 times per person in 2006, the patients' co-payment can be very high, especially for those with catastrophic diseases. Consequentially, the Korean health care system depends on a high share of private funding. Despite the steady increase in the spending on health over the past decade (from 38% of total health spending in 1990 to 53% in 2005), the share of public spending on health is still well below the OECD average of 73%. In terms of the public share of health expenditure, the system ranks at the bottom among the OECD countries.

A national survey conducted in 2006 on the patient's out-of-pocket payment revealed that out of the 38.7% of the total patients' out-of-pocket payment, 23.1% was spent as patients' co-payment (set by insurance terms) and the other 15.6% was the payment for out-of-coverage services. For the in-patient services, the patients' payments for the uncovered services amounted up to 28.7%, which is higher than the patients' co-payment percentage of 16.4%. However, patients with catastrophic diseases bear heavier burden. On an average, they pay 48.6% of their total payment out of their own pockets.

In an effort to alleviate patient burden, recent changes were made to lower the co-payment rates for specific groups of patients or conditions. For instance, for children under 6 years of age, the co-payment rate is 21% for out-patient visits (which is 70% of adult rate). The elderly, over 65 years old, pay a fixed amount of krw 1500 (US$1.5) for clinic visits and krw 1200 (US$1.2) for pharmacy visits. To reduce burdens on patients with certain catastrophic diseases (cancer, heart disease, and cerebrovascular disease), in 2005, the government reduced the in-patient co-payment rate from 20% to 10%. In addition, the government introduced the "Co-payment Ceiling System" in 2005, to protect patients from excessive co-payment. Under this system, patients are exempted from paying further co-payments when the total amount exceeds a certain threshold (krw 2 million, US$2,000) within 6 months.

Table 6 Patient Co-payment Rate

Health care service facility	Co-payment sharing
In-patient	20% of total treatment cost
Tertiary care hospital	Per-visit consultation fee + 50% of the treatment cost
General hospital	50% of (treatment cost + per-visit consultation fee)
Hospital	40% of (treatment cost + per-visit consultation fee)
Clinic	30% of the total treatment cost
Pharmacy	Prescription: 30% of the total treatment cost Without prescription: 30% of the total treatment cost

Source: (NHIC 2007).

Despite these efforts, there are several problems that still remain in the current co-payment scheme. First, for the low-income individuals, the current threshold of krw 2 million, which was recently reduced from krw 3 million (in August 2007), is still too high. A more serious problem is that the ceiling system only applies to the co-payment part, but not to the patients' out-of-pocket payments that are incurred from the out-of-coverage services. As mentioned earlier, about 40% of the total out-of-pocket payments come from the out-of-coverage services.

Furthermore, with rising concerns on fiscal sustainability of the NHI system, policy changes are moving towards retrenchment. As an example, the co-payment rate for the hospital meal cost, which was 20% when it became an NHI benefit in 2006, was raised up to 50% in January 2008. Co-payment for in-patient services for children under the age of 6 years was originally suggested to be zero, but was later increased to 10%.

The co-sharing scheme is expected to work as a device to prevent patients' moral hazard – excessive utilization of medical services. Under the current system, in addition to high co-payment rates, patients often pay an even higher amount for services and fees that are not covered under the NHI scheme. These prices, accumulated here and there, create serious burdens on households for various incidents of care, especially for the most vulnerable populations, such as the unemployed, seasonal workers, the poor, and the elderly people. Considering that the main goal of the social health insurance is the risk transfer to protect the patients in need, by translating out-of-pocket payments to prepayment of defined contributions, the current situation of high patient burden at the point of services makes us wonder if preventing moral hazard is a more critical issue than providing adequate protection. To maintain financial sustainability of the system, discouraging frivolous utilization is a policy objective that cannot be ignored. Nevertheless, to fulfil the core goal of the social insurance system, it is necessary to overcome the insurmountable barrier to health care access. Even if the patients' co-sharing was effective in fulfilling its objective to ensure parsimonious usage of the health care resources as well as to contain public expenditure on health, its effectiveness should be considered in balance with the primary goal of a universal social health insurance program – the protection of vulnerable members of the community with equitable financing and appropriate access to medical care when necessary. Current application of the out-of-pocket payments also raises equity concerns, as the scheme is regressive – paying at the same level regardless of patients' income – resulting in an unequal distribution of the financial burden of illness. Recent proposals include adjusting the ceiling threshold of the out-of-pocket payment based on the income level, to correct regressive feature of the current scheme by setting annual income-related caps on individuals' co-payments.

Geographical barriers

Unequal geographical distribution of medical facilities can also constitute a discriminatory barrier to access to health care. In Korea, government regulation of the supply-side of health care services is still at a minimal level. Other than public health centers, geographical distribution of medical facilities are not centrally planned, but left to private providers. The only requirement governing the opening of hospitals is the minimal number of beds and departments.

This "laissez-faire" policy for the private medical care sector is attributed to be responsible for the skewed distribution of health resources across different regions, particularly between the urban and rural areas. About 92.1% of physicians and 89.6% of hospital beds are concentrated in cities, leading to unequal access to health care services between urban and rural residents. In particular, 44.2% of the medical institutions are located in Seoul metropolitan area and about 81% are concentrated in the six largest cities.

For patients with catastrophic diseases, unequal distribution of health care facilities poses more serious problems. For example, for cancer patients who are particularly in need of timely and long-term treatment, geographical access is critical. In addition, as the treatment involves long-term care, spatial proximity is critical for the patients' family members as well. A study that used the National Cancer Incidence Databases in 1999 and 2002 showed that there were significant regional variations in the regional self-sufficiency of cancer patients. While the accessibility of cancer patients in metropolitan areas was high, some areas had very low level of access, ranging between 13% and 27%. Also, unequal regional distribution of emergency medical centers has been a continuous policy issue. A recent study, which examined the distribution of emergency medical centers in Korea, found a spatial disparity of these centers. On a more serious note, disproportionate disparities in the human capital, facility, and equipment were also identified.

As in most of the other OECD countries, in Korea, the public network of primary health care facilities, including health centers, health sub-centers, and primary health care posts, was established to fill the gaps in private provision in the underserved rural and fishery areas. However, their roles remain insignificant (OECD 2003) and their main activities are limited to specific areas, such as disease prevention and health promotion, vaccination, management of communicable diseases, maternal and child health care, and a few basic curative services. Also, individuals who can afford to pay higher out-of-pocket payments and special treatment charges prefer treatment in private facilities. This may create a two-tier system based on affordability (private vs. public facilities). Maintaining quality and adequate resources within public facilities is an important issue to avoid wider disparities of access.

Consequences of inadequate and unequal access to care

Unmet needs and delayed care

Unmet needs are measured by subjective evaluation, usually using a survey with respondents. Although subjective measures are often criticized for its subjectivity, they help to measure how people perceive the deficiency between their needs and the actual utilization of medical services.

Various methods were used to measure the unmet needs. For example, the BRFSS, a federally funded survey, designed by the US Centers for Disease Control and Prevention (CDC) in collaboration with the state departments to monitor health-related behaviour and risk factors in the US population, used the following two questions to measure the inadequate access to doctor's care: 1) "a time during the last 12 months when you needed to see a doctor, but could not because of the cost," and 2) "not having visited a doctor for a routine checkup during the prior 2 years." In the Medical Expenditure Panel Survey (MEPS), which is a nationally represented survey conducted by the US Agency for Health Care Research and Quality (AHRQ) and the National Center for Health Statistics (NCHS), unmet needs were measured by asking the families if they "had difficulties or delays in obtaining health care" or "did not receive needed care for one or more family members."

In Korea, the National Health and Nutrition Survey, conducted by the Korea Institute for Health and Social Affairs, used a stratified multi-stage probability sample of South Korean households representing the civilian, non-institutionalized population and included a question on unmet health needs. In the survey, the respondents were asked whether "during the last 12 months, if there were times that they could not receive or delayed necessary care" and the "Main reasons for not receiving the necessary care." According to the 2005 survey ($N = 25, 215$), about 13.65% of the respondents reported experiences of unmet needs. Cost barrier was the most prevalent reason for unmet needs. Among the people who reported that they could not receive or had delayed care, about 49.72% said that it was due to economic reasons. Another study that analyzed the same data set showed that the occurrence of unmet needs was more prevalent among the lower income groups. The proportion of people with unmet needs was 33.3% among those aged between 40 and 64 years as well as in the lowest-income group, showing that about one-third of the respondents in the group could not receive the necessary care or delayed the care. A survey that was conducted in 2004 with 1800 families under or near the poverty line provided more detailed evidences on the inadequate access. According to that survey, the Medical Aid beneficiaries who were under the poverty line (17.9%), people who were under the poverty line but not Medical Aid beneficiaries (20.9%), and families within the 120% of the poverty line

(15.7%) reported that they could not visit doctors, because they could not afford it.

Inequality in health care service utilization

Equity in health care service utilization is an indicator that was frequently used in many studies to see if care was available for people according to their needs, rather than by willingness or ability to pay. In Korea, while inequalities in utilization are thought to exist across various population groups according to the socio-economic variables (income, employment status), demographic variables (age, gender, race), and geographic areas, there has not been much research conducted on this issue. Insurmountable difficulties lie primarily in the lack of good data sets. For example, the NHI administrative data or survey data have the typical problems of inaccuracy from over- or under-reporting. Another serious problem in estimating the inequality in utilization is the difficulties in controlling the medical needs. It is difficult to monitor whether disparities in utilization arise from the differences in the needs. The poor and low-income groups are often in the worse health status and thus, have greater needs for health services and tend to use more health care services. For valid interpretation, it is important to correctly measure the medical needs innate in the lower socio-economic groups. For example, Wagstaff and van Doorslear conducted a series of international comparison studies, based on the principle of horizontal equity ("people in equal need of care are treated equally, irrespective of characteristics such as income, place of residence, race, etc.") and estimated the degree of inequality in utilization by the income that remained after the standardization of measurable need differences. Variables like age, sex, self-reported general health, and the presence and degree of limitation of any chronic physical or mental health problem, illness or disability were used as the predictors of need for health care.

In Korea, Kwon et al. (2003)'s study employed the approach of van Doorslear et al., and summarized the degree of inequities in utilization with "HIwv Index."[14] They reported insignificant inequality in the usage of out-patient services and weak pro-poor inequalities (the poor were more likely to use) in the usage of in-patient services. However, they found that health care expenditure was higher among the rich, implying the presence of inequalities in utilization intensity. More recently, Kim and Choi (2007) also produced similar results of insignificant inequalities in the quantitative use, but found that the expenditure for each visit was significantly higher among the higher-income group. This pattern was more prominent among the older age groups.

---

[14] HIvw is a concentration index of the need-standardized utilization. When the HI index equals zero, it indicates horizontal equity: people in equal need (but at different incomes) are treated equally. When the index is positive, it indicates pro-rich inequity, and when it is negative, it indicates pro-poor inequity, signifying that lower-income people use more care than one would expect on the basis of the reported need (i.e., morbidity). For more detailed information, please refer to van Doorslaer and Masseria (2004), van Doorslaer, Masseria, and Koolman (2006), and van Doorslaer et al. (2000).

Inequity in health status

The Korean population is witnessing a continuing improvement in the health status over the past 20 years, reaching similar or even better levels than the OECD averages. Life expectancy at birth rose from 61.9 years in 1970 to 78.5 years in 2005, while infant and child mortality rates decreased from 45.0 among 1000 people in 1970 to 5.3 in 2002, which was almost at the same level as the OECD average (5.4 per 1000 people).

The extent to which better access to medical services actually contributes to health status improvement is not clear though. In fact, most studies have suggested that medical care services by themselves may have limited impact on the health of populations. For example, a study showed that only about 10–15% of deaths in the USA could be avoided with better quality and access to medical care. It is believed that the improved health in England over the previous 200 years mostly came from the improvements in food supplies and sanitary conditions than from medical interventions. Nevertheless, checking whether the gaps in health status between the groups with different socio-economic status are narrowed over the years are undeniably important policy questions to ask while studying the access issues.

In every nation, unequal health status is unavoidable to some extent. People are in different health status owing to many factors, including genetic, behavioural, cultural, and socio-economic differences among them. Therefore, how much inequity exists between groups and if the magnitude of inequity changes over time are the more relevant policy questions than determining whether unequal health status is present between the groups.

Inequity in mortality was one of the indicators that were most often studied. In a study with 759,665 Korean male public servants aged between 30 and 64 years, Song and Byeon (2000) found that the lowest SES group had a significantly higher risk of mortality from most causes, when compared with the highest SES group in the order of external cause avoidable, all cause, and non-avoidable mortality. Khang et al. (2004) using Korea's 1995 Census and 1995–2000 Death Certificate data found that graded educational differentials in mortality were observed among both sexes, with higher mortality rates related to lower educational attainment in most causes of death. In another study, using 10 years' (1990–2000) of data from the Census and Death Certificate data, as well as the Social Statistics Survey from Korea's National Statistical Office, Khang et al. (2004) reported that the relative level of socio-economic mortality inequality remained virtually unchanged in men and women in the past 10 years.

Catastrophic health expenditure

Health care cost is known to be one of the major contributing factors to the increase in poverty in many countries. When available health services are expensive at the point of delivery and when the financial protections are inadequate, the cost of illness pushes people into poverty and deprives their access to necessary health care. Protecting people from catastrophic economic burden is one of the most important goals of social insurance system.

Large health bills do not always result in catastrophic economic burden. A high medical cost may not represent catastrophic health expenditure if the bill does not cause heavy burden when the household has a good health insurance protection or is affluent enough to afford the high bill. On the other hand, even when the charges for medical services are modest, it can become a catastrophic expense, if the frequency of their use is sufficiently high. While there are different opinions on the threshold of defining the amount spent that would be catastrophic, Xu et al. (2003) suggests that at least 40% of the total household expenditure is being spent on medical care.

Recent studies on household health expenditure revealed that the catastrophic health expenditure is more prominent among the lower-income household in Korea. According to a survey that used data from the National Survey of Household Income and Expenditure, a Korean household, on an average, spent € 97,394 (about US$95) per month in 2005, which was about a twofold increase from the € 43,651 spent in 1985 (adjusted to the 2005 price), constituting 4.36% of their household expenditure. The economic burden from health care utilization is unequally distributed with respect to the income level. The low-income households spent a relatively higher share of household income on health services than the wealthy ones. Table 7 shows a trend of the proportion of households with catastrophic health expenditure. From the table, we can observe that initially, it may appear that the implementation of the NHI evidently lessened the economic burden from medical expenditure. In 1985, before the implementation of the NHI in 1989, the proportion of households with catastrophic health expenditure was 1.45%, and it went down to 0.43% in 1990. However, we can also detect that the percentage went up to 1.05% in 2005. The data also suggest that the health care expenditures pose a heavier burden on the lower-income groups. In 2005, among the group with the lowest income, 6.24% of the households experienced catastrophic medical expenditure, which is about six times higher than the average.

Table 7 A Trend of the Proportion of Households with Catastrophic Health Expenditure*

Household expenditure level	1985	1990	1995	2000	2005
Lowest	3.64%	1.76%	4.70%	3.60%	6.24%
2	2.34%	0.76%	1.28%	0.95%	2.08%
3	2.07%	0.25%	0.21%	0.76%	0.64%
4	1.04%	1.01%	0.21%	0.57%	0.32%
5	1.82%	0.25%	-	-	0.64%
6	0.78%	0.25%	0.21%	0.19%	0.16%
7	1.30%	-	-	0.38%	0.16%
8	0.26%	-	0.21%	0.19%	0.32%
9	1.30%	-	0.21%	-	-
10	-	-	-	-	-
Mean	1.45%	0.43%	0.70%	0.66%	1.05%
N	3854	3972	4689	5288	6257

Source: (Huh et al. 2008).
Note: Here, medical expenditure is composed of expenditure on drugs, medical services, and medical appliances. The ratios might be underestimated at least for two reasons: 1) the survey excluding households with one person, and 2) the survey failing to include rural areas before 2003.
*Catastrophic Health Expenditure is defined as being ≥40% of the total household expenditure, net of subsistence (food) expenditure.

While the incidence of household catastrophic medical spending is a good indicator to measure a health system's ability to protect its people from unexpected illnesses, it may not fully capture the impact of inadequate access, as many poor households may choose not to seek health care rather than becoming impoverished. As emphasized by Xu et al. (2003), heavy out-of-pocket payment has a potential dual effect, impoverishing some households that choose to seek health services and excluding others from seeking health care. Xu argues that the prepayment and risk-pooling mechanism, such as social insurance, rather than user fees at the point of need, will provide better protection to households from delaying or giving up necessary medical treatment.

Conclusion

The Korean health care system has been rapidly expanding. During the 1990s, the rate of growth in health expenditure was twofold higher than the average across the OECD countries. Between the years 2000 and 2005, the growth rate in health expenditure per capita in Korea reached 8.7% per year, while the OECD average was only 4.3%.

Despite the remarkable growth, there is still room for further expansion and refinement of the Korean health care system. The GDP percentage of health expenditure in Korea is still at the lowest level among the OECD countries. It has been only 30 years since the inception of NHI, and future framing and value finding of the system is more important than the past achievements or failures.

As a whole, indicators of access to personal health care services provide evidence of continuous progress over the past decade. However, even with the remarkable achievement in establishing the universal health insurance, persistent and better coordinated efforts are still needed to guarantee adequate or equitable access to necessary health care services. The successes in broadening the population coverage are counterbalanced by shallow benefit coverage and high patient co-payment. Underlying most of the access indicators investigated in this study is a growing division between the haves and the have-nots in the society. Protection of health is entitled as a constitutional right in Korea. The 30-year operation of the NHI system, nevertheless, demonstrated that such declaration can remain as a nominal concept than an enforceable right for some groups of people. With respect to geographical access, utilization and health status, the inegalitarian consequences regionally and by social groups are frequent.

In response to persistent demands for better protection, the Korean Government has recently taken several actions, through measures like strengthened benefit coverage, lowered consumer payments, and special coverage for people with catastrophic illnesses. Unfortunately, despite such efforts to expand access to health care, the prospect of meeting these ambitious plans is not bright. Programs to provide better protection to people with selected catastrophic diseases are stalled against the initial promise to expand the list to 10 diseases by 2008, owing to the political and technical difficulties in selecting the subsequent catastrophic diseases. Increasing concerns on fiscal stability has made the government plan to cover 80% of the hospital meal cost to be shrunk down to 50% co-sharing scheme. Similarly, the plan of zero co-payment for children under the age of 6 years was repealed. With the future fiscal pressure and increasing demands from the rising elderly population, and public expectation on medical capabilities, along with the public's unwillingness to pay higher insurance contribution, further expansion of the NHI coverage is predicted to be difficult.

Moreover, recent changes in the government politics and ideological shift seem to further intensify this concern. Under the pressure of global economy and new liberalism, where the state is identified as the cause, rather than the cure of the economic crisis for its inefficiency in managing productive enterprises and services along with its growing social expenses like health, education, and social security, we are facing a policy environment favouring commercialization, decentralization, and privatization. Thus, concepts like efficiency, effectiveness, cost/benefit, freedom of choice, and decentralization are receiving higher attention than ever.

The recent emphasis on biotechnology and medical service industry is a good example. Korea is one of the places where recent advancement in technologies and treatments promises to provide valuable opportunities for guaranteeing and improving the access to medical care for its people. For instance, new technologies in e-health and telemedicine are receiving intensive attention because of their capabilities to provide better access to new technologies and treatments at the right time for people living in the remote areas

As a flip side of this achievement, however, emphasis on the commercial aspect of these new technologies is actually moving the health policy orientation of this country toward an unexpected direction. Framing of medical services and technologies as prominent "commodities" for economic prosperity has brought a major ideological shift, making the government policy emphases lean towards efficiencies and profitability rather than equality and adequacy. Under this backdrop, health care is increasingly perceived as a commercialized sector. This implies that we are facing a hard ideological choice between two contrasting values: health care as a public commodity, based on the state's responsibility to provide social rights for all, or as a market commodity from the economic model perspective. Under the governance that favours commercialization and privatization, health care can no longer remain as the universal right for whose fulfilment the state is responsible, but can be defined as a commodity in the marketplace, where free choice is allowed only for those who can afford. Iriart et al. (2001) points out that "this is a fundamental change in meaning, since health stops being a public good and becomes a private good."

If we are to continue believing that health care should be governed on the basis of public priorities and accountability, rather than efficiencies and market principles, in the current context of expanding commercialization and privatization of the health care system, the challenge is to develop an institutionally and contextually sound policy system that would fulfil the original intent of the health care system to protect people from unexpected illness and economic burden. More specifically, to achieve adequate and effective access to health care among all population, the future task of the Korean government would be to deal with issues like weak regulatory framework, lack of social consensus on governing principle of the system, low premium contribution, and unsustainable financing scheme.

A country's health system reflects its own diverse history, culture, resources, values, and administrative capacities. Health care systems are to be shaped by specific context of national health system development. A more fundamental factor, though, would be to achieve social consensus on the purpose of the health care system – the health system exists to protect and improve the people's health by providing professional and accountable health care for all. Subsequently, policies about the nature and extent of health care provision should be designed to achieve the purpose of health care.

Bibliography

Akileswaran, C., et al., "Lessons learned from use of highly active antiretroviral therapy in Africa", *Clinical Infectious Diseases* (2005)41: 376-85.

Akin, J.S., W.H. Dow, et al., "Did the distribution of health insurance in China continue to grow less equitable in the nineties? Results from a longitudinal survey", *Soc. Sci. & Med.* (2004)58(2): 293.

Andrews, P., S. Ellmann (eds.), *The Post-Apartheid Constitutions: Perspectives on South Africa's Basic Law* (Johannesburg: Witwatersrand University Press, 2001).

Arrow, K.J., "Uncertainty and the welfare economics of medical care", *American Economic Review* (1963)53: 941–73.

Arthur, W.B., "Competing technologies, increasing returns, and lock-in by historical events", *Economic Journal* (1989)99: 116-31.

Atun, R., et al., "A framework and toolkit for capturing the communicable disease programmes within health systems: Tuberculosis control as an illustrative example", *European J. of Public Health* (2004)14: 267-73.

Auvert, B., et al., "Can highly active antiretroviral therapy reduce the spread of HIV?: A study in a township of South Africa", *J. of Acquired Immune Deficiency Syndromes* (2004)36(1): 613-21.

Berlin, I., *Four Essays on Liberty* (Oxford: Oxford University Press, 1979).

Bilchitz, D., "Towards a Reasonable Approach to the Minimum Core: Laying the Foundations for Future Socio-economic Rights Jurisprudence", *South African J. on Human Rights* (2002)19: 1-126.

Bloom, G., X. Gu, "Health sector reform: Lessons from China", *Soc. Sci. & Med.* (1997)45(3): 351-360.

Borzutzky, S., *Vital Connections: Politics, Social Security and Inequality* (Notre Dame: Notre Dame University Press, 2002).

Brameld, K., et al., "Possession of health insurance in Australia - how does it affect hospital use and outcomes?", *J. of Health Services & Research Policy* (2006)11 (2): 94-100.

Burrows, C., K. Brown, A. Gruskin, "Who buys health insurance? A survey of two large organisations", *Australian J. of Social Issues* (1993)28: 106–23.

Butler, J.R.G., "Policy change and private health insurance: Did the cheapest policy do the trick?", *Australian Health Review* (2002)25(6): 33-41.

Buijsen, M., et al., (eds.), *Marktwerking v. Solidariteit. Op zoek naar nieuwe evenwichten in de publieke dienstverlening* (Nijmegen: Valkhof Pers, 2007).

Cameron, A.C., et al., "Microeconometric model of the demand for health care and health insurance in Australia", *Review of Economic Studies* (1988)55: 85–106.

Cameron, A.C., P.K. Trivedi, "The role of income and health risk in the choice of health insurance: Evidence from Australia", *J. of Public Economics* (1991)45: 1–28.

Carney, S., *Australia in Accord. Politics and industrial relations under the Hawke Government* (South Melbourne: Sun Books, 1988).

Carrin, G., C. James, "Social health insurance: Key factors affecting the transition towards universal coverage", *International Social Security Review* (2005): 58.

Carter, S., S. Chapman, "John's $12 tonic: Press coverage of the government's selling of a private health insurance rebate", *Australian and New Zealand Journal of Public Health* (2001)25(3): 265-71.

Castilla, J., et al., "Effectiveness of highly active antiretroviral therapy in reducing heterosexual transmission of HIV" *J. of Acquired Immune Deficiency Syndromes* (2005)40(1): 96-101.

Chaskalson, A., "From Wickedness to Equality: The Moral Transformation of South African Law", *International J. of Const. Law* (2003)1: 4.

Chen, L. and H. Standing, "Gender equity in transitional China's health care policy reforms", *Feminist Economics* (2007)13(3/4): 189.

Chung, J., D. Lee, "An attitudes survey on out-of-coverage health care services", *Health Insurance Forum* (2004)3(3): 72-84 (In Korean).

Collins, S.R. et al., *Rite of Passage? Why Young Adults Become Uninsured and How New Policies Can Help* (New York: Commonwealth Fund, 2006).

Cooper, E., et al., "Combination antiretroviral strategies for the treatment of pregnant HIV-1 infected women and prevention of perinatal HIV-1 transmission", *J. of Acquired Immune Deficiency Syndromes* (2002)29(5): 484-94.

Cruz-Saco, M.A., C. Mesa-Lago, *Do Options Exist? The Reform of Pensions and Health Care Systems in Latin America* (Pittsburgh: University of Pittsburg Press, 1999).

Cueto, M., "The origins of primary health care and selective primary health care", *American J. of Public Health* (2004)11: 1864-74.

Dai, D., "A review of the health care reform (wei sheng gai ge hui gu)", *Chinese Health Economics* (1993)2: 26-28.

Daniels, N., et al., "An evidence-based approach to benchmarking the fairness of health sector reform in developing countries", *Bull. World Health Org.* (2005)83(7): 7-14.

Daniels, N., J. Sabin, *Setting Limits fairly – Can we Learn to Share Medical Resources?* (Oxford: Oxford University Press, 2002).

David, P., "Clio and the Economics of QWERTY", *American Economic Review* (1985): 75.

Davies, G., "Health and Efficiency: Community Law and National Health Systems in the Light of Müller-Fauré", *Modern Law Review* (2004)1: 103.

Deber, R., "Why Did the World Health Organization Rate Canada's Health System as 30th? Some Thoughts on League Tables", *Longwoods Review* (2003)2: 1.

de Jong, E., M. Buijsen (eds.), *Solidariteit onder druk? Over de grens tussen individuele en collectieve verantwoordelijkheid* (Nijmegen: Valkhof Pers, 2005).

den Exter, A.P., H.E.G.M. Hermans, "The Constitutional Right to Healthcare", *European J. of Health Law* (1998)3: 261-90.

den Exter, A.P., H.E.G.M. Hermans (eds.), *The Right to Healthcare in Several European Countries* (The Hague: Kluwer Law International, 1999).

den Exter, A.P., J. Sándor (eds.), *Frontiers of European Health Law* (Rottendam: Erasmus University Press, 2003).

den Exter, A.P., "De Europese kwetsbaarheid van de Zorgverzekeringswet" *NJB*, (2005)2: 87-93.

den Exter, A.P. (ed.), *Competitive Social Health Insurance; Yearbook 2004* (Rotterdam: Erasmus University Press, 2005).

den Exter, A.P., "Patient Mobility in the European Union: Health Spas in Italy", *Croatian Medical J.* (2005)2: 197-200.

den Exter, A, M. Buijsen, "Keuze voor Solidariteit. Kanttekeningen bij het Voorstel Zorgverzekeringswet", *TvGR* (2005)1: 111-17.

den Hartogh, G., *Gift of bijdrage? Over morele aspecten van orgaandonatie* (Den Haag: Rathenau instituut, 2003).

Doty, M.M., et al., *Seeing Red: Americans Driven into Debt by Medical Bills* (New York: Commonwealth Fund, 2005).

Duckett, S.J., "Chopping and changing Medibank part 2: An interpretation of the policy making process" *Australian J. of Social Issues* (1980)15: 79-91.

Duckett, S.J., "Structural interests and Australian health policy" *Soc. Sci. Med.* (1984) 18(11): 959-66.

Duckett, S.J., T. Jackson, "The new health insurance rebate: An inefficient way of assisting public hospitals", *Medical J. of Australia* (2000)172(9): 439–44.

Duckett, S.J., "Private care and public waiting" *Australian Health Review* (2005)29(1): 87-93.

Duckett, S.J., "Living in the parallel universe in Australia: public Medicare and private hospitals" *CMAJ* (2005)173(7): 745-747.

Duckett, S.J., *The Australian Health Care System* (3rd edition) (Melbourne: Oxford University Press, 2007).

Dworkin, R., *Taking Rights Seriously* (London: Duckworth, 1978).

Egger, M., et al., "Antiretroviral therapy in resource-poor settings: scaling up inequalities?" *International J. of Epidemiology* (2005)34(3): 509-12.

Eide, A., C. Krause, A. Rosas, *Economic, Social and Cultural Rights: A Textbook* (Dordrecht: Martinus Nijhoff, 1995).

Esping-Andersen, G., *The Three Worlds of Welfare Capitalism* (Princeton: Princeton University Press, 1990).

Etzioni, A., *The New Golden Rule – Community and Morality in a Democratic Society* (New York: Profile Books, 1997).

Fan, R., "Corrupt Practices in Chinese Medical Care: The Root in Public Policies and a Call for Confucian-Market Approach", *Kennedy Institute of Ethics J.* (2007) 17(2): 111.

Fleuren, J.W.A., *Een ieder verbindende bepaling van verdragen* (Den Haag: Boom Juridische uitgevers, 2004).

Flood, C.M., T. Archibald, "The Illegality of Private Health Care in Canada", *Canadian Medical Association J.* (2001)164: 6.

Flood, C.M., et al (ed.), *Access to Care, Access to Justice: The Legal Debate over Private Health Insurance in Canada* (Toronto: Toronto University Press, 2005).

Flood, C.M. "Chaoulli's Legacy for the Future of Canadian Health Care Policy" *Osgoode Hall Law J.* (2006)44(2): 273-310.

Flood, C.M. (ed.), *Just Medicare: What's In, What's Out, How We Decide* (Toronto: Toronto University Press, 2006).

Fredman, S., "Human Rights Transformed: Positive Duties and Positive Rights", *Public Law* (2006): 498.

Fried, C., *Right and Wrong* (Cambridge: Harvard University Press, 1978).

Gallie, W.B., "Essentially contested concepts", in Proceedings of the Aristotelian Society (1955)56: 167-198.

Gao, J., J. Qian, et al., "Health equity in transition from planned to market economy in China", *Health Policy and Planning* (2002)17(S1): 20.

Gao, J. and S. Tang, "Health insurance and hospitalisation in urban China: bending to the wind of change" *World Hospitals and Health Services* (2000)3: 23-26, 36, 38.

Gath, S., "Enhanced consumer rights in private health care: Have the "Lawrence Amendments" delivered?", *J. of Law and Medicine* (1999)6: 241-252.

George, R., *In Defence of Natural Law* (Oxford: Oxford University Press, 1999).

George, G., "Workplace ART programmes: why do companies invest in them and are they working?", *African J. of AIDS Research* (2006)5(2): 179-88.

Gimbel-Sherr, S., et al., "Using nurses to identify HAART eligible patients in the Republic of Mozambique: results of a time series analysis", *Human Resources for Health* (2007)5: 7.

Hall, J., R. de Abreu Lourenco, et al., "Carrots and sticks - the fall and fall of private health insurance in Australia", *Health Economics* (1999)8(8): 653-60.

Harmon, S., "Solidarity: a (new) ethic for global health policy", *Health Care Analysis* (2006)14: 215-36.

Hindle, D., I. McAuley, "The effects of increased private health insurance: a review of the evidence", *Australian Health Review* (2004)28(1): 119-138.

Holmes, S., C.R. Sunstein, *The Cost of Rights* (New York: W.H. Norton, 2000).

Huh, S., et al., *Strengthening of the NHI Benefit Coverage: Policies and Strategies* (Seoul: Korea Institute of Health and Social Affairs, 2008) (In Korean).

Hunt, P., *Reclaiming Social Rights: International and Comparative Perspectives* (Aldershot: Dartmouth Publishing Company, Ltd. 1996).

Hopkins, S., M.P. Kidd, "The determinants of the demand for private health insurance under Medicare", *Applied Economics* (1996)28: 1623–32.

Huynh, P.T. et al., *The U.S. Health Care Divide: Disparities in Primary Care Experiences by Income* (New York: Commonwealth Fund, 2006).

Institute of Medicine, *Care Without Coverage* (Washington, D.C.: IOM, 2002).

Institute of Medicine, *A Shared Destiny: Community Effects of Uninsurance* (Washington: National Academy Press, 2003).

Ip, P.-K., "Developing Medical Ethics in China's Reform Era", *Developing World Bioethics* (2005)5(2).

Iriart, C., et al., "Managed care in Latin America: The new common sense in health policy reform", *Soc. Sci. & Med.* (2001) 52 (8):1243-1253.

Jheelan, N., "The Enforceability of Socio-Economic Rights", *EHRLR* (2007) 2: 146.

Jost, T.S., *Health Care At Risk: A Critique of the Consumer-Driven Movement* (Durham, N.C.: Duke University Press, 2007).

Kam, S., "The death zone in the national health insurance system", *Health Insurance Forum* (2007)6(2): 60-71 (In Korean).

Kang, M., M. Reich., Priority-setting in the Korean national health insurance benefit package expansion. In 30 Years of Korea National Health Insurance: Celebrating Past Achievements, Planning for the Future. Seoul, 2007.

Kapteyn, P.J.G., P. Verloren van Themaat, *Introduction to the Law of the European Communities* 3rd ed., (London: Kluwer Law Int., 1998).

Kapuy, K., D. Pieters, B. Zaglmayer, *Social security cases in Europe: The European Court of Human Rights* (Antwerpen: Intersentia, 2007).

Kebaabetswe, D., et al., "Barriers to antiretroviral adherence for patients living with HIV infection and AIDS in Botswana", *J. of Acquired Immune Deficiency Syndromes* (2003)34(3): 281-88.

Kewley, T.H., *Social security in Australia 1900–72* (Sydney: Sydney University Press, 1973).

Khang, Y.-H., et al., "Health inequalities in Korea: age- and sex-specific educational differences in the 10 leading causes of death", *International J. of Epidemiology* (2004)33(2): 299-308.

Khang, Y., et al., "Trends in socioeconomic health inequalities in Korea: use of mortality and morbidity measures", *J. of Epidemiology and Community Health* (2004)58: 308-14.

Kinney, E.D., B.A. Clark, "Provisions for Health and Health-Care in the Constitutions of the Countries of the World", *Cornell International Law J.* (2004)37: 285, 287.

Kiragu, K., et al., "Sexual risk-taking and HIV testing among health workers in Zambia", *AIDS and Behaviour* (2006)11(1): 131-36.

Kropotkin, P., *La Conquête du Pain* (Paris: Tresse and Stock, 1892).

Kwon, S.B., et al., "Equity in health care utilization in Korea", *Korean Health Economic Review* (2003)9(2): 13-24 (in Korean).

Kwon, S.M., "The fiscal crisis of national health insurance in the Republic of Korea: in search of a new paradigm", *Social Policy & Administration* (2007)41(2):162-78.

Kwon, S.M., et al., *The Korea National Health Insurance Benefit Coverage* (Seoul: Seoul National University/ The NHIC, 2007) (In Korean).

Kymlicka, W., *Liberalism, Community and Culture* (Oxford University Press, 1991).

Laws, Sir John, "The Constitution: Morals and Rights", *Public Law* (1996): 622, 624.

Lee, A. "The premium subsidy program for the low income families", *Health Insurance Forum* (2007)6(1): 113-31 (In Korean).

Lee, H. "Spatial distribution of the emergency medical facilities and spatial disparity of the demand-supply level for the emergency medical services", *Korean Regional Geography Studies* (2004)10(4): 606-23 (In Korean).

Lim, M.-K., H. Yang, et al., "China's evolving health care market: how doctors feel and what they think", *Health Policy* (2004)69: 329-327.

Liu, C. "The battle against SARS: a Chinese story", *Australian Health Review* (2003) 26(3): 3-13.

Liu, C.J., *Closing the Gap Between Policy and Reality: A study of community health services in Chengdu and Panzhihua* (PhD thesis, 2003).

Liu, G., D. Legge, et al., *Community Health Services. Health Policy in Transition: The Challenges for China* (Beijing: Peking University Medical Press)(forthcoming).

Liu, G., Z. Zhao, et al., "Equity in health care access to: assessing the urban health insurance reform in China", *Soc. Sci. & Med.* (2002)55: 1779-94.

Liu, G. G., Z. Zhao, "Urban employee health insurance reform and the impact on out-of-pocket payment in China", *The International J. of Health Planning & Management* (2006)21(3): 211.

Liu, Y., et al., "Health care in China: the role of nongovernment providers", *Health Policy* (2006)77(2): 212-20.

Liu, Y., G. Bloom, *Rural Health System Reform in Poverty Areas. Health Policy in Transition: The Challenges for China* (Beijing: Peking University Medical Press) (forthcoming).

Liu, Y., W.C. Hsiao, et al., "Equity in health and health care: the Chinese experience", *Soc. Sci. & Med.* (1999)49(10): 1349-56.

Mackintosh, M, M. Koivusalo (eds.), *Commercialization of Health Care: Global and Local Dynamics and Policy Response* (New York: Palgrave Macmillian, 2005).

Marshall, T.H., *Citizenship and Social Class* (Cambridge University Press, 1950).

Mason Meier, B., A.M. Fox, "Development as Health: Employing the Collective Right to Development to Achieve the Goals of the Individual Right to Health", *HRQ* (2008) 30: 259-355.

McGinnis, J.M., W.H. Foege, "Actual causes of death in the United States", *J. of the American Medical Association* (1993)270(18): 2207-12.

McKeown, T., *The Role of Medicine: Dream, Mirage, or Nemesis?* (London: London Nuffield Provincial Hospitals Trust, 1976).

McLean, S.A.M. (ed.), *First Do No Harm – Law, Ethics and Healthcare* (Ashgate: Aldershot, 2006).

Milligan, D., W. Watts Miller, *Liberalism, Citizenship and Autonomy* (Avebury: Aldershot, 1992).

Mills, A., "Mass campaigns versus general health services: what have we learnt in 40 years about vertical versus horizontal approaches?", *Bull. World Health Org.* (2005) 83(4): 315-16.

Mills, A., "Vertical vs horizontal health programmes in Africa: idealism, pragmatism, resources and efficiency", *Soc. Sci. Med.* (1983)17(24), 1971-81.

Mills, E., et al., "Adherence to antiretroviral therapy in sub-Saharan Africa and North America", *J. of the American Medical Association* (2006)6: 679-90.

Moellendorf, D., "Reasoning about Resources: Soobramoney and the Future of Socio-Economic Rights Claims", *South African J. on Human Rights* (1988): 327-33.

Moon, Y.O., et al., "Regional variation in accessing regional hospitals for cancer patients", *Korean J. of Epidemiology* (2006)28(2): 152-61 (In Korean).

Moorin, R.E., C.D.J. Holman, "Development of a health care policy characteri-sation model based on use of private health insurance", *Australia and New Zealand Health Policy* (2005)2: 27.

Moorin, R.E., C.D.J Holman, "Does federal health care policy influence switch-ing between the public and private sectors in individuals?", *Health Policy* (2006)79(2-3): 284-95.

Moorin, R., K.J. Brameld, et al., "Health care financing and public responses: use of private insurance in Western Australia during 1980-2001", *Austra-lian Health Review* (2006)30(1): 73-82.

Moorin, R.E., C.D.J. Holman, "Modelling changes in the determinants of PHI utilisation in Western Australia across five health care policy eras between 1981 and 2001", *Health Policy* (2007)81(2-3): 183-94.

Nabyonga, et al., "Abolition of cost-sharing is pro-poor: evidence from Uganda" *Health Policy and Planning* (2005)20(2): 100-8.

Newdick, C., "Accountability for Rationing – Theory into Practice" *Law, Medi-cine and Ethics* (2005)33: 660.

Newdick, C. "Exceptional Circumstances – Access to Low Priority Treatments After the Herceptin Case," *Clinical Ethics* (2006)1: 205.

Newdick, C., "Citizenship, Free Movement and Health Care: Cementing Indi-vidual Rights by Corroding Social Solidarity", *Common Market Law Review* (2006)43: 1645.

Ngwenya, C., "The Recognition of Access to Health Care as a Human Right in South Africa: Is it Enough?", *Health and Human Rights* (2000)5(1): 27-44.

Nozick, R., *Anarchy, State and Utopia* (Oxford: Blackwell, 1994).

Oliveira-Cruz, V., et al., "Delivery of priority health services: searching for syn-ergies within the vertical versus horizontal debate", *J. of International Devel-opment* (2003)15: 67-86.

O'Loughlin, M.A., "Conflicting interests in private hospital care", *Australian Health Review* (2002)25(5): 106–17.

Peabody, J.W., et al., "Health for all in the Republic of Korea: one country's ex-perience with implementing universal health care", *Health Policy* (1995)31: 29-42.

Pei, L., *Hospital management in a time of change: the need for management training and policy reform in three teaching hospitals in Yunnan* (PhD thesis, 1998).

Pellegrino, E., "The Commodification of Medical and Health Care: The Moral Consequences of a Paradigm Shift from Professional to a Market Ethics", *J Medicine and Philosophy* (1999)24: 243, 258.

Pierson, P., "The new politics of the welfare state" *World Politics* (1996)48(2): 143-179.

Pieterse, M., "Possibilities and Pitfalls in the Domestic Enforcement of Social Rights: Contemplating the South African Experience", *Human Rights Quar-terly* (2004)26: 882-905.

Pillay, K., "Implementing Grootboom: Supervision Needed", *Economic and So-cial Rights Review* (2002)3: 11.

Plant, R., *Modern Political Thought* (Oxford: Blackwell, 1991).

Powers, N., et al., "The effect of increased private health insurance coverage on Victorian public hospitals", *Australian Health Review* (2003)26(2): 6-10.

Raphael, D.D., *Concepts of Justice* (Oxford: Oxford University Press, 2001).

Rawls, J., *A Theory of Justice* (Oxford: Oxford University Press, 1971).

Richardson, J.R.J., L. Segal, "Private health insurance and the Pharmaceutical Benefits Scheme: how effective has recent government policy been?", *Australian Health Review* (2004)28(1): 34-47

Roscam Abbing, H.D.C., "Public Health in the Treaty of Amsterdam", *European J. of Health Law* (1998)2: 173.

Ross, J.S. et al., "Use of Health Care Services by Lower-Income and Higher-Income Uninsured Adults", *J. of the American Medical Association* (2006): 2027-33.

Ryan, A. (ed.), *The Idea of Freedom* (Oxford: Oxford University Press, 1979).

Sandel, M., *Liberalism and its Critics* (New York: New York University Press, 1992).

Segal, L., "Why is it time to review the role of private health insurance in Australia", *Australian Health Review* (1994)27(1): 3-15.

Sen, A., *Development as Freedom* (New York: Anchor Books, 2000).

Sepúlveda Carmona, M.M., *The Obligations of the State under the International Covenant on Economic, Social and Cultural Rights* (Utrecht University (diss.), 2002).

Shen, Y., J. McFeeters, "Out-of-Pocket Health Spending Between Low- and Higher-Income Populations", *Medical Care* (2006)3: 200-08.

Shin, Y., et al., *Medical Needs of The Near Poverty-Line Population in Korea* (Seoul: Korean Institute of Health and Social Affairs, 2004) (In Korean).

Short, P.F., D. Graefe, "Battery-Powered Health Insurance? Stability in Coverage of the Uninsured", *Health Affairs* (2003)6: 244-49.

Shue, H., *Basic Rights, Subsistence, Affluence and US Foreign Policy* (Princeton, NJ: Princeton University Press, 1980).

Sigerist, H., *Civilisation and Disease* (Ithaca: Cornell University Press, 1943).

Smith, J., "Tax expenditures and public health financing in Australia", *The Economic and Labour Relations Review* (2001)12(2): 239–62.

Sonder, L., "The Accord, the communique and the budget", *The Australian Quarterly* (1984) (Winter): 153-162.

Song, Y.M., J.J. Byeon, "Excess mortality from avoidable and non-avoidable causes in men of low socioeconomic status: a prospective study in Korea", *J. of Epidemiology and Community Health* (2000)54(3): 166-72.

Stewart, R., et al., "Emerging threats to equitable implementation of ART in South Africa", *Acta Academica Supplementum* (2006)1: 286-308.

Stjerno, S., *Solidarity in Europe: The History of an Idea* (Cambridge University Press, 2005).

Stoll, M., et al., "Direct costs for the treatment of HIV-infection in a German cohort after introduction of HAART", *European J. of Medical Research* (2002)7: 463-71.

Stone, D.A., "The Struggle for the Soul of Health Insurance", *J. Health Pol., Pol'y & L.* (1993)18: 287.

Suh, N., et al., The Public Satisfaction of the National Health Insurance System (Seoul: NHIC, 2007) (In Korean).

Sun, X.-M., et al., "Survey for the medical financial assistance schemes of the urban poor in Shanghai", *International J. of Health Planning and Management* (2002) 17: 91-112.

Sunstein, C.R., "Social and Economic Rights? Lessons from South Africa", *Constitutional Forum* (2000): II(4): 123, 131.

Swartz, K., *Reinsuring Health: Why More Middle-Class People Are Insured and What Government Can Do* (New York: Russell Sage Foundation, 2006).

Temmink, H.A.G.,"Kroniek van het Europees recht", *NJB* (2001)31: 1502.

Toebes, B.C.A., *The Right to Health as a Human Right in International Law* (Antwerp: Intersentia, 1999).

van Bueren, G., "Including the Excluded: The Case for An Economic, Social and Cultural Rights Act", *Public Law* (2002): 456.

van der Mei, A.P., L. Waddington, "Public Health and the Treaty of Amsterdam" *European J. of Health Law* (1998)2: 135.

van der Wal, K. (ed.), *Vrijheid, gelijkheid en broederschap? Betekenis en huidige relevantie van het devies van de Franse Revolutie* (Budel: Damon, 2004).

van Doorslaer, E., et al., "Equity in the delivery of health care in Europe and the US", *J. of Health Economics* (2000)19(5): 553-83.

van Doorslaer, E., et al., "Inequalities in access to medical care by income in developed countries", *CMAJ* (2006)174(2): 177-83.

Walker, A.E., et al., "Public policy and private health insurance: distributional impact on public and private hospital usage", *Australian Health Review* (2007)31(2): 305-14.

Walzer, M., *Spheres of Justice: a defense of pluralism and equality* (New York: Basic Books, 1983).

Wang, M., "The phase change: Development trend and policy orientation of the Chinese economy (zhong guo jing ji de jian duan bian hua, fa zhan qu si he zhen che fang xiang)", *China Development Review* (2002)4(1): 1-18.

Weiser, S., et al., "The alternative National health programme" *Australian J. Social Issues* (1968)3(4): p. 33-50.

Willcox, S., "Promoting private health insurance in Australia", *Health Affairs* (2001)20 (3): 152-161.

Willcox, S., "Buying best value health care: Evolution of purchasing among Australian private health insurers", *Australia and New Zealand Health Policy* (2005)2(6): 6.

Wolman, D.M., W. Miller, "The Consequences of Uninsurance for Individuals, Families, Communities and the Nation", *J. Law, Medicine, and Ethics* (2004)32: 397-403.

Xu, K., et al., "Household catastrophic health expenditure: a multi-country analysis", *Lancet* (2003)362: 111-117.

Yang, H., et al., *Regional Health Planning. Health Policy in Transition: The Challenges for China* (Beijing: Peking University Medical Press) (forthcoming).

Yu, W., "The medical aid: problems and solutions", *Health Insurance Forum* (2006) 5(2): 86-102 (In Korean).

Zelnick, J., M. O'Donnell, "The impact of the HIV/AIDS epidemic on hospital nurses in KwaZulu-Natal, South Africa: nurses' perspectives and implications for health policy", *J. Public Health Policy* (2005)26(2): 163-85.

Zhan, S., et al., "Economic transition and maternal health care for internal mi-grants in Shanghai, China", *Health Policy and Planning* (2002)17(S1): 47.

Zhang, L., et al., "Social capital and farmer's willingness-to join a newly estab-lished community-based health insurance in rural China", *Health Policy* (2006)76: 233-42.

Zhao, H., *Governing the Healthcare Market: Regulatory Challenges and Options in the Transitional China* (PhD thesis, La Trobe University, 2005).

Zhao, H., et al., *Impact of Hospital regulation policies Health Policy In Transition: Challenges for China* (Beijing: Peking University Medical Press) (forthcom-ing).

Zheng, P., et al., "Public hospitals in China: Privatization, the demise of uni-versal health care and the rise of patient-doctor violence", *J. Law & Medicine* (2006)13(4): 465-70.

Contributors

Silvia Borzutzky is Teaching Professor of Political Science and International Relations at Carnegie Mellon University. She has written extensively on social security and health policies, as well as Chilean politics. She is the author of Vital Connections: Politics, Social Security and Inequality in Chile (Notre Dame University Press, 2002) and co-editor of After Pinochet: The Chilean Road to Capitalism and Democracy (University Press of Florida, 2006). She is also the author of more than 30 articles dealing with Chilean politics, social security and health policies, as well as Latin American politics and international relations. She is currently editing a book on the Bachelet Government in Chile

Martin A.J.M. Buijsen MA, LL M, PhD, health lawyer and legal philosopher, is associate professor at the Health Policy and Management Department of Erasmus Medical Centre (Erasmus University Rotterdam). He currently chairs the health law department.

Stephen Duckett, an economist, heads the Reform Team for Queensland Health. He was Secretary of the Australian Health Department from 1994 – 1996 and has held leadership positions in the Victorian Health Department, at La Trobe University and as Chair of the Boards governing The Alfred and the Brotherhood of St Laurence. He was recognised by his peers in 2004 for his academic excellence by election as a Fellow of the Academy of the Social Sciences in Australia and in 2006 by the University of New South Wales by award of a higher doctorate, the Doctor of Science, on the basis of his published works. He is an Adjunct Professor at Griffith University and the University of Queensland.

André den Exter, is a lecturer in health law at the Erasmus Medical Centre/Erasmus University Rotterdam, the Netherlands. Since returning to the Erasmus University in 2008, his research has focused on international and European health law. Prior to his return to Rotterdam, he was a lecturer in European law at the Radboud University Nijmegen, department of International and European law.

Colleen M. Flood is a Canada Research Chair in Health Law and Policy and Scientific Director of the Canadian Institutes for Health Research, Institute of Health Services and Policy Research. She is also Associate Professor of Law at the University of Toronto, cross-appointed to the Department of Health Policy, Management and Evaluation and the School of Public Policy. Her primary area of scholarship is in comparative health care policy, public/private financing of health care systems, health care reform, and accountability and governance issues. She is the author and editor of five books, including International Health Care Reform: A Legal, Economic and Political Analysis (Routledge, 2000), co-editor of Access to Care, Access to Justice: The Legal Debate Over Private Health Insurance in Canada (UTP, 2005), editor of Just Medicare: What's In, What's Out, How We Decide (UTP, 2006), co-editor of Canadian Health Law and Policy (3rd ed.) (Butterworths, 2007), and co-editor of Administrative Law in Context (Emond Montgomery, 2008).

Lisa Forman is a postdoctoral fellow at the University of Toronto, exploring the right to health, access to medicines and trade rules. She qualified as a lawyer in South Africa with a BA and LLB from the University of the Witwatersrand. She holds a Masters in Human Rights Studies from Columbia University, and a Doctorate in Juridical Science from the University of Toronto, Faculty of Law. Her doctoral dissertation explored the role of human rights in increasing access to AIDS medicines, focusing on South Africa as a case study. Her research interests include the right to health, global pharmaceutical policy, human rights law and theory, and corporate accountability under human rights law.

Timothy Stoltzfus Jost, J.D., holds the Robert L. Willett Family Professorship of Law at the Washington and Lee University School of Law. He is a coauthor of a casebook, Health Law, used widely throughout the United States in teaching health law. He is also the author of Health Care at Risk, A Critique of the Consumer-Driven Movement, Health Care Coverage Determinations: An International Comparative Study, Readings in Comparative Health Law and Bioethics, and numerous articles and book chapters on health care regulation and comparative health law and policy.

Minah Kang Kim, PhD is assistant professor at the Department of Public Administration at Ewha Womans University, South Korea. She is also Assistant Director of the Ewha Leadership Development Institute. After she received Ph.D. in Health Policy Program at Harvard University, Dr. Kang has been an instructor at Harvard Medical School and an Associate Scientist at the Institute of Health Policy of the Massachusetts General Hospital in Boston. Dr. Kim has published articles in journals including Health Affairs, Medical Care and JAMA. Her most recent research interests are on disparity in health and gender issues, and political analysis of health policy.

Vivian Lin took up the Chair of Public Health at La Trobe University in mid-2000 and was Head of the School of Public Health to 2005. From 1997 to then, she was the Executive Officer for the Australian National Public Health Partnership. She has previously held senior positions within the NSW Health Dept, the National Occupational Health and Safety Commission, and the Victorian Health Dept (and its successors). She is the chair of the Australian Network of Academic Public Health Institutions (ANAPHI), the inaugural president of the Chinese Medicine Registration Board of Victoria (since 2000), and a member of the Australia-China Council (since 2006). In 2007, she was elected Vice President for Scientific Affairs for the International Union of Health Promotion and Education (IUHPE). She has co-authored or co-edited a number of key texts in Australia, in health planning, health policy and public health practice. Her qualifications include BA (Yale) in biology and political science and MPH and DrPH from UC Berkeley, where she concentrated on social epidemiology, occupational health, and health policy. Vivian's research interests cover political economy of health and health care, globalisation and health development, policy implementation, and comparative health systems and reforms.

Chris Newdick is a barrister and Professor of Health Law at the University of Reading, UK. He has served on the UK Department of Health's Medicines Commission and given evidence to the House of Commons Health Committee on the National Institute for Health and Clinical Excellence. He is an Honorary Consultant to Berkshire West Primary Care Trust and a member of the Berkshire Priorities Committee which advises health authorities on health care resource allocation. He is an advisor to the British Medical Association's working party on Rationing in the National Health Service. Amongst a wide range of other publications on law and ethics in health care, he is the author of Who Should We Treat? - Rights, Rationing and Resources in the NHS (Oxford University Press, 2005).

Stephanie Nixon, PhD, is an Assistant Professor in the Department of Physical Therapy at the University of Toronto in Canada, and a Research Associate at the Health Economics and HIV/AIDS Research Division (HEARD) at the University of KwaZulu-Natal in South Africa. Stephanie has been an HIV/AIDS advocate, clinician and researcher since 1995.

Paul Schoukens is Professor of Social Security Law (Comparative, International, and European) at the K.U. Leuven (Catholic University of Leuven). He is general coordinator of the European Institute of Social Security. Within the K.U. Leuven, he is working for the European section of the Institute of Social law, organised as the Research Unit on European Social Security (RUESS). He is involved in the organisation of the master in European Social Security and the Summer School on Social Security. He is the programme director of the latter specialised programme, a two-weeks course that gives a general introduction into social protection across Europe from a multidisciplinary perspective.

Nina Veenstra was until late 2007 a Senior Research Fellow with the Health Economics and HIV/AIDS Research Division at the University of KwaZulu-Natal. She graduated initially as a physiotherapist, but later obtained an MPH from the University of Cape Town. She has just recently completed her PhD through the University of KwaZulu-Natal in the field of health policy and HIV/AIDS. Her research interests centre around the impact of HIV/AIDS on health systems in sub-Saharan Africa and appropriate adaptive management strategies.

Sujith Xavier, BA, LL.B. and Human Rights, LL.M., was a Research Associate in Health Law and the Research Manager at the Faculty of Law, University of Toronto. He is currently a PhD Candidate at Osgoode Law School, York University, Canada.

Hongwen Zhao, PhD is currently a researcher and Director of the International Health Department of the National Health Economics Institute, Ministry of Health (MoH, China). He obtained his MD and Master of Biostatistics in China, MPH in the U.S.A. and DrPH in Australia. He has worked as health specialist and project manger at the MoH and World Bank China Office for more than 10 years. He has also been assistant Director-General of the Health Human Resources Centre, and Project Manager of the Health Policy Support Project in the Policy and Legislation Department of the MoH. His research areas include health care regulation, governance and market, and the role of civil societies in the health system during the transition to market economy.

Index

Maklu

Maklu